More Praise for The In

"In *The Intuition Guidebook*, Cyndi Dale shows how to screen others' energies from your own and shift from being 'too sensitive' to 'truly magnificent.' This life-changing, maybe even life-saving book is a masterpiece of sensible and transformational wisdom and exercises, all of which can stair-step you into your divine wisdom."

—Gail Lynne Goodwin, Founder of InspireMeToday.com

"*The Intuition Guidebook* is one of the most comprehensive, readable and practical books I've read on the subject of psychic development. Cyndi Dale is one of my favorite authors, and her vast knowledge and experience shines through in every page. This insightful book is aimed at people with no previous knowledge of the subject, but more advanced students will learn from it, too. Highly recommended."

—Richard Webster author of over 100 books including *Seven Secrets to Success* and *Spirit Guides and Angel Guardians*

"Cyndi Dale's new book, *The Intuition Guidebook*, takes us on a journey through more than just listening to that 'still small voice' that many of us experience. It is an all out, directly written guide to enhancing our psychic/intuitive abilities, whether you are new to this or have walked this path for some time. Through Cyndi's quest to discern her own gifts, she has given us language for the many things we 'feel, see or hear,' that don't seem from the normal realm. The principles in her book help to explain why we feel a certain way around others, hear or see visions that come true, and even how to ground and clear ourselves when they do occur. Cyndi's writing is brilliant, and I highly recommend this book. Believe me, you will walk away with amazing information that will change your life forever."

—Patty Peterson, Award-Winning Singer, Motivational Speaker, and Radio Personality

"*The Intuition Guidebook* is a book of lived experience. Cyndi Dale grew up trying to make sense of her own intuitive gifts and ended up living a life of service. This book is the latest proof of that, as she takes the reader by the hand and leads them to a place of understanding, purpose, and joy in their intuitive gifts."

—Joan Steffend Brandmeier, Radio and Television host and author of *...and she sparkled*

"Are you sensitive to everything and everyone around you? Do you feel you are intuitive, but have had trouble managing these gifts in a constructive way? Have you read other books on intuition or psychic abilities, but felt they just weren't telling the whole story? Then look no further, this is the book you have been waiting for. Quite simply, this book is a gem for anyone that feels they are intuitive and needs guidance on how to live with this, and utilize it."

—Lisa Erickson, Buddhism editor for BellaOnline.com, and Amazon Top 1000 reviewer

"A most timely, comprehensive and valuable resource for so many out there, who feel misunderstood... especially at this remarkable time of the Earth's great changes and human evolution. Cyndi Dale lovingly invites each one of us to fully embody, embrace and understand our gifts, spiritual abilities and divine nature. She teaches us how to not just survive, but to thrive and be ourselves in our fullest expression. Cyndi is truly an expert on the Chakra energy systems and this book most brilliantly exemplifies Cyndi's vast knowledge and experience."

—Evita Ochel, Author, Teacher, and Founder of EvolvingBeings.com

"Cyndi Dale writes with eloquence, passion, and a depth of wisdom that comes only from personal experience. This inspirational and practical book will not only help you to understand and develop your intuitive abilities, but will also guide you to create a life of lasting spiritual purpose."

—Ainslie MacLeod, Author of *The Transformation: Healing Your Past-Life Fears to Realize Your Soul's Potential* and *The Instruction: Living the Life Your Soul Intended*

The Intuition Guidebook

The Intuition Guidebook

How to Safely and Wisely Use Your Sixth Sense

By

Cyndi Dale

Foreword by Deanna Minich, PhD, CN and author of Chakra Foods for Optimum Health

Designed by Anthony J.W. Benson and Barbara Schendel
Layout Design by Anthony Sclavi and Russell Boldt
Cover Photo by Sasha Zukanoff
Edited by Amy Rost

Printed in the UNITED STATES OF AMERICA

ISBN: 978-0-9826687-9-5
Library of Congress Control Number: 2011930662

Published jointly by:
Deeper Well Publishing
and
Brio Press
12 South 6th Street, Suite 1250
Minneapolis, MN 55402

For press inquiries, email: publicity@deeperwellpub.com

Dedication

All my thanks to two very intuitive, splashy, and brave women. Here's to Jessica Hagan, whose insights helped shape, add to, and subtract from this book, and to Amy Rost, whose genius editing—a sometimes thankless job—revealed her brilliance.

Acknowledgments

The Intuition Guidebook has actually been ten years in the making. Through its many transformations, it has been shaped by the thoughts and insights of several incredible people, all of whom have left an indelible mark.

My thanks to Jessica Hagan and Cathy Scofield for earlier manuscript adjustments and Amy Rost for editing this book not once, but TWICE, with flair and grace. In fact, Amy is the reason the book is seeing the light, as one day, she suggested that the world needed this book. Was I not ready to dust it off, polish it up, and finally birth it?

Labor ensued, and a number of other critical and vital players stepped forth. Foremost is Anthony J.W. Benson, my partner in Deeper Well Publishing, who has cultivated all aspects of this book into its current and amazing form. Our other partner in Deeper Well Publishing, William Reynolds of Brio Books, is the other "leg" for getting this book up and running. His tenacious excitement for this new endeavor has encouraged it from manuscript to print.

I must also thank the hundreds of apprentices who have participated in the living version of this book, "The Apprenticeship Program." I have led this program internationally now for years to help participants develop their spiritual gifts. Guess what? The five-star class is based on the material in *The Intuition Guidebook*. Every participant has shared an inspiration critical to this book.

A thank you also to Chantal Monte, whose organizational skills float The Apprenticeship Program, as well as to Wendy Kardia, my assistant of twenty-some years, whose keen wisdom and abilities keeps the entire Essential Energy business operable and enjoyable.

It's also imperative to thank you, the readers, whose innate gifts are changing the world, one person, day, and illumination at a time. If we were all to open our gifts, think then, what this world might become!

EXERCISES

CONTENTS

FOREWORD

Psychic Sense

Like most of you who are about to embark upon reading this book, I spent my childhood enrobed in an ever-changing whirlwind of impressions, feelings, and images that seemed to go farther than pure imagination. Being connected to this realm of possibilities—being too open—only resulted in me feeling what others were feeling, in becoming sick easily with colds, flu, and fatigue, and in continued attempts to untangle myself from a web of sheer emotional overwhelm. For survival's sake, I became an introvert, sequestering myself with books rather than being around people because it felt safer and less taxing.

Looking back, it was almost like I couldn't get out of my own way. It was physically, emotionally, and mentally draining, and even slightly painful, to be so sensitive. Many times, I would walk into a room and immediately become anxious, like I was taking on the energy of the people in a room rather than staying grounded in my own being. Sometimes, I had impressions about people that would later unfold as true. In general, I was constantly overwhelmed.

I had no idea what to call this "condition" or where to turn. Of course, if I had this book in my hands at the time, I could have easily diagnosed myself what Cyndi Dale calls "psychically sensitive." However, being raised in a strict, conservative, Roman Catholic household on the south side of Chicago with a police officer as my father, there would have certainly been no tolerance for using the word "psychic" in my vocabulary! Instead, I recall phrases said to me like "get over it" and "stop being so sensitive."

And if all the stuff on the outside wasn't enough to take in, I was battling the psychic influx of energy with my developing scientific intellect. It was as though both of them were playing a tug of war! Ultimately, my scientific, truth-seeking side got the best of me and I began to search for what "disease" I had, pouring over medical books during my pre-med studies in college. I thought if I could put what I was experiencing into a box, a category, or give myself a label, I could perhaps "treat it" and get rid of it once and for all. The closest I could find to what I was feeling was something along the lines of "social anxiety," but even that didn't feel specific to what I was experiencing, which was much more broad: the extreme tiredness I would feel after being around a group of people, the erratic mood swings when confronted with various people or situations throughout the day, and the deluge of nervousness I felt when I was in certain social conditions like riding the bus to school. As Cyndi says, it's like you become a "sponge" for everything happening around you.

When I couldn't find anything to match, I realized that I needed to look elsewhere. I remember finding myself in a small new-age bookstore in my college town soaking up a flood of "new" information—not on the human anatomical system like I was already studying, but books on the human energy system, and on intuition, energy medicine, chakras, and healing. Quite a different realm than the hard scientific world of facts that I was clinging to for answers! I was drawn in immediately to this new knowledge base because it seemed to provide some explanations for my state of being. What at first was a foreign language began to explain the world that I was living in: "psychic ability," "intuition," "subtle energy," "chakras," "auras," and even "human energy field." I was amazed that I had never seen these terms in my science textbooks or learned about them at school. It felt liberating to embark upon a new territory that seemed from the first glance to provide some answers.

During these days at the university, when I was in my early twenties, I began to meet a lot more people who were like me. I still didn't quite know what to do about "my condition," but I was now exposed to different modalities and therapies that provided some basic coping mechanisms, including yoga, prayer, meditation, and reading self-help books. As I continued down my spiritual path through my mid to late twenties, I met many inspiring teachers who began to teach me about my intuitive abilities, helping me to hone what was in place. I was finally developing better tools around "the condition." Now I set out to become "healed."

Being the scientist I am, I noticed a common thread, or truth, embedded in the teachings of all my mentors. They all referred to a specific practice about protection or establishing boundaries – whether it was a visualization of encapsulating myself in a colored light, using essential oils to keep my aura clear, shielding my body in a cloud of white sage, or even shaking a rattle around my body to "dust off" any energetic residues. When I would practice these techniques on a consistent basis, I started to become more discriminating. I wasn't quite as open to taking things in, and when I did so, my immune system seemed to strengthen. I wasn't as frequently ill. I had stamina. I didn't feel like a leaf traveling on the whim of a gust of wind. Finally, I felt more grounded and present in my body, like an oak tree with thick roots grabbing on to the earth beneath it for stability. I was now becoming able to shake loose all those feelings, images, and impressions which didn't serve me.

In this book, Cyndi talks about not just grounding, but also includes a 5-step approach to harnessing psychic activity, which starts with grounding. I found her approach to be the best and most concise that I've ever come across in my spiritual pursuits.

But back to my story.

Surprisingly, I was starting to rein in my oversensitive nature. I began to enjoy a better grasp on my environment, allowing me to expand my social horizons. When I could see outside of the psychic chaos, I realized that there was a way I could use it to my advantage. Rather than being consumed by the input in my surroundings, I was now choosing what to consume and how to digest it through the conduit of my being.

I could now cast my lifelong study of the scientific and healing properties of food and nutrition in a new light. I would have never thought that I would apply my intuition within the realm of food and nutrition, but I did! I was able to tap into my intuition to uncover tools for people to use in redefining their relationship with food, their bodies, and even their intuition as it related to food choices. I observed that foods people ate tied directly into not just their physical bodies, but also their subtle energy states. Food fed and affected the human physiological processes as well as the human energy system. Either the foods would influence their subtle energy, or their subtle energy would lead to them making certain food choices. Cyndi has also elegantly explained this food-energy connection in her phenomenal two-part book called *The Spirit's Diet*.

One of the most influential teachers I met on my journey to understand the seeming chaos of my life was Cyndi Dale. It was more than ten years ago, when a friend I worked with had told me about her. I was going through significant life changes at the time and my intuitive sense was that she could provide some much needed insight. The first time I met her, I knew instinctively that she was very gifted in her abilities. This woman was jumping with energy, vibrancy, and life—I was shocked that she didn't get drained after seeing clients all day! What was her secret? After just a couple of consultations, she helped me to make sense of my surroundings, the situations I was in, the future I was creating, and to further sharpen and refine my intuition. There is no doubt that she is truly the world's "energetic anatomy expert"—her books have been guiding lights in my deepest periods of questioning. She has such an amazing ability to take mystical, timeless wisdom and turn it into everyday "energy" tips for everybody. She makes sense of that which is difficult to make sense of, and turns the seemingly unreal into that which is real and palpable.

In this wonderful text, *The Intuition Guidebook*, Cyndi takes the challenge of psychic sensitivity head on. The moment you turn the first couple of pages, you will feel the connection and identification with the idea of being psychic. However, Cyndi makes a clear distinction between being "psychic" and "psychically sensitive" throughout the book, helping you to define the difference. When we open ourselves to being psychically sensitive, or not having boundaries on our psychic ability, we can find ourselves on information overload (as I know so well from my childhood days)!

Cyndi will teach you the key practice of psychic discernment, or the invaluable ability to harness your chaotic psychic ability to work *for* you rather than feel it is working *against* you. With her guidance, you will get your life back; you will experience a life that is manageable, nourishing, and fulfilling rather than out-of-control, depleting, and outright draining.

In fact, she will take you beyond being "psychic" into being "intuitive." Nowadays, the term "intuition" is tossed around loosely; it means different things to different people. Cyndi explains it clearly and beautifully as involving the "conscious management of psychic activity." Essentially, this amazing book is about the shift from being psychic to being intuitive—it's much like taking a wild animal and taming it, as the psychic moves into the filtered ability to be intuitive. What is great about this skill is that it's like running your unconscious psychic energy through an energetic sieve so that you can manage it rather than it taking control of you.

Not only does Cyndi's approach make sense, but she guides you through this seemingly daunting process with the help of questionnaires and easy-to-follow exercises. She makes the esoteric profoundly real and true to life with her ability to maneuver through the labyrinth of the energetic, intuitive world.

I see this book as a continual reference and resource, a go-to book to remind you of what you need to make your intuition bloom and flourish. Personally, I wish I had it years ago as I struggled through my own journey. It's the ultimate guide to helping you distill your psychic ability into the essence of your spiritual purpose—and if you are a truth seeker, chances are there is no greater quest than this. And for this great quest, there's no better person to take you on this journey than Cyndi Dale through the paths outlined in *The Intuition Guidebook*!

—Deanna Minich, PhD

INTRODUCTION

Are You Too Sensitive? A Profile of the Gifted Psychic

Do you ever feel as if:

- You have a lot in common with the kitchen sponge? You are always absorbing everyone else's feelings.
- You know things you aren't supposed to know? And it's hard to prove yourself right!
- Your megashopping days are over? Being in a mall is like being in a theater with Surround Sound. You can sense, hear, and feel what's going on with everyone around you.
- You're crazy? You have bizarre dreams and visions, hear voices in the night, make predictions that come true, have an ability to heal, receive spirit visitations, and experience other really abnormal events.

Before I finally figured out what was going on, I lived with similar issues. I still remember trying to sleep as a child. I would say my prayers and snuggle with my doll, but as soon as I closed my eyes, the "movie," as I called it, would start. Some of my experiences were wonderful. At times, I believed that I could hear the angels singing in the wind. Other moments were terrifying, like the time a ghost visited me. One night, I watched shadows on the wall, while a dark being told me how he would hurt me if I went to wake my parents.

Some experiences were more normal, yet just as challenging. My stomach would hurt after my parents argued, and I might lie there in my bed, struggling not to throw up as I continued to see their fight in my mind's eye. Not only did I perceive the invisible world, but I could also pick up on others people's issues, feelings, and thoughts.

It was a little like being at war. All day long, I would run the gauntlet. Instead of being targeted by arrows and darts, I was attacked by an invisible arsenal. While I didn't experience all of the following scenarios every day, they occurred often enough to trouble me:

- Being so overwhelmed by everyone else's unspoken needs that I sometimes forgot my own
- Receiving predictions and dreams that I didn't want and that frightened me
- Having insights about people I just met
- Shorting out light bulbs or computers when I was upset
- Hearing voices from an invisible realm
- Seeing colors, energies, and entities that didn't make sense to me

Was I just imaginative? Was I crazy? Why did I seem so different from other people and see the world so differently than others did?

If I had been just imaginative, I presumably could have created more beneficial and less unusual experiences. I could have imagined winning a lottery and then actually won it! If I had been crazy or mentally ill, I might have responded to the never-ending parade of therapists I visited and "codependent no more" groups I attended as an adult.

As it was, I knew there had to be some explanation for these unusual occurrences, and maybe even something good behind them.

After all, I frequently saw some of the following things happen:

- Dreams would come true.
- People would actually heal when I placed my burning hands on them.
- Spirits that others could not see would provide me information that was true, and I could often help people with this information.
- Visions would accurately describe the reality of a situation.

Even though I spent years telling myself that there was something positive about these apparently unique sensitivities, I didn't really believe it. I couldn't focus on the good instead of the bad because I didn't have a label for my sensitivities. All I knew was that I didn't particularly *want* to know why someone at the grocery store was angry. I didn't *want* to sense that another student had cheated on his test. I didn't *want* to be visited at night by my dead great-aunt Hazel, nor did I *want* to be privy to information about when someone close to me might die. Certainly, I didn't *want* to be so physically vulnerable that all I had to do was hear about someone having a cold, and I'd begin sneezing.

Despite the fact that my world was populated by unseen sources of voices, noises, visions, and knowledge, I was very alone. Like Helen Keller, I often felt wrapped in a dark world that was impenetrable from the outside. I didn't think, especially when I was a child, that anyone could relate to the reality of my life. Some people told me these sensitivities were evil, and often I felt guilty and bad about myself. Other people told me I was too sensitive emotionally and that I should just "buck up," which I took to mean that I should ignore my sensitivities. But when I did, my life would fall apart. It seemed I either had to play along with my sensitivities or even worse things would happen.

Do you understand what I'm talking about? Do you sometimes feel too sensitive? Do you seem to be invested—or cursed—with supernatural gifts that make life unnaturally difficult? Then you might be what I eventually decided to call myself:

Psychic.

Psychic Versus Psychically Sensitive

The truth is, we are all psychic. Being psychic simply means that we pick up and send off information that moves so fast that it's hard to measure. We use our psychic gifts on a daily basis, sometimes to figure out what our children are saying—and sometimes to know what they are not saying! We use our psychic abilities to select our route to work, to sense if we should stay home, to predict the weather, and sometimes to avoid life altogether. Natural psychic sensations provide information to guarantee that you survive life's challenges, dangers, hassles, and struggles. Being psychic is normal, and like everything normal to us, we tend to disregard its importance.

For many of us, however, being psychic is a problem. While some enjoy the subtle effects of this sixth sense, going about our day-to-day business with no notion of the extraordinary, many of us are inundated, moment-to-moment, with the overwhelming information available psychically. Some of us are so psychic, so bombarded with psychic information, so lacking in energetic boundaries, that it becomes hard to function in at least one area of life. We can't choose dish soap without being aware of the repercussions of selecting the blue gel over the white powder. We can't hum without unlocking voices that are not our own. We can't sigh without being compelled to speak the truth. We can't close out the world, for even then the pictures will not stop coming.

If the invisible, inaudible, and unexplainable are too much for you, then you aren't only psychic. You are also **psychically sensitive.**

Quite simply, being psychically sensitive means that you lack the psychic boundaries necessary to tune out harmful or unnecessary psychic information and tune into just the good stuff. You are picking up—or picking up on—physical, spiritual, visual, or verbal information that isn't meant for or isn't helpful for you.

Psychic sensitivities are often misunderstood and misdiagnosed. They are frequently considered personality disorders rather than psychic gifts. There is also little formal training or education for those with psychic abilities, and the training that does exist don't always help. Many psychic-development classes and books concentrate on the explosive opening of the psychic senses. But for those of you who are already psychically sensitive, this approach is parallel to lighting a stick of dynamite under an already lit stick of dynamite. The psychic must be expanded in line with your everyday needs and life. You not only want to survive, but also to more fully flourish!

Even though there are now books, movies, and philosophies that are more accepting of the spiritual, the unusual, and the invisible, psychic sensitivity is still culturally underdeveloped. Psychically sensitive individuals often grow up feeling alienated, strangers in a strange land whose quest becomes adaptation. Examples of problems that stem from psychic sensitivities can include everything from physical addictions and diseases to spiritual attacks and invasions.

If you're sensitive to that which doesn't fit the label of "normal," then the only solution lies in accepting and training your personal supernormal gifts.

From Psychic Victim to Empowered Intuitive

It's one thing to be invested with certain abilities; it's another thing to be able to direct them. What you can't control controls you. The good news is that you can transform these, your sensitivities, so that they work for you, not against you.

The key is to shift from being psychic to being **intuitive.** Intuition involves the conscious management of psychic activity. For example, the psychically sensitive might literally absorb someone else's illness and become sick. Upon evolving from psychic to intuitive, this gift can help its owner sense another's illness and figure out how to help or treat it, or the gift may be used in a number of other positive ways.

Intuitive abilities are different from psychic sensitivities. That fact is clear to intuitive expert Philip Goldberg, who says that "telepathy and clairvoyance are not intuition; they are ways of bringing in information that intuition may then work on."[1] While psychic sensitivities are natural and unconscious, developed intuitive abilities are consciously managed. While the psychic individual breaks rules, flees constraint, and has no limits, the intuitive individual follows guidelines, seizes control, and uses boundaries.

In this book, you will find all the information needed to shift from being psychically sensitive to being intuitive and to forge a path to your spiritual purpose in life.

In Part I, you will become acquainted with the reality of the psychic world. You will read about the basics of energy, the core information you need to understand your psychic abilities. You will also be introduced to your energy system, specifically the auric fields and the chakras, which assists you in working with psychic energy. You'll also explore the energetic programming that may underlie your psychic sensitivities and how you can undo that programming. Through the exercises at the end of the chapters, you will begin to decode your own psychic gifts, analyzing how they are working—or not—for you. The exercises will also show you how to go from being too psychic to safely intuitive.

Then you will be ready to leap into Part II, which is designed to help you make the shift from being survival oriented to being consciously intuitive, so you can benefit from being psychic. You will be introduced to a vital aspect of becoming intuitive: discernment. It's not enough to know that you are psychic; you must know *when* and *how* to be psychic—and under what conditions! The concepts of integrity and sourcing will lay the groundwork for transforming your innate psychic sensitivities into the gifts they can be. You'll learn how to set up a gatekeeper, a filter for psychic energy. Building on the chakra knowledge you obtained in Part I, you'll discover the eleven major psychic gifts, each of which is housed in a different chakra. And the exercises in this section will enable you to pinpoint your exact psychic gifts (your gift order).

As you enter the doorway of Part III, you will have a solid sense of your particular psychic gifts, know how they are affecting you, and have gathered a number of useful intuitive tools. Part III is structured so that you can delve directly into your strongest gift area, whether it is kinesthetic, visual, or verbal. A chapter is devoted to each of these three main gift types, and depending upon your gifts and desires, you can walk through one, two, or all three of these chapters. Within these pages you will find the "red flags," or warning signs related to being too psychic in each gift area, and techniques for using this gift safely. You'll also find exercises and tips for personalizing the intuitive development process.

Part III concludes by addressing the important question, what's next?

What's after the sixth sense?

What about the "seventh sense"?

For some of you, this book will point out the need to seek counseling or medical care before you undertake intuitive development. It may also show you why you may need to ignore the psychic universe altogether. Life is a series of steps, not a compilation of leaps. Always lean toward safety before satiety.

Having said that, I offer you this book because it might save you from some of the pitfalls I've undergone in learning how to manage my psychic abilities. This is the guidance that I wish I'd had earlier on during my own intuitive-development journey. This is my intuitive development bible—the book that I would like to have read years ago.

Part I

The Psychic as Real

Chapter 1

Living in Two Worlds

> *Knowledge has three degrees—opinions, science, illuminations. The means or instruments of the first is sense; of the second, dialectic; of the third, intuition.*
> ~Plotinus, Egyptian philosopher

There is a world within the one we call reality. This is the **extrasensory world.** It is also called the supernatural or spiritual world. Some people just call it the "other side." The truth is, the other side is on this side! It's right here, inside and outside each of us. I call this reality the **psychic reality**. It's not a reality taught in school or considered polite to talk about at dinner parties, and yet it is the reality that underlies the one within which we usually function. The psychic reality often determines the concrete world, or **sensory reality**—the world that most of us think is "real" and normal. The sensory reality is actually composed of and created by the psychic reality, although most of us tend to ignore this progenitor.

Everything in the sensory reality begins as an idea. The art on your walls, the shoes on your feet, the food on the table, as well as the table itself, all started in someone's imagination. Ideas are invisible. The imagination is intangible. The intangible is the psychic. Even a child was once a wisp of air, a desire, or a dream.

Whoosh—something happens to make the idea or desire a work of art, a shoe, or a baby. That *something* is an alchemical process between the psychic or idea-based world and the sensory world of particles and waves. Holding the idea as the goal, the psychic dimension transforms the hard-core stuff of neutrons, protons, electrons, and fast little particles called positrons to create what you can see, touch, taste, smell, and hear.

At first, the psychic reality doesn't seem to work by sensory rules. But the truth is that sensory and psychic realities have much in common. The normal five senses can be used in both sensory and extrasensory realities. Moreover, the basis for communication is the same in both sensory and psychic reality. **Communication** involves receiving, encoding, translating, and transmitting information. This information, regardless of the reality, is packaged into small portions or packets. These bits of information can be called **information-energy**.

The Mechanics of Information-Energy

All energy contains encoded information, and all information is encoded into energy. Everything in the world (and outside of it, by the way) is made of energy. **Energy** is really *information* in *motion*. I like to use the term *information-energy* in order to emphasize the fact that all energy contains information that tells that energy what to do or be.

All energy travels in one of two forms: **particles**, which are small and measurable units, and **waves**, which are rippling energies. There are some particles that can transform into waves and some waves that turn into particles. This ability to transform is important because psychic information, like sensory data, can start as a packaged, localized thought and spread in waveform for great distances. Waves or moving particles that have an impact on the physical or spiritual universes are called **energetic forces** and type of psychic energy. Psychic data can be carried on or within energetic forces, in addition to being an energetic force in its own right.

The real difference between psychic and sensory data isn't the form each takes, but the speed. **Sensory-based information-energy** is carried within slow-moving energy particles and waves. **Psychic-based information-energy** is carried within fast-moving energy particles and waves.

In the world of energy, speed is everything. Sensory information moves slower than the speed of light, and psychic information moves faster than the speed of light. (I discuss the scientific evidence for this statement in my other books, including *Advanced Chakra Healing*.) Due to its relatively slow speed, sensory energy is susceptible to physical forces, including gravity and electromagnetic fields. Physical forces can bond or glue together sensory energies and hold them tightly enough to enable, for example, a table to be a table. The trained nature of these forces in the sensory world also explains why it's easy to predict what happens to energy in the sensory world. Time marches forward, and action-reaction remains fairly constant. Hence, the sensory reality is a seemingly stable one, at least from a human perspective.

Because of this predictability, sensory reality can be shared or communicated. A table is a table. A rose will smell like a rose to everyone who has previously been exposed to roses. It is commonly expected that we can communicate with and be understood by others who share our sensory reality.

But in psychic reality, the energy of a table might also be encoded with messages from the past. It might still contain the spirit of the oak tree from which it was hewn. And the scent of a rose could be from a future garden not yet in form.

Compared to physical, sensory energy, psychic energy seems unpredictable. Because it moves faster than the speed of light and faster than natural physical laws, psychic energy is particularly malleable from a quantum perspective. The smallest particles in psychic reality move really fast and can literally jump from one reality to another, one dimension to the next, and even from the idea to the solid state—instantly. Because psychic information-energy can move so fast, we can potentially hear someone's thoughts before they even think them, see an event that is occurring two thousand miles away, or smell a flower garden that will flourish fifty years from now.

Psychic energy, as explained by physicist Fred Wolf, occupies that space beyond light speed where "an object or a consciousness would be completely free of the shackles of space and time. It could 'drop in' at any time, past or future. It could visit anywhere at an instant. All points in the universe would be its home."[1]

How We Detect Information-Energy

All individuals are born with the potential to understand and the ability to use both sensory and psychic energy. We are all designed with special equipment that is able to access both sensory and psychic information.

People capture and send sensory communication through their physical organs: ears, skin, nose, tongue, and eyes. There is another set of organs that works with both sensory and psychic data. These are called **energy organs,** and they are part of a larger **energy system,** a complex set of fast-moving bodies of light that can translate psychic information-energy into sensory information-energy and back again. The energy system is as physical as it is spiritual. Each organ within it is constructed of the same chemicals, ions, minerals, proteins, and other organic materials that compose our physical existence. But these energy organs are also composed of energies that move at higher vibrations, such as emotional truths, beliefs, and spiritual forces.

The most important energy organs for psychic gifts are called chakras and auric layers. **Chakras** are swirling bodies of light that help regulate the inside of your body, while the **auric field** is made of bands of energies that manage our relationship with the outside world. (The individual chakras and layers of the auric field are described in detail in chapter 3.)

These psychic centers react to different stimuli, based on the type of danger coming at us. One of the chakras, for instance, regulates psychic information pertaining to life-and-death situations. This psychic center relates to the physical adrenal organs. Upon receiving the psychic warning of life-threatening danger, the adrenals pump out adrenaline, and we either "flee" or "fight." Yet another chakra perceives our own and others' feelings. What do we do when we feel a loved one's sadness? We comfort her, not only helping her, but also reinforcing an important relationship.

We are all sensitive enough to receive the information-energy necessary to keep us alive. How practical for a caveman to psychically "hear" a dinosaur coming long before it steps on him! Humans thrive in community. How vital it is to sense how others feel or what they need! The nature and strength of our various sensitive gifts differ from person to person, but the gifts exist for the good of all.

The Challenge for Psychic Sensitives

We all use our chakras and auric layers for communication. Some of us, however, are more affected by the psychic than the sensory. We might perceive way too much of the psychic world, such as strange visions, intruding voices, fleeting touches, inexplicable smells, or unusual tastes. We might also collect and hold onto psychic energies that don't suit us. The psychic can transform into the sensory; thus, emotions, beliefs, and other energies that can become physical toxins or diseases. There are dozens of ways we can be overwhelmed by the psychic, which is why we must become maestros instead of mice in relation to our innate gifts.

The psychic is often defined as supernatural or paranormal. Note that there are two operative parts to each word: *super* + <u>*natural*</u> and *para* + <u>*normal*</u>. While it's great and even sometimes glamorous or sexy to live in the *super* or the *para*, we're here in body to function in the *natural* world in a *normal* way. It's never enough to merely linger in supernatural realms; we must link them with physical, sensory reality.

> *The challenge of being psychically sensitive? To live in both realities—the psychic and the sensory—simultaneously.*

> *The goal of living in both worlds? To create a third reality, one that combines the best of the psychic and the sensory.*

Creating this third reality—the one that is the sensory plus the psychic, that is heaven and earth, that is practical and spiritual—is the real goal of psychic development. It is the end result of using the psychic and the sensory in such a way as to unfold your true self, your inner nature, and your divine and human beingness. This is where the sixth sense transforms into something even greater: the seventh sense.

Taking Responsibility

Some people think it's unwise to tamper with native psychic sensitivity or ability. Perhaps they value and rely so heavily on the information they receive. Perhaps the extraordinary information they receive makes them feel special. Whatever the reason, they fear that making any changes may mean giving up their sensitivity all together.

While psychic sensitivity can lead to amazing insight and revelations, it can also overwhelm and cripple the uninformed person. Psychic sensitivity can be dangerous because it exposes you to any and all psychic information available at any given time. Being naïve in regard to the psychic or the intuitive is careless, especially when there's something you can do to protect yourself.

When you cloak your psychic abilities mindfully and watchfully, you don't lose your sensitivities. You don't stifle your gifts. Instead, you paradoxically become more open to psychic information—the right kind. Intuitive boundaries also aren't fixed in stone. They move in and out and up and down, depending upon need. They are permeable and allow freedom with safety. They also allow in people, information, ideas, and sources that are of love and that send you messages of love. As an intuitive person, you can manage your psychic abilities and thus tap into universal powers. You get to decide how, where, and when to direct these forces.

Many psychic individuals shy away from learning about the psychic world because they think it's frightening or even evil. Others won't develop their psychic powers because they are scared of power; they think they'll hurt someone or perhaps open themselves to evil influences.

Psychic sensitivities are powerful and can, in unethical hands, become the basis of misused sorcery, mind control, manipulation, black magic, and the occult arts. But in their more ethical guises, psychic sensitivities are at the core of all religions, creativity, spiritual revelations, and miracles. The distinction between using psychic abilities versus not using them is simply how much you control the psychic information—and for what reasons you use it.

We are not responsible for the information that we receive psychically, but we do need to act responsibly with such information. And you don't need to pick up all psychic data just because it's available. You don't *need* to act like a kitchen sponge or a one-way receiver just because you *can*.

This is where training comes in. It's almost impossible for untrained psychic individuals to see the difference between using a psychic gift responsibly and being responsible for what the psychic gift reveals, simply because they are unaware of the gifts and assume the way they receive information is just "the way things are."

> *If we don't use an innate psychic ability, we will become used by it. What we don't manage eventually controls us or allows others to control us.*

It's not enough to see psychic pictures in your head or hear voices inside of your mind. You must decide which types of pictures, messages, insights, and sensations are safe, ethical, and supportive for your life and ultimately feed your spiritual purpose. The psychic senses are gifts, and they are to be used purposefully. In fact, they might hold the key to living a meaningful and fulfilling life. And I emphasize the word *life*. The true psychic master links his or her abilities with the "real world." You don't need to choose between psychic and sensory-based perceptions. Both are real, and both are you.

To become intuitive rather than purely psychic can be difficult. Change usually is. As an intuitive individual, however, you go an extra step, from being psychic to being intuitive, and in doing so, you can find your purpose, coax it to life, and prosper.

Exercise 1

The Psychic Sensitivity Quiz

The following questionnaire will help you assess your own psychic abilities, especially those that might cause you problems. You will be referring to your quiz results several times in this book, using the results as a springboard for other exercises. So hang on to the results!

This quiz will help your determine:

1. In what areas of psychic sensitivity you may be the most gifted.
2. Which areas of psychic sensitivity may cause you the most difficulties.
3. How these areas of sensitivity can be transformed into strengths for use in everyday life.

Directions

Select the number that indicates how strongly you agree with each numbered description. Zero means the statement doesn't fit at all. Five indicates an absolute fit. You'll score your results at the end. Each description is a way of finishing this statement: "I have experienced the following."

1. Illnesses or physical problems that in some way, don't feel like my own or that don't make any sense.

   0 1 2 3 4 5
2. Feeling others' physical issues in my own body.

   0 1 2 3 4 5
3. When someone tells me about a gruesome event or physical trauma, I feel the sensations of the event in my own body.

   0 1 2 3 4 5

4. Strong addictions to substances such as stimulants, alcohol, or hard drugs, or to sex; it seems that nothing helps me recover.

   0 1 2 3 4 5

5. Life struggles centering on money, housing, or getting my basic needs met.

   0 1 2 3 4 5

6. Chronic or episodic headaches, skin problems, or viral or bacterial infections in the genital or lower renal/elimination tracts—none of which respond to professional help.

   0 1 2 3 4 5

7. Feel others' feelings as if they are my own.

   0 1 2 3 4 5

8. The inability to separate my own emotions from others' emotions.

   0 1 2 3 4 5

9. Being stuck in feelings that I can't ever get rid of.

   0 1 2 3 4 5

10. Difficulties in feeling how I "should." For instance, I don't feel sad when someone dies or angry when someone is being mean.

    0 1 2 3 4 5

11. Loss of creativity or an inability to be creative when I need to be.

    0 1 2 3 4 5

12. Physical problems with my intestines, premenstrual syndrome (PMS) or other "female" problems, prostate issues, or other abdominal difficulties. Nothing seems to help.

    0 1 2 3 4 5

13. Knowing information that I have no reason to know.

    0 1 2 3 4 5

14. An awareness that hits me suddenly.

    0 1 2 3 4 5

15. Complete loss of energy under stress, like I'm "leaking."

    0 1 2 3 4 5

16. Constant problems with my stomach or any other digestive organs.

    0 1 2 3 4 5

17. Addiction to caffeine, coffee, soda, beer, corn products, or work.

    0 1 2 3 4 5

18. Lamps, street lights, computers, and other electrical devices often warp or stop working around me, especially when I'm stressed.

    0 1 2 3 4 5

19. Knowing, without explanation, that someone is ill or disturbed. Sometimes I even understand the reasons for and solutions to the problem.

    0 1 2 3 4 5

20. An almost uncontrollable urge to heal someone or help him or her fix a problem.

    0 1 2 3 4 5

21. The ability to perceive the health or lack of health in others' relationships.

    0 1 2 3 4 5

22. Burning or tingling sensations in my hands that seem to occur when I'm around or thinking about an ill person.

    0 1 2 3 4 5

23. Difficulties in separating myself from those who are very ill, needy, or disturbed.

    0 1 2 3 4 5

24. Dreams that tell me about others' illnesses or problems.

    0 1 2 3 4 5

25. Physical problems with my heart, breasts, or lungs that seem to increase when I'm having relationship problems or when I'm around sick or needy people.

    0 1 2 3 4 5

26. The ability to hear others' thoughts or to know what they are going to say.

0 1 2 3 4 5

27. Hearing voices, noises, or sounds from sources that "aren't there."

0 1 2 3 4 5

28. When writing, a flow of information coming from something outside of myself.

0 1 2 3 4 5

29. Overwhelming difficulties in asserting myself or saying what I need.

0 1 2 3 4 5

30. The sensation of having my thoughts or words guided or controlled by something outside of myself.

0 1 2 3 4 5

31. A tightening or constriction in my throat, neck, or jaw, especially in reaction to what someone is saying or has written. A susceptibility to throat viruses or mouth ailments, frequent laryngitis, or thyroid problems.

0 1 2 3 4 5

32. Seeing visions, colors, or shapes with my mind's eye or sometimes my physical eyes.

0 1 2 3 4 5

33. Getting answers to questions or issues in pictures, shapes, or visions.

0 1 2 3 4 5

34. The ability to understand or interpret the meaning or symbolism behind information that is visually presented.

0 1 2 3 4 5

35. Extreme self-image or related problems, such as body-image issues, anorexia, bulimia, suicidal tendencies, or self-hatred.

0 1 2 3 4 5

36. Visions that have revealed possible future events.

0 1 2 3 4 5

37. Physical ailments involving the eyes, sight, or visual perception.

0 1 2 3 4 5

38. A sense of higher or spiritual right and wrong.

0 1 2 3 4 5

39. A sense of knowing my own or another's "true destiny."

0 1 2 3 4 5

40. Susceptibility to brainwashing, cults, or extreme ideas, which could include difficulties in walking away from a distorted family system.

0 1 2 3 4 5

41. Awareness of or problems with negative entities or demonic influences, or a hyper awareness of evil forces.

0 1 2 3 4 5

42. Major depression or high anxiety, paranoia or schizophrenic tendencies, possession or similar experiences, or seasonal affective disorder (SAD). Professional or chemical assistance has not helped.

0 1 2 3 4 5

43. The sensation—not drug induced or enhanced—of being "lifted out of my body" or seeing or being "in the white light."

0 1 2 3 4 5

44. The sense of having lived before or occupying a different time right now.

0 1 2 3 4 5

45. The ability to move through time; knowing about places I've never been or people I've never met.

0 1 2 3 4 5

46. The ability to know someone else's past.

0 1 2 3 4 5

47. The thought that I can change shape or become something else either in body, mind, or soul.

0 1 2 3 4 5

48. The urge to live in another time or space; not feeling like I'm always "here."

0 1 2 3 4 5

49. Difficulties in staying in one time or of connecting in the here and now.

0 1 2 3 4 5

50. The ability to see or work with symbols or patterns.

0 1 2 3 4 5

51. The ability to perceive others' soul issues or problems.

0 1 2 3 4 5

52. Sometimes inexplicable knowledge about someone's enduring self, soul, or higher spirit.

0 1 2 3 4 5

53. The ability to work with archetypes or cosmological truths.

0 1 2 3 4 5

54. The sense that I must offer global assistance around a cause.

0 1 2 3 4 5

55. Challenges in accepting the evils and problems of the earth.

0 1 2 3 4 5

56. An attraction to natural medicine or treatments.

0 1 2 3 4 5

57. Sensations that mirror what is occurring in the natural world.

0 1 2 3 4 5

58. Sudden changes in my physical or emotional state in reaction to astronomical or geophysical changes, such as barometric shifts or planetary movements.

0 1 2 3 4 5

59. Problems in my house, yard, or residence when I'm being challenged in life.

0 1 2 3 4 5

60. Extreme environmental sensitivities or highly allergic reactions that don't seem to respond to treatment.

    0 1 2 3 4 5

61. The sense that some of my ancestors are with me.

    0 1 2 3 4 5

62. The movement of objects or materials in response to my thoughts or conscious direction.

    0 1 2 3 4 5

63. Reactions in the physical universe that seem tied to my state of mind. For example, a storm comes up when I'm angry.

    0 1 2 3 4 5

64. The ability to change others' negative attitudes or energetic charges into positive ones—and vice versa.

    0 1 2 3 4 5

65. The experience of being drained when I touch a needy or negative person.

    0 1 2 3 4 5

66. The sense that I absorb natural or supernatural forces.

    0 1 2 3 4 5

67. The ability to direct natural or supernatural forces.

    0 1 2 3 4 5

Totaling the Results

Add together the numbers you have circled. This total will help you assess how sensitive you are in general. It may also help you determine if you are "too psychic" in certain areas and need to develop better psychic boundaries.

Note: You may have circled a number indicating a sensitive experience that is causing significant problems; you qualify as "too sensitive" based on that situation alone! If this is the case, pay special attention to descriptions in Part III that might help you pinpoint a particular gift area or over-sensitivity.

Total:

Interpreting the Results

General Psychic Potential

Highly Psychic	200 to 335 points
Medium Psychic	100 to 199 points
Low Psychic	30 to 99 points
Underpsychic	29 points or fewer

If Your Potential Is Highly Psychic

You probably relate to many conditions described in this book.

Highly psychic individuals spend a great deal of time in other worlds. As a child, you may have frequently daydreamed about or even *visited* another reality for comfort, education, or insight. Highly psychically sensitive children often relate to invisible playmates, angels, and spirits for companionship. Frequently, they understand relationships in terms of how another person psychically feels, smells, seems, or appears to them. Dreams, predictions, spirit visitations, an enhanced sense of others' feelings or needs, a connection to nature—there are many ways that the psychic reality permeates the world of the highly sensitive child.

As an adult, you may continue to have this psychic sense of reality, or perhaps you have developed your paranormal senses since childhood. If so, you are probably sensitive in many areas rather than just one. You might notice another's illness and long to help, and then sense another person's emotions as the day continues. Overwhelmed by the person's sadness, anger, or fear, you might spend the next few hours sorting what is real from what isn't real.

In school or at work, you are bright, but perhaps not always "on cue" with the day-to-day learning or work processes. Rather than trust what you hear or read, you have an inner sense that guides and motivates you. It can sometimes be hard to prove just how you know what you know! You might even prefer sensing reality through your gut, visions, or dreams instead of other, more "normal" ways of knowing.

Being this psychic can seem like a disease. You might long for more personal space. You might yearn for more quiet in your own mind. You might desire separation from others. Have hope! You can learn to better manage or control your gifts.

Begin first by affirming the beauty of your psychic senses. You are gifted for a reason. Learning about your strongest gifts can be the key to uncovering and living a purposeful and happy life.

You will benefit from a better understanding of how the psychic world augments the physical universe. While we all live between these two universes, your life purpose involves merging psychic with sensory realities to bring more heaven on earth. Defining the strengths and downsides of your particular types of psychic gifts will enable you to use them for the greater good.

If Your Potential Is Medium Psychic

You probably have one or more very strong psychic gifts that would benefit from intuitive development. The mid-sensitive person tends to have a few strong suits. When applied personally and professionally, these gifts can catapult you into great success.

As a child, you were at least somewhat aware of a reality that stretched beyond the "norm." However, you probably also were fairly comfortable operating within the laws of the status quo. The question is, were you able to use your paranormal insights to assist yourself? Alternatively, did these insights detract from your life, maybe even distracting you from your goals?

Sometimes, medium psychics are scared of their innate psychic sensitivities because their strongest gift has taken over. When this occurs, you can be plagued by constant visions, senses, knowledge, or verbal messages. The key to changing the situation is learning how to integrate your strongest gift(s) in your life. You can do so through intuitive development, therapy to deal with underlying stress, and insightful career and relationship planning. Obtaining guidance about developing your specific gifts can alleviate any annoyance or even danger, and help you apply your psychic sensitivity for your own and others' well-being. Your gifts are critical to your survival, as well as your ability to thrive in the world, and understanding your strongest gifts will greatly enhance your effectiveness in the world.

If Your Potential Is Low Psychic

You are probably comfortable operating within sensory reality, but would find your life enhanced by developing your innate psychic abilities.

Everyone is psychic, but not everyone needs to use their psychic gifts to achieve their spiritual destiny. Some people are by nature more sensory than psychically based and prefer to understand the world through their normal five senses, leaving psychic exploration to others. It might be more critical to develop your personality than your psychic senses.

People who are sensory tend to thrive in the everyday reality. If you're one of these people, you are probably known for your common sense, practicality, and pragmatism. You are effective at getting results, understanding the obvious, and motivating others to meet reality-based goals. At times, you may have doubted the existence of alternative ways of knowing, but certain experiences may have taught you that there is more to the world—and to you—than meets the eye.

Developing your own gifts will enhance your sensory, reality-based nature and could greatly assist you in transforming any area of confusion. The key is to first better understand what psychic sensitivity and psychic boundaries are all about. Then you can evaluate your own gifts for practical application.

If Your Total Is Less Than 29 Points

You fall into the category of underpsychic, which paradoxically means that you are probably highly psychic. Perhaps your psychic sensitivities are so raw that at some point in your life, you shut them off completely.

Why would someone surrender or hide his or her psychic gifts? The list of reasons is endless and could include trauma and judgment, sexual abuse or injury, prejudices and criticism, or childhood or societal abuse, including neglect, addictions, religious brainwashing, and poor parenting. You might not have realized that psychic sensitivities even existed.

If you tested as underpsychic and think that the reason stems from trauma or other tragic, difficult circumstances, read this book, but please don't do the psychic-development exercises until you work with a trained professional, such as a licensed physician or therapist. You don't want your innate psychic abilities to suddenly explode—and then have your life implode. If there is a good reason that you unconsciously hid your gifts, you must respect this reason. A therapist will be able to help you discover why you thought that you had to hide your abilities.

Chapter 2

Understanding Your Sensitivities

> *Be fit for more than the thing you are now doing. Let everyone know that you have a reserve in yourself; that you have more power than you are now using. If you are not too large for the place you occupy, you are too small for it.*
> ~James A. Garfield

Being psychic is about being powerful. But if we don't know how to manage these powers, we become powerfulness to them, rather than empowered by them.

Here's a practical example. You have to chop down a dead tree. A friend starts up a chain saw and hands it to you. You know that this awesome machine can get the job done, but you don't know how to work it, much less turn it off! Let's compound the scenario by imagining that the chain saw weighs one hundred pounds, and you haven't worked out in, oh, ten years. Common sense says that the chain saw has more power than you do.

Psychics who are barraged with floods of unfiltered information-energy are in an equally tangled mess, a situation that brings about the **psychic victimization cycle.**

The Psychic Victimization Cycle

The psychic victimization cycle, the communication sequence that hurts the psychic sensitive, has five steps. Do you recognize them?

1. A psychically sensitive person inadvertently absorbs outsiders' issues, feelings, diseases, or problems. Or she is afflicted by visitations, images, noises, voices, or senses from non-apparent sources. These situations arise because her psychic sensitivity has been misunderstood, misdiagnosed, or untrained, causing her to have poor or virtually nonexistent psychic boundaries.
2. Because the psychically sensitive person cannot stop or control the flow of this information, she begins to feel powerless and bad or worthless.
3. The perception of being powerless leads to fear, which sometimes results in feeling angry at circumstances that seem out of control.
4. This anger can turn into hopelessness, shame, and depression, and the gifted individual thinks she needs more information-energy to restore security.
5. The psychically sensitive now opens to more psychic information-energy, but instead of guided answers, she receives a flood of non-relevant—or even harmful—information.

Psychic sensitivity, which could be enhancing physical security, is now causing anything but real safety. Too much data only overwhelms us, creating more fear.

Because of this cycle, it is common for the psychically sensitive to have a hard time coping with typical life issues. Undiluted psychic gifts can:

- Flood you with feelings that you can't sort through,
- Distort your perceptions of relationships,
- Dampen your enthusiasm for life,
- Lead to low self-esteem and cynicism,

- Cloud your personal vision of the future,
- Make it difficult to hold faith,
- Lead you to misuse your gifts in an attempt to get at least some needs met.

Being sensitive doesn't need to be a curse. In fact, a healthy and spiritually based use of the psychic gifts can:

- Connect you to your true self,
- Provide needed information,
- Enable healing,
- Give you the right words at the right time,
- Clarify choices and opportunities,
- Link you to higher planes of spirituality, adding meaning and purpose to your life.

We are all psychically sensitive—some of us more than others. If you feel plagued by your gifts, then it's time for you to know that you don't deserve to be victimized by your own abilities. There is purpose in the psychic, and there's a way to harness it. But first, you have to become conscious of what you're doing.

The Unconscious Sensitive

The power latent in psychic sensitivity is magnificent and can make you shine. What good are these abilities if you don't know how to wisely use them—or worse, if you allow them to use you? To benefit, you must become conscious rather than unconscious of their use.

Pure psychic sensitivity is an automatic process run by your unconscious or subconscious. There's nothing wrong with having parts of your life run by your unconscious or subconscious. Do you want to concentrate every time you brush your teeth or breathe? Do you really want to think about every word that comes out of your mouth or count how many bites of food you eat at a meal? No. You can trust your unconscious and subconscious with these and millions of other habitual activities.

But what if you hold the unconscious belief that you are bad? Psychic information flows not only from the outside world to you, but also from you to the outside world. That means if you harbor the unconscious belief "I'm bad," you will send that message to the world, which, in turn, will treat you that way. You will ingest the negative experiences and psychic messages that you receive in return, and that information-energy will then share the thought of being bad with all parts of your inner self. This complicated mess will leave you wondering just who or what is "making you feel bad." Left in charge, your unconscious and subconscious won't sift through your psychic mail—they will rip, tear, shred, mutilate, and toss until you won't know who sent what message or why!

What's the solution? It is to become *intuitive* rather than psychic.

Intuition is the conscious management of psychic communication. The **intuitive sensitive**, in contrast to the psychic sensitive, has learned to control and manage his or her inherent psychic abilities.

> ***Psychism*** *is the ability to receive and send energy information that moves faster than the speed of light.* **Intuition** *is the ability to screen out and select information that is useful and relevant to you and your purpose.*

Separating the Wheat from the Chaff

The first step of intuitive development is learning how to separate good from bad and helpful from harmful information. Just as you can't make bread without winnowed flour, you cannot properly use your psychic abilities without undergoing a winnowing process. Flour doesn't begin white and soft. It starts life as a wheat stalk, and only parts of this stalk can be processed into flour. Winnowing involves separating the usable grain kernels from the inedible husks.

There is psychic data that is necessary and fruitful, and psychic data that is unnecessary and even toxic. We need to separate the wheat from the chaff, or kernels from the husks, if we want to reap bountiful lives. Picking up all the psychic debris weighs us down and prevents us from finding the good kernels. Just as the tastiness of bread depends upon working with purified ingredients, so is a quality life contingent on taking in only beneficial psychic data.

Talking about this point always makes me think of John, one of my favorite clients. John was a very spiritual twelve-year-old who had been hearing a voice since he was a small child. He was sure that the voice was God because it said that it was. I was ready to believe him, until he told me some of the messages given by this voice.

John recounted a dream in which "God" had told him to kill his parents. John had actually gone to bed the next night with a knife, intending to stab his mother or father if they entered his room. Neither did. Another time, John heard the voice telling him to hurt his dog. John, a loving boy, had instead run crying to his mother, but had been unable to tell her what was really going on. From this point on, when he went to bed, he would shake, asking this voice to say nice things instead of mean things. Everything he heard scared him. Finally, John told his mother what was going on, and she called me.

John's story demonstrates the cycle of the psychic victim. He was overwhelmed with negative psychic data to the point of feeling powerless. In my office, he shared how scared and guilty he felt, especially at the thought that he could have killed his parents. While he wanted the voice to stop, some unconscious part of him instead opened to more psychic information, seeking data the only way he knew how. John had an innate gift, one that was, unfortunately, harming rather than helping him. What could have provided him love, solace, and guidance was instead creating trauma, agony, and self-hatred. Should John have felt guilty for his murderous plans toward his parents? Would he have been helped if I had shamed him or told him he was bad because he was hearing bad things?

I worked with John for several sessions on discernment techniques, which I will share with you in chapter 5. I helped him establish a gatekeeper, a divinely appointed spiritual guardian, to keep him safe, and I taught him the basics of psychic boundaries. I also showed his parents techniques for keeping John safe. Almost immediately, the bad voice stopped; in fact, all voices stopped. John began to enjoy life, made new friends, and began a fun school baseball career. Years later, he came to see me and told me that he had finally heard the voice of the real God, which spoke only to tell him that he was loved.

Like John, you have the right to decide exactly what type of information you want coming into your life.

Do You Have to Be Spiritual to Be Intuitive?

After twenty years at the Stanford Research Institute, psychic researchers Russell Targ and Jane Katra found that, "It is not necessary to hold any particular beliefs about spirituality or anything else in order to be psychic." Rather, their experiments "clearly demonstrate that psychic abilities are part of our inherent nature."[1]

I find, however, that most people who walk the path of intuitive development eventually find the sought or unsought

Holy Grail of belief—an Absolute Power, a Greater Good, an All, a Greater Consciousness that cares. Once we've learned to consciously manage raw psychic data in order to live a fruitful and healthy life, our now-conscious abilities usually stretch one more step: into the spiritual. If there is psychic communication, there must be some source worth hearing. Even many individuals in science, long held to be a bastion of atheists, are suggesting, "The true reality is the spiritual background, which is the purposive cause of the material manifestation."[2] This "spiritual background" is the Divine, the Greater Mystery, the Holy Spirit that is greater than the sum of its parts.

Christian author Charles Swindoll says that all humans are "equipped with sufficient 'internal machinery' to connect with the living God," but we have to learn how to "plug in."[3] This machinery is the psychic. The plugging-in process is called intuition. The goal is the indescribable connection of being one with "the All," the creative consciousness that some call God, others the Goddess, the Divine, the White Light, the gods, Nature, the Higher Power, the Mother, Allah, Krishna, the Great Spirit, the Creator.

Whatever you call this supreme source, know that its main interest is to help you develop your psychic sensibilities as tools for communication so that you can receive more from life—and offer more to it. When transformed from the sixth to the seventh sense, these gifts are more than means of conveying data; they are the means for giving and receiving love.

What Is Really Yours?

Most negative or destructive psychic information-energy stored in your body or psyche isn't your own. I believe that more than

80 percent of all life problems, in fact, are caused by energies not our own. Our own information doesn't harm us. You might have beliefs that are wrong, feelings that are repressed, or issues that indicate misunderstandings, but these are ultimately challenges to work through, as each presents an opportunity for understanding and growth. Others' information-energy, on the other hand, causes real damage, for several reasons.

From a scientific perspective, all information-energy is frequency or vibration based. The energy that makes a chair a chair runs on certain bands or vibrations. The energy that creates your ears runs on its own unique set of frequencies—frequencies that are different than the energies of your kidneys. **Harmonics** are the full set of vibrations that make up who we are. Personal energies will "match" our harmonics, or personal vibrations. We can fail to release or recognize personal vibrations, such as feelings and ideas, or we can misplace them inside or outside of our body. Unreleased, unrecognized, or misplaced vibrations will cause blocks, misperceptions, holes, muddy spots, rips, tears, and congestion in our energetic fields. In turn, those energetic problems will create physical, emotional, mental, and spiritual challenges. If we shift our misunderstood or misplaced energies, however, they will heal rather than harm, instruct rather than restrict, help rather than hurt.

Energy internalized from others won't match our own frequencies and will always harm us. Imagine that your face is burned, and surgeons graft skin from your thighs onto your face. The frequency of your own skin will match that of your facial skin, and this transplanted skin has a good chance of "taking." Now think what might happen if you undergo heart surgery, and the surgeon leaves an instrument in your body. The metal tool doesn't synchronize with your physical tissue, and results in all sorts of problems!

As close or desirable as the energetic match might be, others' energies are not your own. They will not "take" and will cause problems. These **psychic toxins**—others' energies that you acquire psychically—can transform into physical energies. You can actually psychically absorb energies that can turn into a disease or a tumor in your own body!

In addition to creating negative physical effects, absorbed energy can also adversely affect your personality and spirituality. *When we internalize information that isn't relevant to us, we become someone that we are not.* Psychic energy can carry all sorts of information, including instructions about careers, money, ideas, feelings, emotional states, attitudes, prejudices, religious ideals, body-image standards, and more. What if a ten-year-old girl internalizes the culture's model of the "perfect body?" Well, many of them do, which is one of the reasons so many girls in our culture experience anorexia. Certainly there is a genetic predisposition to alcoholism, which involves inheriting the inability to produce a certain liver enzyme necessary to fully break down alcohol. The template for alcoholism, however, is a family matter and is energetically passed from parent to child. If you chronically experience an issue that never seems to change, no matter how much you work on it, you may have internalized or been imprisoned by a psychically transferred energy that is affecting your integrity.

Why do we psychically absorb ideas that conflict with our spiritual wisdom? The psychic is designed to enable survival, and we innately believe that the key to surviving is to adapt. To adapt means to fit in. By adhering to—and suffering from—norms that don't necessarily support our real self or spiritual purpose, we actually think we are assuring our own survival.

But running our lives with others' psychic energy prevents us from living in integrity with ourselves. This is not a judgment; it is a fact. The word *integrity* means integration of integrals—or in plain language, making wholeness out of parts. Most people list these parts as physical, emotional, mental, and spiritual. You could also say that you are composed of your body, mind, soul, and spirit. If any one of these parts is programmed or run by psychic data that doesn't match up with your "real self," you will be out of integrity.

What does it look like to be out of integrity because of psychic sensitivity? The list of symptoms is endless. Really sensitive psychics will be constantly afflicted by the psychic victimization cycle, stressed by a seemingly endless succession of thoughts, voices, ideas, pictures, sensations, images, orders, or visitations that are unwelcome at best and dangerous at worst. Even so-called normal people are adversely affected by unwanted psychic instructions. Just about every person who comes to see me is experiencing the negative affects of others' psychic information. Typical scenarios are:

- Hating your profession—because you've accepted someone else's idea of what type of work you should do
- Not having enough money—because you are living out someone else's "poverty mentality" or religious beliefs that being poor is virtuous
- Physical maladies—because of energies inherited from the family
- Depression—because you are repressing parts of your real self
- Anxiety—because you've accepted familial fears of the future
- Relationship problems—because you keep dating or marrying people who remind you of a family member
- Dissatisfaction—because if you are living for others, you aren't living as yourself
- Oppression—because parts of your self are being repressed by another

These and other issues can be caused by any number of problems for which it's important to see a licensed professional. In addition, the origin of some of your problems may be psychic energies that are not yours. Running your life on others' concepts will keep you from integrating the various parts of yourself needed to live a full, happy life. It can also cloud your perceptions so much that you don't even know who you really are, which not only affects your life, but also can keep you from becoming full of the spirit that you are.

It's time to separate the wheat from the chaff, the useful from the useless, and the helpful from the harmful. And it's time to put up boundaries so the harmful can never enter again.

Who Are These Children? (And Who Are We?)

Souls incarnate in groups. As our planet is preparing to evolve, we are attracting souls that are more mystical, refined, and spiritual than ever before. My own children prove this point.

My oldest son, who is in his twenties, functions great in the world, but exhibits a silent, calm approach to its frenetic craziness. He is already writing a book, a commentary on the world as it is—and needs to be. He is an indigo being, one of the young adults whose instinctive and intuitive wisdom imbues all that he does.

My youngest is a spirit child. When he was four years old, I received this comment from one of his daycare providers: "I am pleased to have met one of the world's greatest humanitarians." Not only would Gabe zoom in on a difficult situation or troubled person, but he also would also naturally formulate the most loving response—all the while talking to angels, sensing others' feelings, and performing any other number of heroic supernatural maneuvers.

Other children and young people today share some of my childrens' capabilities. I can't count how many of my clients make comments like these about their children:

"He sees spirits. I'm not sure how to handle it."
"She can tell how I feel, even when I try to hide it."
"He was born with a heart for peace."
"She seems to remember past lives and memories from other times."
"He can tell what's going to happen before it does."
"She's so sensitive, I wonder if she'll survive in this world."
"He's autistic, but I have a sense that there is a gift within that condition. If only I could understand it."

Through my personal life and work, I've come to believe that our world is being blessed with a new set of guides—earth guides, clothed as today's children. Depending on their particular soul type, their attributes range from practical and astute to hyperpsychic and saintly. Each type is psychically sensitive in a unique way. And each type begs for a different sort of parenting, a range of interactions that assure these children's extraordinary abilities continue to develop.

Following is my rendition of the soul groups currently alive today, with an emphasis on those filled by children. (The list describes these groups from oldest to youngest.)

Construct souls. This "grandparent generation" is represented by souls that have come to earth to share very specific ideas or goals. Their world, which is passing away, required specific knowledge and expertise, as well as fundamental values. These souls came to be mothers or factory workers, farmers or accountants, men or women. They arrived to fill the ranks of definitive social and religious groups, becoming capitalists or communists, Muslims or Christians, and so on. Their psychic gifts were forced into categorical representations of these specific groups. For instance, a born-again Pentecostal Christian might be supported in displaying hands-on healing abilities, while a tax collector had to "tune out" to remain analytical. These individuals and their collective groups created our nations, places of worship, and institutions. Unnecessary spiritual gifts were simply ignored—or punished.

Bridge souls. The baby-boomer generation bridges the old with the new, the material with the spiritual, and all other opposites, as well. Part of their job has been to separate the wheat from the chaff, to eliminate the harmful viewpoints and behaviors of former generations and make room for new spiritual wisdom. This mission has required serious self-work, often conducted through processes such as Twelve Step programs, family-systems therapy, spiritual expressionism, emotional maturation, feminism, gay rights, adventure seeking, and living the "purpose driven life." The so-called New Age and other revolutions actually reawakened principles and activities from the times of the ancients, thus inserting higher ideals into the place of those being eliminated. This is the reason for the upward and exponential interest in "what was," including yoga, meditation, and mysticism. The goal of the psychic in this group is to actualize the individual's gifts and purpose.

Indigo souls. This twenty-something generation, which actually includes children currently their teens and people now in their thirties, is wisdom-based. They want experience and freedom, but are also learning to accept responsibility. Many of them are driven to save the planet and help the world. Their representative color—indigo—combines blue and purple, the colors of chakras five and six and their gifts of communication and vision. The ultimate objective of these souls is to establish higher goals for this world and decide how to achieve them. Many members of this group opened their psychic gifts as they matured, naturally supported in this endeavor by their "seeker" bridge-soul parents. They naturally developed the means for screening out harmful information and could, therefore, be considered natural intuitives. Unfortunately, some of their parents operated more like construct souls than seeking souls. Indigos in these situations act more like hippies than "happies," and must struggle with learning how to be responsible. In general, however, indigos are attracted to mystical practices that support their life goals. Holistic concepts encourage their ongoing pursuit of the mystical.

Crystal souls. These souls have incarnated several times on earth and in a variety of existences. They are roughly twenty years of age and younger. Having tasted earth—and being desirous of heaven—most are here to accomplish one of two goals:

1. Reveal what must still be changed, such as entrenched prejudices, areas of discrimination, family dysfunctions, religious intolerance, and "isms" like ageism, sexism, and other wrongful attitudes.
2. Open the doorways to love.

Those crystal souls here to accomplish goal number one are often diagnosed as having learning disabilities, special needs, ADD, ADHD, autism, or Asperger's syndrome. I believe their conditions are present to force society to change its views. Autism, for instance, invites us to respect and honor feelings and figure out ways to support emotional health.

Attention-deficit disorder (ADD) asks that we pay tribute to the kinesthetic—the drive to move and learn creatively—within us all. Part of the "plan" is unfortunate, however, for these children lack psychic boundaries and pick up way too much psychic data from others. Some compensate by remaining too open, as those with ADD or ADHD do, or by shutting down, as occurs with autism and Asperger's syndrome. Whichever way they respond, the goal is to assist them in developing strong auric fields.

The second group of crystal children isn't characterized by what's wrong with them, but by having too much "right" with them. These are the kids with the wildly out-of-control psychic gifts. They see ghosts, are able to astral travel, know too much, have stomachaches for others, or exhibit just about every one of the red flags covered in this book. In general, these children are mirroring adults' issues back to them and are often plagued by the issues the adults are not dealing with. Their psychic protection plan? Boundaries, boundaries, boundaries.

Spirit souls. And then there are souls that are incarnated angels, avatars, or visitors from the very highest planes of existence. Some haven't been here before. By and large, these are our youngest children, although a few are spaced out among the other generations as well. These souls lack strong protective boundaries, but because they are implicitly wise and spiritual—and enjoy a strong bond with the Divine—they don't need such boundaries. They arrived with clean souls and intact spiritual insight. Highly psychic, they most often tune into helpful rather than harmful information and often serve as their parents' teachers, rather than the other way around. These souls show us what we could be.

Chapter 3

Psychic Boundaries and Energy Bodies: The Key to Functioning

If you hear a voice within you say "I cannot paint," then by all means paint, and that voice will be silenced.
~Vincent Van Gogh

To benefit from the psychic, it is crucial that we have boundaries. Boundaries don't hold us or imprison us. Instead, they form a perimeter that determines what information-energy we will let in and what we will keep out. We don't want to keep out all psychic information; being sensitive isn't a bad thing, but is necessary for our survival. Instead, **psychic boundaries** are an energetic means for *filtering* psychic information-energy. Establishing psychic boundaries is equivalent to setting up a fence with a gate or a house with a door. You might want to be able to open the door or the gate to let in your friends or loved ones, but you also want to be able to close and lock it to keep out thieves or murderers. You get to decide whom or what to let in—and when. Everything else has to stay out.

Psychic boundaries are necessary to control your access to:

- Others' physical diseases and problems
- Others' feelings
- Others' needs, problems, or drives

- Visiting spirits
- Information about the future
- Ideas that don't suit you
- Visions, messages, and senses that scare or hurt you

Energy Bodies: Our Natural Psychic Boundaries

We have a built-in filter system designed especially to deal with psychic information-energy. This system is composed of **energy bodies**, fast-moving organs that convert psychic information-energy to sensory information-energy and back again. There are hundreds, if not thousands, of different energy bodies in and around your physical body.

Energy bodies are just like physical organs except it's difficult to see them, even with modern medical technology. The liver, for example, is an important organ in the human body. It cleans the blood, helps process fats, and serves to regulate certain digestive processes. The liver is also part of an energy body called the third chakra. The third chakra, like all the chakras and like the liver itself, deals with cells and tissues. Because this chakra is an energetic organ instead of a physical one, however, it has a broader reach. It also manages the psychic data serving certain emotional, mental, and spiritual concerns.

Energy organs have to move fast enough to catch and disseminate psychic data. They also need to be slow enough to access and transform sensory data. To serve their important functions, all energy organs affect you physically, emotionally, mentally, and spiritually, using psychic and sensory data to ideally create well-being and health.

The Auric Field: The First Line of Psychic Defense

The best-known energy organ is the auric field (or the aura) which consists of graduated layers of light that manage the energy outside your body. The aura can be visualized as a complex layer of energy bodies that surround your entire physical body. The auric layers number twelve in all, and each has a different physical, emotional, mental, and spiritual purpose. All of the auric layers set boundaries, screen psychic data, and regulate your relationship with the outside world.

Artists and other sensitive people have long seen auras, usually as bands of color around a person or other animate being. Angels, Jesus, the Virgin Mary, Krishna, avatars, and the saints are frequently depicted with halos or other glowing lights around their heads or bodies; these lights are depictions of their auras. Indigenous healers from hundreds of cultures have also worked with the aura to perform healings. In contemporary times, certain types of photography can actually capture these auric layers on film. The most well-known process is Kirlian photography, invented in the 1930s and now used by some holistic professionals to perform personality and even disease diagnosis.

Some physicists and scientists believe that the auric field is similar to the electromagnetic (EM) field that surrounds each of us. One particular researcher, Victoria Slater, contends that energetic manipulation or psychic-based healing is nothing more than "consciously regulating what physicists call quantum and EM energy." She sees EM energy itself as frequencies of light waves that carry particles called photons. While we can only see the visible light with our primary senses, Slater asserts that "it is not unreasonable that some will have developed the ability, the skills, or both to see the limited range of visible light into the infrared and ultraviolet ranges."[1]

Psychics who can see the aura usually describe multiple energetic layers, each with a different color or pattern. I, as well as many others, perceive auric layers with my psychic senses. While most psychically gifted people see seven bands of energy, I have pinpointed twelve. I believe the inability to see the higher five bands has to do with cultural programming—we see what we are conditioned to see—as well as training. It's difficult to see the higher vibrations, unless you use your pineal gland, as well as the pituitary gland. Most visual psychic activity is done through the pituitary, but only the pineal gland enables full sensing. Because most societies enable pituitary rather than pineal psychic visioning, it's difficult to obtain information that depends upon pineal viewing. To help you expand your gifts, I reference the pineal as often as possible throughout this book.

Each of the auric layers performs several vital functions, screening and emitting specific types of psychic information-energy. Each layer can be depicted as a certain color, which reflects the frequencies it operates on; is located in a different place; and performs a unique set of functions. The following chart describes the color, location, and function of each auric layer.

Auric Layer	Color	Location	Function
First	Red	In and around skin	Protection of life energies
Tenth	Clear or brown	Outside of the first layer	Mirrors programs, serves as a second self
Second	Orange	Outside of the tenth layer	Screens feelings and emotions
Third	Yellow	Outside of the second layer	Filters ideas and beliefs

Auric Layer	Color	Location	Function
Fourth	Green	Outside of the third layer	Attracts and repels relationships
Fifth	Blue	Outside of the fourth layer	Attracts, repels, and sends guidance
Sixth	Purple	Outside of the fifth layer	Opens to choices, projects decisions
Seventh	White	Outside of the sixth layer	Connects with spirits and Spirit, broadcasts spiritual decisions
Eighth	Black or silver	Outside of the seventh layer	Broadcasts karma and absorbs powers
Ninth	Gold	Outside of the eighth layer	Connects with others based on soul issues
Eleventh	Pink	Linked with the eleventh chakra	Commandeers forces
Twelfth	Clear	Linked with the twelfth chakra	Links with the energy egg; connects our human and divine selves

Each auric layer is in charge of certain psychic frequencies, or information-energy packets. The various layers filter everything from physical sensations to intellectual understandings to others' spiritual beliefs. For instance, the second auric layer filters emotional psychic data. Based upon conscious, unconscious, and subconscious programming, this layer energetically decides what feelings to allow into your body and what feelings to send into the world. Feelings, like all aspects of life, are frequencies. Sadness vibrates at a different rate than does anger or fear. If you are programmed to perceive fear but ignore anger, you can psychically read when someone is scared, but not necessarily notice when someone is angry. (Chapter 4 explores unconscious programs in more detail.)

When all your auric layers are up and running, they are like the offensive line of a football team protecting you, the quarterback, so you can throw the psychic "ball" and gain some yardage in your life. As long as each of your players stays lean and mean, you're protected and able to move forward. Good auric boundaries also ensure that you don't "tip off" the other team, accidentally informing other people of your plans or moves.

Individuals with difficult or crippling psychic sensitivities, however, have poor psychic boundaries. Usually, their auric fields have holes, extended areas, or weak spots—the equivalent of missing members of a football team. Lacking a protective front line, they can't screen out the psychic information that is useless or harmful. Thus, they can't make life happen for them.

The Energy Egg

The energy egg is a three-layered energy body that lies outside of the twelfth auric field. It regulates the flow of spiritual energies into and through the body. The inner layer manages processes that are physical in nature. The middle layer stretches into the realm of possibilities and, based on our programming (see chapter 4), introduces new energies and ideas. The outermost layer reaches far beyond the known dimensions and brings the unknown into our lives.

Chakras: The Control Switches of Psychic Data

The auric layers, the energy bodies around your physical body, connect to **the chakras,** the energy bodies within your physical body, creating a symbiosis between what happens inside and outside of you.

The chakras house your life experiences and conclusions. They are actually circling units of light that regulate your internal body. The word *chakra* comes from Sanskrit meaning "wheel of light." Chakras can process all frequencies of information-energy. Consequently, chakras can convert psychic information-energy to sensory data and back again.

Most of us can't see chakras with our "normal" eyes, because our eyes aren't trained to perceive subtle, faster-moving energies. Richard Gerber, author of *Vibrational Medicine*, notes, "Subtle energies at the etheric level are merely at a higher octave than the physical."[2] Throughout the ages, however, psychic individuals have been able to see beyond the everyday, and they have perceived the chakras.

Hundreds of cultures have worked with a chakra system, and contemporary studies at major universities, including Duke and the University of California, Los Angeles, are actually documenting the existence of chakras. Valerie Hunt of Stanford University, author of *The Science of Human Vibrations*, has produced striking documentation, and healer Rosalyn Bruyere describes applications of Hunt's work in *Wheels of Light*. Bruyere explains that chakras aren't simply New Age or mystical phenomena but actual organs, the sounds and locations of which can be located within the body.[3]

There are dozens—in fact, hundreds—of chakras. The chakras that we'll consider in relation to psychic data include seven based in the body and four of the five around the body. As with the auric bands, I perceive more chakras connected to the body than many other psychic individuals do. Since I was a child, I have been able to see chakras not noticed by other psychics. I could see what I could see because I didn't know I wasn't supposed to! I encourage you to work with the system that is comfortable for you, but to consider the additional chakras, as they provide an incredible depth of natural and spiritual material.

The following is a chart showing the body-based locations, colors, and basic missions of the primary twelve chakras.

Chakra	Color	Location/Body Connection	Governs
First	Red	Genital area, adrenal glands	Security and survival
Second	Orange	Abdomen, ovaries and testes	Feelings and creativity
Third	Yellow	Solar plexus, pancreas	Mentality and structure
Fourth	Green	Heart, heart	Relationships and healing
Fifth	Blue	Throat, thyroid gland	Communication and guidance
Sixth	Purple	Forehead, pituitary gland	Vision and strategy

Seventh	White	Top of the head, pineal gland	Spirituality and purpose
Eighth	Black	Above the head, thymus gland	Karma and universal linkages
Ninth	Gold	Above the eighth chakra, diaphragm	Soul programs and plans
Tenth	Brown	Below the feet, bones	Legacies and nature
Eleventh	Pink	Around hands, feet, and body, connective tissue	Forces and energy conversion
Twelfth	Clear	Around body and thirty-two points in the body	Personal mastery; the ending of human self, access to the energy egg

One of the most important jobs of a chakra is to transfer and translate psychic information-energy between the body, the brain, and the auric field. Based on the programs instilled by your brain and other aspects of yourself into the various chakras, your chakras will determine what messages you're going to give the world and which messages you are going to allow in. If you don't like what's happening in your life and think that the cause might be your psychic boundaries, you must restructure the boundaries in your chakras before your life will change.

I believe that each of the first eleven chakras is paired with a specific layer of the auric field. Information-energy enters our system through the layers of auric field and gravitates to the chakras that run at a similar vibration. These coupled energy bodies are responsible for the eleven main types of psychic sensitivity, or psychic abilities. The twelfth and outermost chakra and auric field is personal to each individual and represents the abilities related to achieving your higher purpose.

Of these chakras, the seven that are based in the body are particularly important because they regulate vital physical functions of our endocrine system, as well as running energetic functions. Think of the seven in-body chakras as prisms. Cosmic energy enters the body and breaks into bands of different colors, each with its own frequency. These separate bands then drift to the chakras that run on equivalent frequencies. The psychic energy "knows" which chakra to enter based on frequency; each chakra deals with certain bands and intensities of vibrations and rejects other frequencies. The information and vibration of the incoming energy strike programmed chords within each receiving chakra, which in turn translates the data for dissemination through the spine and into the brain. The brain decides how to deal with this encoded information and informs the appropriate chakra how to best communicate with the outside world. Packaging a message within a packet of light, the active chakra now refracts the message back into the world. And all of this happens within a split second.

Our programming decides what kinds of psychic information we will pay attention to, as does our spirit, our vital, whole, infinite essence that determines our true self and directs us toward our higher goals.

Each chakra has a front and a back side. The front side is attuned to certain bands of light—those that relate to our external and conscious reality. The back side regulates information from our own unconscious and subconscious, in addition to information from external sources, such as the Divine, other entities, nature, our own soul, and others' unconscious, subconscious, and soul aspects. You might say that our front sides form reality out of what we inadvertently and unknowingly bring in through our back sides.

Each chakra also has two wheels associated with it. The inner wheel is most frequently programmed by spiritual energies and truths from our own spirit. Your spirit always wants the best for you and others. The outer wheel is most affected by issues carried in by our soul and our negative subconscious beliefs, as well as programs indoctrinated by family, culture, religion, and peer groups.

In most cases, incoming psychic energy first meets the outer rim of the outer wheel. Why mainly the outer wheel? Why can we not simply operate from the higher-functioning inner wheel? Unfortunately, our soul believes that it needs to conform to familial, societal, and religious standards in order to assure survival. It thinks, "If I let my spirit take charge, I'll be crucified/killed/ridiculed/ignored/rejected/unloved/unsafe." So rather than letting us operate from the healthier, more spiritual inner wheel, our soul intervenes and forces all incoming psychic messages through the outer wheel. It wants to fit into the "tribal community" and won't leave anything to chance!

Once a psychic message clears the entrance wheel (again, usually the outer), it passes into an empty space in the middle of the chakra, which is linked to a major endocrine gland and to spinal vertebrae. In this way, the information is encoded straight into your hormonal system and fed through the spine to your brain, which reacts and encodes a rebuttal based on programming or memory. The rebuttal is psychically encoded and sent to the middle of the appropriate chakra, which releases this message into the world at large, primarily through the corresponding auric layer. Now others can "read" our psychic response through their own chakra system. Simultaneously, the brain might encode a sensory response, which could appear different than the psychic one. We might verbalize "yes," while we're psychically thinking "no." Our programming might make us believe that we'll be unloved, rejected, appear foolish, or be unsafe if we share our true response. Hence, our thinking will be different than our behavior.

The psychic sensitive tends to be aware of these differences in others, which can result in many challenges. Your "gut sense" says one thing, and your ears hear another. Your "inner knowing" reveals one story, your eyes a different one. These discrepancies can make you feel crazy, like you live in your own reality. The truth is that everyone lives in two realities, the one that they show, and the one that they feel.

More in-depth information about the chakras can be found in my books *The Complete Book of Chakra Healing, Advanced Chakra Healing,* and *The Subtle Body.*

Special Energy Bodies

There are other energy bodies that can be especially useful in intuitive development. **The Akashic Records** are an energy body that contains everything you have ever thought, said, done, felt, or considered throughout time. The Akashic Records also contain **Shadow Records**, which reflect everything you could have been or done in the past and possibilities in the present or the future. The easiest place to access these records is through your eighth chakra.

Where the Akashic Records show you every possible outcome, be it good, bad, or neutral, the Book of Life shows you only the positive experiences and learning gained through everything you have ever done or could ever do and say. It appears as a film that surrounds the Akashic Records, as well as every aspect of the self.

The morphogenetic fields are fields of energy which surround every animated being, body, organ, or cell. Morphogenetic fields link similar beings together and provide a means for sharing information and learning. English biologist Rupert Sheldrake proposes that morphogenetic fields are actually organizing fields that "act across both space and time."[2] They are created from systems or categories of beings, objects, and energies that are similar in critical ways. An animal species is a system, so it has its own morphogenetic field, as does all of humanity. Likewise, a particular family, such as a pack of dogs or a human family group, is a system. The universe, the planet earth, individual continents, and specific population groups also have their own morphogenetic fields. Morphogenetic fields are also capable of shaping and even creating systems.

Exercise 2
Five Steps for Safe Psychic Activity

Here is a five-step method for staying safe when consciously accessing psychic information. I encourage you to learn this method now, as you will be actively using your psychic abilities throughout the remainder of this book's exercises.

Step One: Grounding

Grounding involves rooting your soul in your tenth chakra and, through that energy center, into the earth. When you are traveling around the psychic dimension, being grounded ensures that you are safe because it keeps a part of your soul in your body no matter where the rest of it is flying. Think of your soul as an astronaut journeying outside of his or her spaceship. You want a cord keeping you connected to the ship—or else!

To ground, first close your eyes and focus on your breathing. Bring your attention to your feet. Continue to extend your awareness, which is really your conscious self, out past your feet and even further down into your tenth chakra, which resides about a foot and a half below the ground. Lock into this chakra and feel the strength of the earth's core within your body.

Do this grounding technique when you rise in the morning, when your head touches the pillow at night, and especially when you want to enter any sort of meditative or trance state.

Step Two: Centering

There is a center point to your body, a spot that gravity holds in equilibrium. This same body center point serves as a psychic center; basically, it is the homeostasis point for your chakra system. When you're in your center, there's as much psychic energy above as below you. When you're **centered**, you are in this locus of control. You can't be shaken, because you're balanced and in touch with yourself.

Not everyone has the same center point. The most common center points are the solar plexus or the heart, but I've seen centers as high as the sky and as low as the ground. Your center is determined by your spiritual purpose. If you need to draw from the psychic and sensory strengths of the seventh, eighth, and ninth chakras, for instance, in contrast to the lower ones, your center might be higher—say, in your sixth center—rather than lower, such as in your third center. Conversely, a football player—someone more dedicated to the physical reality governed by the first chakra—might have a lower center, perhaps the second chakra.

To center, take a deep breath in and hold it for a moment. As you exhale, let your awareness/conscious self travel to the center point of your being. If you are reluctant to center, command that your conscious self locate and lock you into your center.

Step Three: Assuming Safety

When you **assume safety**, you are assuming that you are divinely loved and protected—and given the way that energy works, what you assume to be true actually becomes true. When you claim your divinely established right to be safe and secure, your cells and body align with the Divine—and therefore, you are safe!

When you're physically safe, it's safe to be psychically open. Know that your psychic faculties can alert you to physical or psychic danger if need be.

Step Four: Opening

You want your chakras (now safe in the assumption of divine love) to be open at all times. Sometimes they close down. It is natural for them to contract when you are fearful, tired, or angry. When **open**, our chakras can best receive, evaluate, and emit the information-energy required to keep us in tip-top shape.

We often want to receive psychic information in response to a provocative question or to help us with a particular issue. If you follow the first three steps and then set your chakras and auric layers on open for a response, you will eventually attract the required guidance. The Divine (or your gatekeeper, a divinely approved spiritual connection, which you can discover in exercise 5) will send a message, a messenger, and an interpretation. As long as you affirm divine protection and companionship, you can remain open. Then, simply make an effort to notice the information-energy responding to your request.

Step Five: Closing and Protection

Closing

To **close** is to reseal or renew your energetic protection or boundaries. You usually do this after you've prayed, meditated, engaged in contemplation, or operated in an altered state. *Closing* is really a misnomer. You want to seal yourself energetically while keeping your chakras open. Imagine zip-locking yourself into a plastic bag sturdy enough to protect you, but meshed or filtered so you can still absorb and eliminate psychic information-energy.

To close, reassume safety and ask that the Divine (or your gatekeeper) help hold your chakras and auric layers in a state of safety as you continue through life. Often, I close by reaffirming the Divine's protection and imagining a harmonic light around me. You can also use any number of psychic protection techniques based on your particular psychic sensitivities. Protection is a main focus in Part III.

Protection

There are times that we want our intentions, feelings, or perceptions cloaked. Perhaps you're going to be with someone who constantly pries into your business and uses the information against you. Perhaps you believe you're being bothered by a demon or a negative entity, and you don't want to be located. You can, through imaging, commanding, praying, or sensing, disguise either your entire being or a particular aspect of yourself. You can imagine a bubble of light, ask for Divine protection, or simply acknowledge that you deserve to be safe at all times. The easiest technique is to surround yourself with a white or pink light or ask your gatekeeper to protect you (see exercise

5, "Finding a Gatekeeper"). You can personalize your psychic defense through the suggestions in Part III.

Exercise 3
Centering in Your Centers: The Most Effective Energetic Protection

Now that you have grounded, centered, and opened to divine love and protection, you can locate the centers of your chakras and function from these powerhouses.

A chakra has an inner and an outer wheel. The outer wheel, front and backside, holds the programs gathered in this and other lifetimes. It generates the psychic energy that creates our concrete reality. The inner wheel carries our spirit's essential programs. It channels the energy we need to fulfill our spiritual mission and live as our real selves.

The most effective way to break out of a psychic victimization cycle and operate intuitively is to operate from the inner wheels of each chakra. By doing this, the energy of your own spirit merges with the Divine Spirit and bathes the outer wheels with healing energies, thus releasing you from harmful programs. This practice also assures complete psychic protection, as the internal energies will only disseminate messages, attract energies, and interpret data for your highest good. Here is a simple way to start living your life from this wellspring of wholeness.

1. Ground and center.
2. Breathe into the center of your heart (fourth) chakra, consciously directing your self into the innermost sanctum of this energy body.
3. Spend a few minutes bathing in the spirit energy of this centermost place in your heart. How do you feel in here? What types of energies dwell in this heart space?

4. Intuitively observe the outside rim of your heart chakra, noticing the differences between this place of peace and the swirling energies that compose the outer chakra. What types of core beliefs lie within each space? Feelings? Spiritual ideas? Ask yourself: how might my life change if I generate psychic activity from the center of my heart, the inner wheel of my fourth chakra, rather than the outer wheel?
5. If you desire, ask your spirit to enhance the energies of your inner heart chakra wheel. Gently but quickly expand this energy flow in a circular fashion, pushing it outward until you perceive a 360-degree circle of energy around your entire body and throughout your auric field. Watch what happens to the negative programs and energies.
6. Decide to continue this process no matter what. Know that your innermost spirit generates the created energy field with the Divine Spirit's assistance, so it requires no further thought or effort on your part. Rather, this resulting field will work like the sun. It will burn out or deflect harmful energies before they reach your field and will usher in energies supportive of your well-being.
7. Now ask that your heart chakra share this process with all other chakras. Breathe into each chakra until they are all spinning from their centers.
8. Acknowledge that you are now grounded in your own spiritual truths, and breathe your way back into a conscious relationship with your body and the external world.

Chapter 4

Programming: Why You Receive the Psychic Energies You Do

Remember that what you believe will depend very much on what you are.
~Noah Porter

You can buy the best computer in the world, the one with all the bells, whistles, and expensive price tags, but all the pretty packaging doesn't do a thing for you unless you've installed software that makes it work—and work for you. A professional ball player isn't going to get much use out of a program that helps a writer create romance novels; neither will tomorrow's bestselling fiction author get far if working with a program for getting to bat.

The basis of all psychic issues—whether the problem lies in your auric field, your chakras, or any other energy body—is in your programming. A **program** is a belief that controls our thoughts, emotions, activities, and reactions to life events. **Programming** determines your sense of self, your sense of the world around you, and therefore, your actions. If our psychic communication runs on a program such as "I am a good person," we will attract sensory and psychic information that supports our well-being. We will make decisions that fortify us and allow us to prosper.

And we will probably like other people; if we think that we are essentially good, then we'll grant grace to others. But how about a program like, "I am bad"? Think of the psychic data you'll attract if you believe you are a bad person. If someone else is thinking a negative thought—even if it's not about you—you'll think it's about you, and that thought will support your low self-image. You'll magnetically attract friends, bosses, companions, and situations that further convince you that you are bad. Thinking you are bad, you might act badly and create additional complications in your life.

Using our football analogy from chapter 3, imagine that one of your opponent's receivers is headed down the field, carrying the football and hoping to make a touchdown. You want to block him and are in position to do so, but he flashes a psychic note at you saying, "You're stupid." This message completely debilitates you, and you stop in your tracks, unable to block him. Someone else might not have read the psychic message, much less perceived that there even was one. However, because your dad always called you stupid when you were growing up, you are susceptible to sensory or psychic words of that sort. The auric layer governing mental messages was unable to screen out the message, and because of your sensitivity, you and your team lost the opportunity to score.

Childhood violations, negative family beliefs, ungodly spiritual dogmas, and stuck emotions can all work together to keep your auric layers from filtering unwanted psychic information. Because your aura lets information *out,* as well as takes it *in*, auric holes, weak areas, or deficits may be both attracting negativity and leaking positive energy. The bottom line is that if you're psychically telling yourself that you're stupid, you might be psychically telling the world the same thing.

Whatever programs run your life will run your psychic responses. Negative programs are the ones that create the psychic victimization cycle

Our programming sets rules for our psychic powers, and negative programming means we will attract information, people, and events that reestablish the so-called truth of the programs. Therefore, programs lead to **patterns**, which are set ways of reacting. These patterns can severely restrict our personal growth, success, and happiness. You have to change the program to change the pattern.

Let's take a look at different types of energetic programming that can affect your psychic boundaries.

Beliefs: The Energy that Sets Direction

At the most fundamental level, the accuracy, effectiveness, and usage of the psychic reduce to the matter of beliefs. You are what you believe.

If you believe that you are a good person, you will psychically attract people and situations that will support that point of view. And guess what? You'll probably have a pretty good life. If you believe that you are a bad person, you will attract people and experiences that underscore your belief. You will have a pretty bad time of it in life. Of course, there's a limit to the power of belief. I might believe that I am a bee or a ballerina, but my belief won't help me sprout wings or stand *en pointe*. Still and yet, thinking I'm a bee or ballerina will certainly shape my life and actions!

Beliefs are the programs or concepts that run our minds and brains. They are the cornerstones of communication, and everything in life depends upon communication. Our mind depends upon beliefs to make instant decisions, just as the energy bodies depend upon beliefs for psychic communication.

In and of themselves, beliefs aren't bad. They are useful. Having the belief that "hot things are dangerous" saves us time, energy, and repeated pain. Once this belief is locked within your system, your psychic and sensory senses will perceive heat of a hot stove and tell your body to protect itself. Your psychic senses can even alert you if you leave a stove burner or an iron on when you leave the house. Thinking, however, that all hot items can hurt you is a harmful belief. What if it prevents you from ever using a stove for cooking? (Okay, that might not be the worst thing in the world.) What if it keeps you from enjoying a sunny day or helping your child if her clothes have caught on fire? Beliefs can be dangerous if applied universally or misapplied in the wrong situations.

There are positive and negative applications of beliefs. Many therapies involve analyzing self-destructive behavior to uncover the errant beliefs underneath. The idea is that if you change the detrimental belief, you can more easily change a negative behavior. The trouble with this approach is that it is endless. There might be a thousand beliefs woven throughout a fear of flying, for instance—anything from "It's bad to be out of control" to "Airplanes can crash; therefore, any airplane I am on will crash." *Much psychic sensitivity reflects inaccurate or negative beliefs.* Why would we keep tuning into others' negativity unless we held a belief, a program, that made us do so?

Through my own process and in working with sensitive clients, I have found that all belief systems reduce down to two fundamental beliefs, one accurate and one not, and six add-on beliefs, which can be framed as positive or negative. The two fundamental beliefs are:

I am love.
I am separate.

From the two universal beliefs, we create these secondary ones:

Belief	Negative Aspect	Positive Aspect
Worthiness	I am unworthy.	I am worthy.
Deserving	I don't deserve.	I do deserve.
Power	I am powerless.	I am powerful.
Value	I have no value.	I am valuable.
Love	I am not lovable.	I am lovable.
Goodness	I am bad (or evil).	I am good.

When we believe ourselves to be made of love, we are open to the Divine and the endless succession of energy and light that fuels our bodies. Science is showing that the body runs on the flow of photons, wave particles of light that generate from our DNA and infuse our entire bodies with healing energy. Disturb the flow of photons and the result is illness. I believe that photons (and their subunits, which I call rabbits) are encoded with the basic message of creation, which is love. We are literally made of and fed by the love that began the universe. If we know this truth, we will work with the positive aspects of the six secondary beliefs, all of which stimulate the inner wheel of our chakras and our spiritual programs. Our psychic activity and communication will support our true selves and authentic interaction with the world; thus, we will enjoy rich, fruitful, and prosperous lives.

Thinking ourselves separate from the Divine, we interrupt the flow of photons needed for health and vitality and for clear and accurate thinking. The resulting fear and shame lead to negative perceptions and distorted thinking, which in turn sets us up to attract and disseminate untruths. Our psychic senses will, therefore, attract people, experiences, and problems that resonate with the negative aspects of the six secondary beliefs, all of which feed off the initiating thought "I am separate."

Beliefs provide consistency. Because an accepted belief becomes automatically triggered by certain stimuli, it keeps you from having to recreate all the decisions and thoughts associated with it. But when they become rigid, or they generate from the negative aspects of the secondary beliefs, they become mental or emotional strongholds.

Mental Strongholds: The Prison of Paired Beliefs

Mental strongholds are beliefs that keep us from thinking, acting, or reacting independently. A mental stronghold is made of two or more beliefs that are glued together and remain partnered long after the event that bonded them. A mental stronghold will keep you imprisoned, psychically and physically, in walls as concrete as those of a jail.

Let's say that your first dating companion broke up with you. What are you going to think? Well, one thought might be, "I'm in love." The second thought is, "My lover hurt me." Both are true statements. Knowing that you are in love and that your lover hurt you can actually help you process what happened and, over time, move on. But what happens if you keep these two ideas cemented together and from them form a third opinion, such as, "Being in love hurts." Chances are that you'll continually protect your heart from love and choose only unloving partners. You'll never get "hurt" again, but neither will you love again! You have just adopted one of the secondary negative beliefs, that correlates to love, and, in turn, establishes separation between you and others.

The resulting wall you put around your heart is constructed of thoughts, which are made of psychic energy. No matter how much therapy you undergo, you won't loosen the bonds that secure you. No matter how hard you try, you'll continue to send psychic messages to the world that reinforce the mental stronghold. You'll send away potential lovers before you even meet them! And chances are, you'll attract people guaranteed to hurt you in your relationship because both your and their psychic programs call for it.

A mental stronghold isn't only going to affect your daily life. It will alter your way of being on every level of reality. As I explore in my book *Advanced Chakra Healing*, you exist on four separate levels of reality simultaneously. These four levels of awareness, called pathways, hold your ability to function physically, supernaturally, creatively, and through your divine nature. Thoughts that imprison you in one arena might very well limit you in every other. Believing yourself undeserving of love from human beings, you might refuse the love of the Divine, allow your imagination to create reality-based nightmares, and attract supernatural entities more than happy to victimize you. Mental strongholds inform your psychic self at every level, which is why it's so important to weed out the negative ones and reinforce the positive.

Emotional Strongholds: When Feelings Hurt Us

There is another form of stronghold that is just as potent and potentially destructive as a mental stronghold. **Emotional strongholds** are similar to mental strongholds, but with one major difference. Whereas mental strongholds are composed of at least two beliefs, emotional strongholds are made of at least one belief and one feeling.

There are five basic feeling constellations. They are happiness, fear, anger, sadness, and disgust.

Each of these basic feelings serves as a vital fuel for your body. Each carries a message from your inner self to your conscious self, instructing you about a need. The basic messages of the feelings are:

Happiness: Keep doing what you are doing. It is bringing you love.

Fear: Stop! Slow down or speed up, go forward or backward, or get out of the way altogether. Something is happening that isn't good for you.

Anger: Put up a boundary. Something or someone is violating a basic boundary, and you must deal with it.

Sadness: Look for love. You are sad because you perceive a lack of love. Look for the love in the situation, and you will regain joy.

Disgust: Spit it out. You have consumed or been exposed to a poison—a toxic idea, property, food, or person. Get rid of it.

When we join two or more feelings together, we create an emotion. The word *emotion* presents us with a formula: *e* equals "energy" and *motion* equals "movement." Emotions, therefore, energize you into movement. They are the gas that makes a kid run if he or she has broken a window playing baseball. They are the force that makes you say "No way!" to someone who mistreats you. They are the propellant that says "Great!" when you're offered a raise. But emotions create disruption if the feelings involved stick together past their "expiration date"—past the original time or situation for which they were needed.

Let's say you are a child. What might happen if Mom is fired from a job, but instead of looking for work, she stays home and drinks. You are going to have any number of feeling-reactions. Typical ones might be fear and anger. You are scared about money and wonder if you will soon run out of food, and you are angry that your mom isn't doing anything to remedy the situation. These are normal and healthy feelings. The fear tells you that something has to change, and the anger tells you that your mom isn't being a good parent.

The problem is that you might join these feelings with any number of thoughts (and not always rational or helpful ones). Instead of thinking, "My mom should be more responsible," you may think, "My mom doesn't love me; that's why she is drinking." You've now partnered fear and anger with the thought of being unloved. From this point onward, you will tend to interpret others' self-destructive patterns as pertaining to you. You will think they are acting poorly because they don't love you. Every time someone is being self-destructive, you will be hooked into fear and anger. The kicker is that whenever you feel both fear and anger, you might assume that everyone around you is being unloving to you!

Regarding psychic activity, emotional strongholds will cause you to attract and send out information-energy that tells the world to support your internal lie. Using our example, your psychic centers will actually tell the world that you aren't lovable, that you only deserve to be treated poorly. You'll attract situations that create impoverishment, and stimulate fear and anger. You'll perceive others as always sending you unloving messages, which in turn will make you angry or scared—but you won't know why!

The world of the supernatural is full of forces and entities that would love to keep you angry, because they literally feed off anger. You might experience nightmares in which entities or ghosts threaten or scare you, or voices instruct you to hurt yourself or your mother. The self that is capable of creative magic might imagine all sorts of troubles. "If Mom doesn't love me," you think, "how can anyone else?" You won't trust loving people, but because you're comfortable with alcoholism, you'll attract friends or mates that abuse alcohol. Mistrusting your mother, you might refuse any notion of a feminine aspect of the Divine, perhaps idealizing only the male version of the Divine so predominate in the world or disavowing the idea of a Higher Power altogether. If the Divine didn't save me from my mother, how can there be one?

When we internalize or create strongholds, we train our energy system to operate negatively in life situations. The Universe, or the Divine, is designed to adapt to us. When we hold onto programs and patterns that support separation-based beliefs, the Universe complies by providing us situations that reinforce our beliefs. It isn't that the Universe is bad or wants to see us suffer; the Universe is benign and non-judgmental. We have free will, and if we want to think of ourselves as bad, the Universe will let us, though the Universe/the Divine won't think of us that way or judge us for it.

As long as you operate from either mental or emotional strongholds, your psychic senses will continue to reinforce the negativity that, consciously or unconsciously, you've come to regard as true. Either stronghold enables a dysfunctional energetic program that can carry into every situation of your life: the codependent bargain, which is a type of energy cord.

The Codependent Bargain: A Classic Energy Cord

The psychic transforms into the physical. All strongholds eventually lead to the development of an energetic prison of both psychic and physical energies that lock us into our mental or emotional aberrations. The most dangerous of these energetic structures is called the **codependent bargain**, a term used first by Cathryn Taylor in her book *The Inner Child Workbook*. Seen energetically, a codependent bargain is a certain type of energy cord that costs the holder everything and the recipient nothing. An **energy cord** is a tube of energy that transfers information from one person or place to another. Psychically, cords look like garden hoses. They usually represent agreements or an understanding between two people and are usually limiting and destructive in nature.

For instance, a newborn child might subconsciously perceive that he is unwanted by his mother. The child's subconscious might forge an energetic agreement with the same part of his mother, using psychic communication to negotiate and seal the contract. The child might psychically say, "Mom, I'll take on your emotions, and in exchange, I'll give you my life energy." Mom psychically agrees. She's getting rid of her negative and scary feelings and, in return, receiving an endless source of energy. Why would a child even subconsciously agree to this loss of life energy? He subconsciously perceives that Mom might not even feed him if he doesn't become a source of strength.

On the energetic plane, agreements like this result in an energy cord. The baby receives Mom's unacceptable feelings and loses his life energy. Like strongholds, a cord might be only a temporary problem, but once established it is seldom released. The child is now setting up a lifelong pattern. Until this cord is transformed or broken, he will continually absorb his mom's feelings and give away his power; not only that, he will transfer this cord into other primary relationships and in all likelihood form the same agreement with employers, mates, and even children.

Cords determine the flow of our psychic energy. As our infant grows, this patterned response to relationships will cause him to refuse others' positive feelings while absorbing their undesirable ones. Though help is present, the growing child will reject it—and probably won't even perceive he is doing so! Instead, he will attract circumstances that continually weaken him. His chakras and auric layers will gather psychic data that reinforces this corded commitment. Thus, cords lead to the psychic victimization cycle by their very nature.

There are a few cords that are healthy. When pregnant, a mother unconsciously creates an energy cord between her womb space and the child's lower energy centers. While feeding the baby physical nutrients through the umbilical cord, Mom also transfers information, teaching, wisdom, and love through the energetic cord. She also perceives the pulse of the child's heart and thoughts through this cord. This incoming psychic information helps her to adapt to the child and supply it with all its needs.

When the child is born, this first energy cord is the basis of an intense emotional and spiritual bond. Because of it, the mother is alert as to the child's feelings and needs. She can sense when the child is endangered or threatened, no matter the physical distance between them. The child, too, develops a necessary trust in its mother, which is later applicable to all relationships. The cord disintegrates to 75 percent intensity when the child is three months old, to about 50 percent at six months, to about 25 percent at eighteen months, and then finally falls away between the ages of three and four. During these first years, the father's energy primarily enters through the mother's cord, making him a secondary figure in the child's life. As the mother's cord falls away, the father, if present, forms an increasingly personal relationship with the child and, therefore, becomes more directly influential. (In the case of absent fathers, lack of presence is also an influence, often leading to abandonment issues and pain, and ultimately to the child questioning why the father doesn't love him.)

Frequently, however, the mother either pulls more energy from the child than she returns or shoves her problems and issues into the child. Some mothers never release the energetic bond, creating a smothering effect. Sometimes, such as when the woman plans to give up her child for adoption, she psychically prepares for the upcoming trauma of separating from her newborn by never establishing an energy cord; as a result, the child usually has lifelong deprivation or abandonment issues. Sometimes the mother never psychically releases the child to the adoptive parents, and the natal energy cord stays in place, so the child always feels like something—or someone—is missing.

The cord or codependent bargain, seen through an energetic viewfinder, is established when we give away energy because we want something back. However, we don't get something back. Instead of backing out of the deal, we give more, thinking that will solve the problem. And we still don't get anything back. This effort leads to a loss of energy, despair, resentment, and unrealistic expectations. In the case of our infant, his mother is more than happy to take his life energy, but the nature of the agreement makes it impossible for her to meet her end of the bargain and love him unconditionally. The problem is that she doesn't unconditionally love her child! No amount of energy or input from this baby is going to change that. If she wants to learn how to love him, she's got to make the decision herself. Bribery, quite simply, doesn't work.

The child, however, thinks it will. In fact, no matter our age, if we're making codependent bargains, you can bet we believe they will work. And they don't. We give everything and get nothing back.

The real danger of these bargains or cords is that over time, they sublimate into our own energy system. We don't even need a partner to keep our bargain going because we uphold it within ourselves! As baby becomes Junior, he subconsciously folds this agreement into his own body. He thinks, "I'll keep giving my energy away (to people, things, places, and concerns I don't care about), but I'll never give myself unconditional love." This inner agreement now programs all his psychic undertakings. Because he won't give himself unconditional love, he won't attract or accept it from outside of himself. The psychic activity he does allow will be unloving, cruel, and will rob him of energy.

If you were stuck in a psychic victimization cycle, I would guess you have at least one cord, one codependent bargain. Lovingly dealing with this bargain will make more difference in your psychic health than anything else.

By examining for mental and emotional strongholds, as well as energetic cords and codependent bargains, you can go far in setting yourself free from negativity that might enforce a victimization cycle.

The Programming of the Spirit

Beliefs cause all our problems. Then again, beliefs can also do the opposite. They can open us to the heaven that continually enfolds us all. By examining the energetic nature of beliefs, you begin to see that everything comes down to **spirituality**, the expression of our spirit into the world.

There are many parts to each of us, and each part runs on a program of beliefs. Beliefs influence each aspect of yourself: your spirit, soul, mind, and body.

Your spirit is your core essence or self, that part of you that expresses a unique and well-defined spiritual truth. It's your job to express this truth through all that you do, in order to create more heaven on earth. This expression constitutes your **destiny**. The spiritual truth that defines your purpose or destiny is really a belief. This belief is encoded into every aspect of your being. If you access this core belief and only those beliefs that align with it, your psychic abilities will always reflect the Divine and your own divine nature. They will access only information-energy that will bring you closer to your spiritual destiny and disseminate only psychic information-energy that will allow others to support your destiny. You have the choice, however. You can believe either what your spirit knows or what the world teaches. Your spirit, always connected to the Divine, retains the pristine picture of destiny, no matter what happens to other parts of you.

Your soul is the part of you that moves through time and space, collecting experience. While your spirit knows all energy as spiritual, your soul can separate sensory from psychic energy. While the soul carries all the information needed for destiny to be expressed in sensory reality, the soul can also be wounded. The wounding and damage sustained by the soul affects your choice of beliefs, emotional health, relationship choices, and everyday actions in the sensory world. Negative soul programming can also prevent you from psychically accessing the information or guidance needed to achieve your destiny. In addition, negative soul programming can block the spiritual forces required for you to assert yourself in a purposeful life.

Your mind is an extension of your soul. It plays an integral role in the selection of your beliefs. There are many parts to your mind, managing both the sensory and psychic systems. You have a higher mind, which links to spirit, your consciousness, and the higher learning processes in your brain; a middle mind, which connects you to your unconscious and daily self and to the mammalian parts of your brain, which, in turn, manage your emotions and thoughts; and a lower mind, which links to your soul and subconscious and the reptilian section of your brain, which, in turn, regulates your limbic system and the fight-or-flight reactions in your body.

Your body is the physical expression of your spirit, soul, and mind. Ideally, it is an extension of the Divine and the mirror of your spirit. In everyday reality, the body is also programmed by your soul and run by your mind. Soul damage and strongholds can keep your body from linking with your spirit, which can warp natural psychic sensitivities, prevent wise use of psychic abilities, or perhaps prevent you from using them at all.

Spiritual Genetics and Spiritual Gifts

If your spirit were allowed to run the show, your psychic abilities would guarantee success. Psychic energy would link your physical chromosomes to your **seed of destiny**, a set of energy structures and constructs that would, if opened and vitalized by the Divine, program your body to match your spirit. This seed is similar to a collection of chromosomes or genes wrapped within an energetic nucleus. It holds your **spiritual genetics**, which are similar to your physical genes except that they regulate all the spiritual forces and abilities you need to achieve your destiny. As the spiritual genes activate, so do your psychic gifts. By age twenty-one, you are pretty much prepared to begin your life path. At this point, the seed-of-destiny genes fully awaken within your body, as does the spiritual truth that you represent. Now you can fully access all your psychic abilities, which are customized to carry out your purpose. Now you can live in the seventh sense! (You can read more about the seed of destiny and other related energetic bodies in my book, *Advanced Chakra Healing*.)

If you were to really activate your psychic senses this way, each chakra would unfold a **spiritual gift**, a transformed psychic ability that enables psychic energy to support your spiritual purpose. I also call these gifts the genius gifts, as they enable you to be the genius you really are! You won't have need of every type of spiritual gift, as you are here on earth for a specific purpose. Why activate the ability to paint paintings if you're a construction worker? If your life purpose calls for a great deal of physical strength, you'll probably have a strong first chakra, which is in charge of physicality. The psychic gifts associated with this chakra will also be intense. (See chapter 10 for more on how psychic and intuitive abilities become spiritual gifts.)

Your chakras are designed to always use the psychic. They will transform from a sixth-sense means of using psychic energy to a seventh-sense usage as you mature. Even after your spiritual transformation, you would still display stronger and weaker spiritual gifts, according to your destiny.

Want to Know What Really Happens?

Unfortunately, most of us never get to the seventh-sense stage because we're stuck in the drama of negativity. Negative energies and strongholds keep us from transforming our psychic gifts into spiritual gifts, the sixth sense into the seventh sense. They also keep us from activating our seed of destiny and, therefore, living a purposeful and fulfilling life.

A false belief is any thought or concept that fails to match the spiritual truth carried in your spirit or fails to align with divine truths. These lies can come from millions of sources. Most common are:

- Genealogical patterns of hatred and failure
- Issues and misperceptions carried within your own soul
- Cultural prejudices and standards
- Lies modeled or taught by your family
- Untruths taught by various institutions, including school, the media, and religion
- Genetic influences and cellular memories
- Personal interpretations of life events
- Deceit from psychic sources, such as entities or other energetic influences

These various forms of negative beliefs convince us we have no right to own our spiritual destiny, to use powerful psychic forces for good, to apply our imagination to change reality, or to access the Divine directly. We might not even feel deserving of our psychic gifts or be willing to fully use them! The power of belief can prevent us from becoming our real selves.

The good news is that you can do something about it. By becoming intuitive rather than psychic, you invite the transformational process that leads to the goal—your true self. You are invited into the world of the chakras and the gifts of your spirit. You are invited into your true self.

Exercise 4

Your Psychic Difficulties

This exercise is designed to help you uncover what might have occurred in your life to adversely affect your psychic boundaries. While not conclusive, it might help you begin to see what you are sensitive to and why. Pay special attention to figuring out if your problems might arise from mental or emotional strongholds, codependent bargains (energy cords), or a mix of these. By perceiving what has caused you problematic psychic programs, you can take the right steps to heal yourself.

Part One

Get a paper and pen or, if you prefer, coloring tools. Ground and center and assume divine protection (see exercise 2). Now ask the Divine to bring you into an energy body called the Akashic Records.

We will further explore this energy body in chapter 6, in the section about chakra eight. (A definition of these records can also be found in chapter 3.) For now, know the Akashic Records are the place within yourself that holds the information about everything you've ever done, said, or thought. It is the place of your story, the tale of how you came to be whom and what you are.

Assume the Divine in holding you in this place. Now ask to read or be shown an experience that clearly overloaded or damaged your psychic boundaries or has caused your psychic sensitivities. The answer may come in the form of a memory of your childhood, or it may involve a story with characters you've never met. In the Akashic Records you are accessing all time, and you may be glimpsing a past life, long forgotten, in which you shut down your gifts. While watching or reading this experience, assume the role of neutral observer. Refrain from assessing, judging, or evaluating what you learn for the next few minutes. Just watch and listen. Record your experience with your writing or drawing materials.

Part Two

It's time to evaluate your story and draw conclusions from it. How could you have responded differently to the wounding experiences? Could you have left a bad situation? Not blamed yourself? Expressed your feelings? Discussed your feelings with someone else? Composed different beliefs? Called on an authority figure or the Divine in the midst of the trauma? Dealt with the problem yourself instead of waiting for intervention? Or were you too young to do anything at all? If necessary, forgive yourself for any misguided behavior.

Know that the purpose of reexamining these situations is not to blame or shame yourself or other people. It's to really look at what's happened to you from an adult perspective. Some of us get trapped in a psychic victimization cycle because we couldn't see the choices available to us when we were younger. After all, we were young! Some of us erroneously believe that we could have stopped or changed a situation that we really couldn't control. Either way, the truth is that life is different now than it was. By perceiving a situation accurately, through mature eyes, we can better see the choices available to us today.

Part Three

Look back at the experience you just described and qualify it. Was this violation primarily physical, emotional, mental, or spiritual? Did it primarily result in a mental or an emotional stronghold, and if so, what were the beliefs or feelings that were involved? Did you create a codependent cord, and if so, with whom or what? How did this situation and your perceptions of it affect your psychic gifts, your psychic boundaries, and your perceptions of yourself as a spiritual being?

Part Four

When you feel that you fully understand the situation and your reaction to it, decide if you are ready for healing. To heal is to make whole. The truth is that you are whole and have always been whole, but in failing to realize it, you haven't been able to act accordingly. What might it mean to be "made whole" following this experience? How might your psychic abilities now return to greatness or be transformed in order to provide you with healing? After making your decision, resume the five steps of safe psychic activity (see exercise 2) and ask the Divine to establish safe psychic parameters for daily life.

Part II

Preparing to Be Intuitive

Chapter 5

Discernment: Following the Path of Safe Travel

> *I don't want to see them, my feet are cold. What do I want seeing stars for?*
> ~Niall Williams, *The Fall of Light*

The ancient Greeks had a story about a great and famous man named Daedalus. An inventor, Daedalus fashioned wings of wax with which to journey across the seas. Leaving Crete on wings one day, he brought his son, Icarus, with him on his sojourn.

Though Daedalus understood the virtue of caution, he had forgotten the impetuousness of youth. In awe of his newfound power to fly, Icarus began to wonder just how high the sky might be. As his curiosity and daring drove him higher and higher, Daedalus called to him, warning him to fly lower. But Icarus continued upward, until he was too close to the sun. The heat melted his wax wings, and he tumbled to his end.

Aren't we all a little like Icarus, wanting to fly higher and higher—until we too are burned? Being too psychic is a little like flying too close to the sun's flames. Psychic information-energy is real energy. Energy creates everything on this earth and in the heavens—including fire. Lacking solid psychic boundaries, we can easily burn ourselves with others' psychic energy, or hurt them with our own. This is where discernment comes in.

In this chapter, we're going to discuss the basics of discernment, the art of learning intuitive control and boundaries. We're all different. My psychic boundaries will operate a little differently than yours. However, there are basics that everyone can and must learn in order to benefit from, rather than be hurt by, psychic energy. At the end of this chapter are exercises to assist you in assessing your own discernment needs and conducting safe psychic communication for daily and meditative purposes.

The Value of Discernment

The worlds of psychic reality are many and varied, bold and beautiful. Psychic sensitivity is our means of soaring in and between different levels of reality and our own imaginations. But doing so can be dangerous, if we don't follow the rules.

Many people wonder where the rules are supposed to come from. From an external authority? From an internal sense? From the Divine? The truth is that safety rules come from all sorts of sources, external and internal, from the natural and the spiritual planes. And no, you don't have to believe in the Divine to be an ethical or spiritual person. Rather, you need only acknowledge your intrinsically personal values, as well as the fact that, as a human being, you are a communal being. What others do affects you. What you do affects others. To be safe and to invite safety for others, the psychic sensitive absolutely must develop and live within a set of standards that invites goodness for all. This involves discernment.

To **discern** is to understand something that is not at first clear or obvious. The **act of discernment** often involves distinguishing between two or more choices in order to decide what is fitting. The **laws of discernment** are about how we treat our own selves and others when it comes to using psychic data and energy. These laws ultimately boil down to being kind, supportive, honest, and loving.

When you fly, you don't want to worry about landing too hard—or in the wrong place. This means it's important to learn the rules of flying. The ground below is as hard as the sun is hot above. You need to know how to discern—how to quickly and easily make decisions that enable safety and love for all.

Let's look at the kind of character traits that attract the Icarus within us to danger:

- Over-eagerness: Icarus's eagerness led to a rash mistake.
- Lack of planning or forethought: Icarus charged off into the sky without thinking ahead to the potential consequences.
- Pride: Icarus assumed that he could handle anything that came his way.
- Failure to self-monitor: In contemporary terms, Icarus was out of touch with himself. He was so excited, he ignored the increasing heat and his father's concern as he rose higher and higher.
- Refusal to take others' advice: Daedalus wisely cautioned Icarus, but the boy didn't listen.
- Love of the thrill: Like many of us, Icarus loved the power, the control, and the zing of getting his own way or living on the edge. This thrill is seductive, but ultimately unsustainable.

Discernment is not about being judgmental. **Psychic discernment** is actually a process that leads you out of judgments held about yourself or others. To psychically discern, you must first be okay with deciding what thoughts and actions hold integrity for you, not just for other people. After finding this clarity, you can then decide what actions you need to take or want others to take.

The Role of Integrity and Altruism

An apple pie that is missing a slice isn't whole anymore. It lacks integrity. If that same apple pie were given a slice of pecan pie to fill in the missing piece, it would still lack integrity with itself. There's a piece of something not like itself in the middle of it. To have **psychic integrity** means that you are using your psychic abilities to:

- Better define and become your true self.
- Get rid of energies that don't fit with your true self.
- Fill up with energies that reflect your true self.

Your true self is your spirit. You are here to express your spirit. If a teacher or role model, or a system of knowing such as tarot cards, actually helps you better define and become your own spirit—great! If they no longer lead you further into your real self, then you have to stop consulting them.

To lack psychic integrity is to disavow your spiritual nature. You are refuting your strengths. You are allowing others to put a slice of pecan pie into your apple-pie self! If you use your psychic abilities to manipulate others, you are underscoring the mental stronghold, "I am more than." You are refusing to heal places where you are weak or hurt. You are pretending that you are a pecan pie when you are an apple pie. Lacking integrity, you ultimately fail to take care of yourself. You also fail to live up to your responsibility to others.

The other side of integrity is **altruism**, the unselfish regard for others' needs. An altruistic person is devoted to others' welfare. At first thought, altruism could cause problems to psychic sensitives. Isn't "giving ourselves away" how most of us psychic sensitives get into so much trouble in the first place? But if we act like our true selves, we'll be expressing our spiritual truths. We will naturally act, talk, and feel altruistically toward others. Put in a psychic context, altruism screens psychic sources or information that doesn't fit with our true self. Being psychically altruistic also forces us to send or disseminate only psychic messages that are good for others.

Altruism often follows an intense spiritual experience. A **spiritual experience** is one that forces us to look beyond our programs, patterns, and strongholds to our true spiritual nature for answers and greater truths. Spiritual experiences aren't always fun. Sometimes they come in the form of a job loss, a bout with illness, the death of a loved one, or a divorce. I have a friend who says that most good change occurs after a spiritual *breakthrough*, which can all too often seem very similar to a spiritual *breakdown*. Science will tell you, however, that you have to break apart a current order to create a new or healthy order. Sometimes we have to tear ourselves apart all the way to our foundation if we're going to move our base and start over. And if we've built our life on sand, our foundation is unstable and will usually come apart whether we want it to or not.

Life hands all of us ample opportunities to grow spiritually—to move from the psychic to the intuitive, from the intuitive to the spiritual. The consciousness that most call God is unconditionally accepting and loving. We can learn about life—and love—any way that we want. Once we stop searching through the wreckages of our lives—or thinking that others are the wrecking crew—we're ready to get down to it and accept the responsibility for creating our own lives.

Like Icarus, though, we have choices. We can choose to accept responsibility or not. We can choose to learn from our mistakes or make them again. We can learn to read the signs or ignore them and end up falling to the ground. Anything is acceptable; there are simply paths that are more or less enjoyable.

If we really want to be integrated, to lead lives of altruistic integration, we need to become discerning. Discernment is the key to leaving behind the psychic victimization cycles and writing our own life stories.

A Matter of Source

A **psychic source** is exactly what it sounds like: the origin of psychic material. There are many types of energies and beings that can contact or communicate with you. They might be animate or inanimate, aware and conscious (whether dead or alive) or not. They include:

Entities: beings with a soul, but not a body or form. Entities might also be called *spirits*. (In this book, I use the word *spirit,* in singular form, to describe the eternal, divine aspect of the self.)

Ghosts: souls of deceased people or animals that linger in this world because they didn't finish what they wanted to when alive, are angry and want justice, still want to serve or protect the living but are afraid to die, or don't know that they are dead.

Phantoms: beings that appear in this world from another plane. This world is like a movie screen, and they simply project an image of themselves onto it.

Energies: the charges that compose anything, inanimate or animate, and make it recognizable. For instance, a living plant emanates electromagnetic charges. After it dies, the space it used to occupy can still reverberate with these charges. A living person is composed of countless energetic charges and can be discerned from all other beings by his or her unique set of charges, even after death. When using the word *energies,* most psychics are referring to the sense, feeling, or impression of the charges involved, rather than the tangible presence of something.

Consciousness beings: animate beings that operate in waveform only, like liquid colors or lights. They usually represent a certain cause or belief system. An example is someone like a Martin Luther King, Jr., who, upon death, might be offered the job of continuing his mission by serving as a spiritual guide. These beings often appear as balls of light rather than human in form.

Demons: energies, entities, or beings that hurt others or prey upon others to serve their own ends.

Angels: a class of beings that have spirits but no souls, unless they choose to incarnate in a body. There are many subgroups of angels, including **archangels**, which are a master class; **power angels**, which convert material energy into spiritual energy; **shining ones**, which transform heavenly energy into physical energy; and various teams of angels that provide assistance for specific ends, such as the **clean-up angels**, which perform repair services after you've been injured by negative beings.

Beings from the Natural: All nature beings have personal spirits, but they also connect into a greater, group spirit that holds the template for all of their kind. Some, but not all, also have souls. Think of two tigers. One might be a spirit only, keyed into the greater group spirit of "tiger." It wouldn't have a personal mission or sense of self; rather, it would perform in a purely "tiger" manner. The second tiger might also have a soul, as it desires to serve a specific mission. It would, therefore, have a highly developed personality and employ this for a higher end. Thus, it would exhibit behaviors that aren't normal for "tiger," in addition to typical tiger behaviors.

Natural beings include **devas**, natural spirits that work with plants, animals, and the elements to help the natural world grow and repair; the **elementals**, fire, water, air, metal, earth, wood, stone, light, ether, and star beings that provide healing and guidance; **totems** or **power guides**, which represent the spiritual nature of various animals, reptiles, and birds and help specific people with specific needs; and various other natural beings and forces.

Planetary beings: guides from—and in—the stars, other planets, and space itself and that provide guidance and love.

Masters: living or dead beings who assist humans according to a certain specialty or perform a specific type of service. They may or may not have ever been alive.

Avatars: beings that retain their body but didn't die in order to keep it. One example is Elijah, a prophet from the Old Testament. He rose to the heavens without dying, thereby retaining his physical body even while leaving the earth plane.

Aspects of the self: subparts to our personalities, including the **spirit** or eternal and always-healthy self; the **soul**, the part of the self that accrues learning—and injury—through experiences, lifetime after lifetime; the **mind**, the aspect of self that holds beliefs and thoughts; and the **body**, which is the sensory self. (See chapter 4 for more on these aspects of our selves.)

Within the body and affecting all other aspects of the self are other component selves, including **inner children**, aspects of ourselves that are usually still held within a traumatic situation and require rescue and healing; **innocent children**, representing the childhood we would have had if we hadn't been injured; the **God self**, the inner self that knows it is a child of the Divine and can live from that belief; the **primal self**, representing our basic physical nature and survival needs; the **ego**, which reinforces our personal identity and needs (also called the personality); the **master self**, which understands and has already fully completed our soul mission; and the **higher self**, which links with our spirit.

The most personally beneficial and present sources fall into the category of **spiritual guides**, entities or forms of energy from another plane, dimension, or energy realm that enable us to fulfill our spiritual purpose.

I believe that everyone is born with at least two lifetime spiritual guides. Often one is an angel. The other is sometimes a relative or someone known and trusted in a **past life**, a life experienced by your soul in another time period. Many children report experiencing the presence of their guides, whom they trust and derive great benefit from. As we proceed through life, new guides are assigned or attracted to us, sometimes for the duration of a project, term, or lesson, sometimes for longer periods of time. New guides often appear just before a big transformation or important event, and their appearance can be startling if you don't know what their purpose is.

You can read more about these and other types of contacts in my book *Advanced Chakra Healing*. Sources, both positive and negative, can originate from any of the five levels of reality.

The Five Levels of Reality

There are five basic levels of reality, each of which can serve as a source for psychic or sensory information.

The Natural is the world that works mainly with the sensory, although the psychic still functions as a sped-up version of the sensory.

The Spirit is the Greater Spirit, God, the All, the Divine.

The World of Spirits consists of dimensions, planes, and spaces or times within or outside of this timespace. These worlds house entities, energies, consciousnesses, or other beings or forms that are animate and can communicate.

The Antiworlds are the dimensional folds that oppose or hold that which isn't found in the physical universe.

The Energetic consists of (1) planes or dimensions that operate only energetically and (2) the beings or consciousnesses that dwell in these places. This reality interfaces with the larger World of Spirits and at some levels, is a subset of it; however, there are energetic wave platforms that are void of conscious beings and, in fact, might convert entering beings to pure energy.

In addition to these five levels of reality, we each exist on **four pathways,** four levels of *awareness* that add up to a Greater Reality, in which heaven and earth are the same. The Four Pathways encompass all five levels of reality. The Four Pathways are the **elemental** or **physical,** the power or supernatural, the **imagination** or creative magical, and the **divine** or heavenly. (These pathways are described in greater detail in any of my three *Advanced Chakra Healing* books.)

Sourcing: A Key to Breaking the Psychic Victimization Cycle

Breaking the psychic victimization cycle begins and ends with being clear about the source of the information you're receiving. I've heard many clients accuse other people of sending them negative messages or energy, only to figure out that the voices came from their own heads! If we do track a psychic source to something or someone that isn't us or isn't working for our highest good, we want to break off contact. We want to be connected to only loving sources that give us guidance that is in keeping with our spirit and helps us fulfill our spiritual destiny.

If we're experiencing psychic victimization, at some level, we inadvertently hooked into or connected with a negative source. Without shaming ourselves, we need to figure out how this happened and if some part of ourselves is actually "benefiting" from the harmful relationship. We are all guilty of performing negative behaviors for a hidden payoff or benefit. We might not consciously perceive a benefit in eating a chocolate cake every night, but perhaps it's a way to avoid our feelings. Likewise, we might hook into a dangerous entity because we obtain some sort of benefit. Maybe it empowers us. Maybe we prefer battling an entity than taking a chance on relationships or finding our true purpose. To accomplish our real life goals and end the psychic victimization cycle, we need to distinguish between healthy helpful sources and interference.

Interference is detrimental psychic intrusion. An interfering source wants to keep us from fully expressing our spiritual self. These forces might be living or dead beings. If something or someone that is dead—or from another planet or plane—insists on talking to you, figure out if it's really worth listening to. Just because someone is dead or invisible doesn't mean he or she knows anything more than you do. I like to tell people that figuring out whether or not to heed a psychic source isn't any different than figuring out whether you want to answer your doorbell. Don't you first look through the peephole or the screen door before opening up the door and inviting someone into your home?

Never merely accept a guide as a positive influence or a spiritual guide on its word alone. There are many beings, such as ghosts or beings just passing through our world, who, because they were human, don't know anything more than you do. There are also those sources that might delight in harming you, as that is how they obtain their energy.

To the unprepared, all sources can sound good or like the voice of the Divine. That doesn't mean they are. Here are the general differences between helpful and hurtful sources.

Harmful Source	Divinely Ordained Sources
increase fear	decrease fear
shame you	never shame
encourage you to blame others; discourage personal responsibility	increase personal responsibility
use hateful, unjustified opinions	use facts
put forth illogical ideas based on a false assumptions	are logical, if not always understandable
highlight your gifts and make you feel better than others because of them	highlight your gifts, but don't make you feel better than others because of them

Harmful Source	Divinely Ordained Sources
encourage you to ignore obligations, or release you from duty	emphasize duty and obligations
decrease wisdom	increase wisdom and truth
discourage hard work	encourage hard work
force insight	offer insight
leave you feeling elated or giddy (Note: extreme feelings are indicative of lies.)	leave you feeling uplifted
demand that you worship them and surrender your personal values	invite responsible worship and living by personal values
say they are the key to your growth	promote self-growth
if giving you a warning, will show you how you can benefit from another's demise or tell you that you are a helpless victim	if giving you a warning, will tell you what to do

Self-Discernment Principles: The Basic Laws of Discernment

I have developed a long list of discernment principles that help me distinguish between helpful and harmful sources and perform what I call **sourcing,** the act of qualifying and selecting what psychic sources I want to receive information-energy from. These principles reflect my own walk through life as a psychic sensitive and my work with people who are also psychically sensitive.

Sourcing always starts with you. Are you willing to live from an ethical value system? Before you can evaluate others, including the invisible sources, you must have a code of ethics for evaluating yourself.

1. Seek integrity above all else.
We want to be one within ourselves. To do this, our words need to match up with our actions, and our actions must be motivated by the spiritual truths within us.

2. Seek righteousness, and know that decisions will be right.
Righteousness is about being right with the ultimate creative consciousness of love. It's about doing what we perceive what love—and the highest, divine source of love—wants us to do and having faith that if we do, everything will turn out all right in the end.

3. Know that there is atonement.
To **atone** is to be "at one," a basic tenet of the philosophy of Pythagoras, a great Greek mathematician. Atonement involves recognizing that no matter what we've done, we are one with all that is and we are completely loved and already accepted. Even though we act without integrity, it is not forever lost to us. To find it again, we have only to atone or reach for the most altruistic attitude or behavior, and we will regain our sense of inner peace.

Requesting and Receiving Signs

One of the most important tools in the intuitive toolbox involves **signs,** or encoded messages. Asking for, recognizing, and interpreting signs is an ancient method for receiving guidance, accepting healing, and divining messages.

There are a few types of signs. An *omen* signifies something that will happen in the future, positive or negative. A *portent* indicates an unpleasant future event. A *warning* reveals something unpleasant that might occur, but could possibly be changed. An *indication* alludes to a possible positive or negative event, but one that isn't yet locked into place. A *prophecy* divulges divine plan. A *premonition* forecasts part, but usually not all, of the scope of a possible future, and a *message* provides insight, inspiration, or advice about action to take in the present time to create a positive future.

We receive signs all the time, although most of us are unaware of them. The most commonplace signs come in nightly dreams, from nature, or through other people, but there's an endless plethora of sources. Some signs come bidden; others are unbidden. Signs are important because while we are embodied, our spiritual gifts are limited. It's pretty hard to obtain a bird's eye view of reality when we're walking with two feet on the ground. Signs can alert us to danger, reveal choices, instruct us on decisions, provide instruction, and assist in healing. They can come from any of the five levels of reality, from sources helpful or harmful; therefore, it is important to discern the meaning and trustworthiness of the sign.

How do we recognize signs when we're getting them? How do we interpret what we're receiving? How do we actually ask for one when we want one? Here are a few tips.

Recognizing signs. To follow a sign, you have to first see it. The basic rule is that you'll receive signs according to your psychic gift type. In chapter 6, you'll begin to differentiate your gift types, the ways in which you communicate psychically. Your gift types determine if you'll receive signs that are primarily verbal, visual, or kinesthetic—through hearing, sight, or sensing. *Verbal signs* could include psychic voices or songs that pop in your head. You might be meditating on a question, then turn on the radio or television and hear a spot-on response. You could read a meaningful phrase in a book, write a message to yourself, or reflect on something that someone said seemingly out of the blue.

Visual signs involve inner and outer sight. Visual psychics might receive images, shapes, or colors in their mind's eye, in response to a question or problem. Spiritual guides often send visions, revelations, or messages in nighttime dreams or sometimes through daydreams. You might also perceive signs through normal sight. Do you keep seeing the same person on the same street corner, day after day? Read the same words on street signs, no matter where you are in the city? Repetition often indicates a sign.

My favorite vision story involves my oldest son, Michael, whom I was driving to the dentist. He was scheduled to receive his first filling, and he was not excited; in fact, he was belligerent and angry. "You don't understand!" he kept shouting to me, as I insisted that I'd been through this, so I knew he would survive. Exasperated, I finally said, "Well, God understands. "

"He does not," Michael insisted.

Just then, we pulled up alongside a huge bus. Imprinted on the advertisement that ran alongside the entire bus were two words: "I understand."

Michael got the message.

Kinesthetic signs are concrete and sensory. The main types are nature based. We are natural beings and members of the animal kingdom. Why wouldn't nature assist us? We affect it; it affects us. Most native spiritualities honor the unexpected, obvious, or repetitive presence of certain elements, animals, birds, reptiles, or climactic shifts, believing that the spirits of these things or beings are sending messages. There are many books about reading nature signs, and I encourage you to investigate this area if you're interested.

Other kinesthetic signs include any other sudden or repetitive occurrence. Do rocks keep falling on your head? I had that happen three times during a hike, and I finally sat down to figure out what, in real life, had been "hitting me on the head," but that I'd been purposely missing. I figured out that I was ignoring some major relationship issues that were sure to cause disaster, if I didn't deal with them.

In general, I label an occurrence a sign if it meets any of the following criteria:

- It happens three times. If something occurs three times, pay attention.
- It is sudden or unexpected.
- You are filled with a sense of meaning upon receiving it.
- The event is out of synch with "normal reality."
- Others tell you it's important.
- There's a supernatural or paranormal sense to the event.
- You feel initiated into an evolved or mystical state.
- The potential sign stays in your mind long after it happens.

Interpreting signs. Once you've recognized a sign, you have to figure out what it means. Interpreting signs is actually an ongoing and lifelong process, and one that can involve all of your sourcing and discernment skills. In general, know that you can always use prayer, meditation, or contemplation to gain the Divine's perspective of the sign. Source the sign following the "Five Stages of Practical Discernment" found in this chapter. Develop skills particular to your psychic style, as covered in Part III.

The following questions will help any psychic type in interpreting signs:

- Can I trust the source?
- Is this sign important?
- Is it for me or for someone else?
- Is this sign an omen, portent, warning, indication, prophecy, premonition, or message?
- Does it show me something that will happen, could happen, might happen, or should happen?
- Does it show me something that I must do to create a good future for myself or others?
- If I ignore it, could something bad happen?
- If I pay attention to it, might something good happen?
- Does it indicate a decision I must make in the present?
- Would the Divine support me in following the message of the sign?

Most important, rely on your inner self. Signs can be confusing and confounding. You might be shown a vision of the future that seems disastrous, for instance, and be told you cannot change it. Why, then, are you told? I have faced this situation many times, in my personal life and at work. The most challenging experience involved a vision of a friend's death. The Divine told me that I couldn't change the outcome or tell him. The revelation was specific, right down to what clothes he was wearing and who attended his deathbed. His death occurred exactly as revealed. What then, was the point? I was able to quietly and gently minister to my friend's needs and, later, his children's pain, because I had already grieved his death. There was a purpose in knowing, and it was good.

We are all spiritual beings, and the innermost aspect of self already knows all the answers. Trust your own instincts; they won't lead you wrong.

Asking for signs. In the Bible, Jesus says that we only have to ask, and we shall receive. You can ask for a sign for anything and for any reason. There's no issue too big or too small for the Divine. The key is to pray directly to the Divine for a sign. Verbal psychics, pray aloud or write your requests for a sign. Tell a friend about your problems and that you are requesting a sign, and have them hold faith with you. Select a song that reflects your need and sing it aloud. Be verbal, and the sign will come.

Visual psychics, imagine that you are typing your request and handing the note to the Divine or an angel. Clip a picture from a magazine that reflects your need or query, and tape the picture somewhere obvious. Circle a date on a calendar, and ask the Divine to send you a sign by then. Conduct an everyday vision quest: give the Divine a certain amount of time—say three days—to help you, and then pay attention for signs during those days.

Kinesthetic psychics can trust their bodies, environments, and nature. Wear a certain piece of jewelry or an accessory, or carry a blessed rock or talisman, having "charged" it with your request. Decide that until you receive a sign, you'll wear a certain item of clothing. Set up a talisman, plant, rock, or picture—something that you can see every day—that represents your request. Whenever you pass by it, thank the Divine for the sign you'll receive. Spend time in nature, and invite it to share its knowledge with you.

And all psychic types, know that inevitably, the Divine decides how to get a message to you, not the other way around. Stay open and encouraged. The Divine will provide a sign in a way that you can recognize, so know that you won't miss it! I always say that the Divine knows how stubborn I am. If the

Divine has to hit me on the head to get me to pay attention to something, that will happen. (And it has.)

The Five Stages of Practical Discernment

Once you understand that you have to apply the laws of discernment to yourself first and foremost, you can apply them to others with integrity. Of course, you can't change anything or anyone else. Just because you're willing to be honest doesn't mean that you can make anyone else honest. This fact is the rationale for being discerning, for figuring out who or what sources, living or dead, you want to engage.

The need for discernment is especially strong—and easiest to achieve—at the points of psychic contact. These points are five stages at which we make decisions about what to do psychically. The **five stages of discernment** are:

The Opening: deciding whether to receive psychic information or to open to a psychic source
The Method: selecting what process or methodology to use for psychic communication—verbal, visual, or kinesthetic
The Assessment: deciding whether to believe the information received and/or what parts of it to trust
The Deciding: looking at choices and deciding the best response
The Doing: taking action through psychic activity or protection

To help you with psychic discernment, the following are some questions you can ask at each stage.

1. The Opening

- Am I in the right mental, emotional, physical, or spiritual shape to receive psychic information at this time?

- Am I psychically safe enough to receive at this time?
- Would it benefit me to open psychically at this time?
- Would it benefit anyone else for me to open psychically at this time?
- Would it injure others or me if I opened at this time?
- Would opening psychically create more wholeness within me at this time?

2. *The Method*

- Is there a better method for receiving psychic data at this time?
- Is there a safer method?
- Is there a safe chakra or set of chakras to use at this time?
- Would the Divine support my choice of method? This question might take some time to answer. Pray, meditate, contemplate, or ask for a sign until you're sure. Ask yourself, "If I were the Divine, would I sanction this process?"
- Does this method support my spiritual path or not?
- Does this method have integrity to me?
- Does this method offer integrity to others?
- Does this method align with my value system?
- Does this method call undue attention to me?
- Is this method easy for me to use?

3. *The Assessment*

Is the information you're receiving:

- **Loving?** Loving information-energy is progressive, practical, and encourages compassion. Fear-based sources or information lead to increased terror, alarm, or powerlessness. Good or godly psychic messages will increase love, not terror—even if they include a warning.
- **Change oriented?** Warnings or other threatening psychic messages

can be valid. The key to their validity is this: can you do something with the information? Spiritual sources will try to warn you about impending disaster if you can somehow change the outcome or if knowledge of the event will prepare you to better handle it. Credible psychic warning messages leave room for growth, change, or response.

- **Personalized?** If a source gives you a message demanding a change in another person, raise the red flag. First, you are not responsible for anyone else, nor can you change him or her. Second, the Divine can usually find a way to get a message to someone else by itself. Third, if it is clear that you are supposed to pass the message along, know that the means and reasons to do so will also be provided.
- **Empowering?** You must immediately retreat from any source or psychic message that insists that you are a better or more important person than anyone else. Stop all the communication at once and turn to a trusted spiritual source to disengage from the empowering source. If you discover that you really miss the special feelings of these communiqués, see a therapist. Find out why you feel so inferior that you need psychic elevation.
- **Ethical?** Ethics are a body of values that, when followed, result in a positive and altruistic outcome. Does a message encourage an ethical response?
- **Respectful?** A truly spiritual source will show respect toward you and other people in its tone, message, and actions.
- **Universal?** Divinely sanctioned messages will uphold universal standards of belief and ethics, applying these same principles across the board to all peoples, not just certain groups. For example, a godly source will never tell a Christian it is okay to break Christian principles to hurt an Islamic person, or vice versa.
- **Accepting?** The Divine accepts us as we are, and we should accept

each other and ourselves the same way. This doesn't mean that we stop growing or allow others to abuse us. However, permanent change occurs only through **grace**, the giving of love where it is believed to be undeserved. Are we offering grace to others and ourselves? Viable psychic sources increase our awareness of grace, not inhibit it.

- **Enlightening?** Does a presented psychic energy offer a breakthrough or only a breakdown? We can't allow ourselves to be torn down unless it is part of the process of being built up. Nor can we can allow others to be torn down.

4. The Deciding

- What are possible ways to respond? It's usually easy to determine two options to a problem. But black-and-white thinking lacks creativity and usually results in differentiating between a "bad" and an "even worse" response. There are always more than two choices. Examine possibilities until you can see at least three options.
- Which choices are ethical, and which might not be? At one level, we're called to look at choices through the lens of our value system. Our values, however, might be particular to us and not universal. We might value monetary success; while this value is not "bad," it could lead us to treat others poorly for our own gain. The answer is to be values based and also ethical.

  To be **ethical** means that we look beyond our personal good and treat others with love, honor, and respect. Reflecting upon the ethics of our choices is key to differentiating better from worse, not just bad from worse.
- Does one particular action step emerge as more loving than the others? Loving is an action verb. The ends never justify the means. The means actually affect and determine the end. This is especially

true in psychic and spiritual matters. Is there an action step that avoids manipulation and leads toward goodness? Finding this action step is the basis of being ethical.

- What choice will create balance? Your psychic process, no matter how spiritual, should not take over your life. If you follow the advice given or the choice you are considering, will you still have time for relationships, healthy eating, exercise, work, sleep, rest, and play?
- Does my choice increase humility? Would the action you take in response to psychic input make you more humble or more grandiose? Following a valid psychic message doesn't make you more or less holy than anyone else, nor should it give you bragging rights.
- Does my choice emphasize learning? Would the process involved in a potential choice leave you feeling fresh, renewed, and peaceful, yet stimulated for change and growth? If the ultimate connection increases your knowledge and education, you are on track.
- Is the choice altruistic? Would the responsive behavior motivate altruistic actions or results? A grace-filled response to psychic input always helps the self, but also leads you to becoming a better person who, in turn, helps others.
- Does the choice challenge me? Psychic processes that are truly spiritual make you face your issues. Whether your spiritual communication assists you personally, professionally, or both, it must lead to self-growth.

5. The Doing

- Will sharing this message or taking my chosen step lead to a greater good?
- Do I feel good about carrying out this decision? Relieved? Unhappy? Remorseful? Guilty?
- Do I need to adjust my role, thinking, or behavior to be more ethical?

- Is there anything else I need to do to be loving or altruistic?
- If I know that I am doing the best I can do, and following the highest spiritual guidance possible, am I willing to release the outcome?

It's important to ask others if they want to hear the intuitive information that you've received. If they say yes, ensure that they mean it by first offering a little bit of data and seeing if they ask for more.

Note: There are a few times I have received a message for someone else and been instructed to get it to them, only to find it impossible to do so. At these points, I have asked my gatekeeper to place the energetic message in the other person's auric field, so that they can receive it independent of me. (See exercise 5, at the end of this chapter, for more about establishing a psychic gatekeeper.)

Synopsis: A Guide to Sourcing

Here is a chart to show you the basics of evaluating a psychic source. You want to discern between righteous information, which prompts good will and benefits, and questionable information, which can lead you or others astray.

Righteous information is . . .	*Questionable information is . . .*
Love based. It leads to progressive, practical change for yourself or others. The message may be difficult to hear, but is ultimately loving.	***Fear based.*** It leads to increased terror, alarm, hopelessness, or powerlessness.

Righteous information is . . .	*Questionable information is . . .*
Ethical. It doesn't call for breaking your own values or more universal standards of ethics. The process by which you received the information lines up with your ethical and moral codes.	***Ethically doubtful.*** It calls for or leads to avoidable injury of others. The process by which you received the information conflicts with your ethical and moral codes.
Moral. It subscribes to not only specific, but also universal moral principles; there is a greater good achieved.	***Morally doubtful.*** May be moral on the surface, but will lead to remorse, guilt, or complaints from your conscience.
Personalized. You would be willing to apply the message to yourself as well as others.	***Ego oriented.*** It includes accusations or advice that puts you in a superior position.
Universal. If the message were applied, it wouldn't benefit one group more than another.	***Discriminatory.*** It would benefit one group or person more than another.
Flexible. Free will is maintained; you and others have choices about how to apply the information.	***Forced.*** It uses coercion or manipulation to increase the belief in the message or the messenger; the message might initially seem nice, but ultimately feels violating.
Accepting. The core of the message is about being loved and accepted just as you are.	***Judgmental.*** The message insinuates that the receiver must take its advice to be lovable.

Righteous information is . . .	*Questionable information is . . .*
Enlightening. The messages can lead to spiritual breakthroughs, even if the messages are tough in nature. Warnings or predictions leave room for change, learning, or growth.	***Damaging.*** The messages might lead to permanent psychological or spiritual breakdowns.

The Role of Feelings in Psychic Discernment

Feelings are difficult, but they are also humanity's salvation. Feelings move physical matter into the psychic realm and help us shift psychic energies into the physical world. They are also present when you work with and/or receive psychic information. In order to be a safe sensitive, you must learn how to read your own and others' feelings. Your feelings can also tell you if sources are spiritual or not. In fact, one of the most dependable ways to make discerning psychic decisions is to work with your feelings.

There are two basic types of feelings, each of which can emanate from or recognize any of the five basic feeling constellations, introduced in chapter 4. The first are **sensory feelings**, which emanate from your body. They are not bad! Rather, they tell you how your bodily self is doing, and they often speak for your soul or mind as well. They can tell you if you like a certain brand of ice cream or trust a person you've just met. Body-based sensory feelings exist only to assure survival. These feelings, however, can be manipulated by outside sources, as well as internal parts of yourself. People commonly give in to fear, for instance, in order to hide from a deeper issue. Or you might cloud your sadness with anger so as to not seem vulnerable.

You might also have ingested so many feelings from other people or beings that you can't even distinguish your own personal feelings. Do you really desire that thousand-calorie hamburger, or are you eating to cover up the way your dad's rage feels inside of you? Programming or trickery from others can manipulate your natural feelings. You might feel fear when you ought to feel excited, or angry when you ought to be happy. Are you really too scared to interview for a job you deeply want, or is an external entity projecting fear into you? Do you really want to interview for that job, or are you doing so only because you're operating from your family's beliefs about success?

The second type of feelings, **spiritual feelings**, can work through the body—and usually do—but they come from your true self. They are open only to input from your own spirit or from divinely inspired sources. A spiritual feeling might induce you to cry during a kid's cartoon, but that's because you are receiving an important message through the show. Your spirit might prompt you to yell, but only at an appropriate time, such as when a mugger is attacking and you need to scare him off. Not only do spiritual feelings fuel your spiritual purpose, but they also enable you to receive true spiritual guidance and discern motives in others.

Spiritual feelings are highly attuned to the Divine and reflect your spiritual purpose. The key is that they harmonize rather than harm. I perceive them more like awarenesses than raw emotions; while they might cause me to respond to a situation with sharp words, tears, a handshake, laughter, or a no, they always feel *right*. They make me feel better about myself, more connected to a greater truth. They never leave me feeling judgmental or terrorized, shameful or wrongly guilty. I am a better, rather than worse, person for having felt them.

Here's how to distinguish a spiritual from a distorted sensory feeling, and how to determine the message behind a spiritual feeling.

Spiritual Feeling: Anger
Your boundaries have been violated, and you need to set better ones. With love, you can establish physical or psychic parameters that work for you and others.

Distorted Sensory Feeling: Rage
You are angry and hurt. Your boundaries have been violated, so you feel deeply sad. Rather than take care of yourself or confront the original violator, you get angry with innocent people in ways that are out of proportion. You don't want to accept the responsibility of feeling your sadness and moving to forgiveness.

Spiritual Feeling: Sadness
You recognize deep inside that love is at the core of this relationship or situation. You need to own that love and allow it to heal you.

Distorted Sensory Feeling: Sorrow or Grief
You have "frozen" a loved one or a positive situation or memory in time and space and refuse to move on. If you keep sorrowing, you don't have to get on with your life and accept new love.

Distorted Sensory Feeling: Despair
You think that you can move through sadness by giving up on love or by holding on to your pain forever. You are not allowing yourself the healing promise of love and the excitement of new adventures.

Spiritual Feeling: Happiness
You are unified within yourself and the Divine. Keep doing what you are doing!

Distorted Sensory Feeling: Bitterness
You are allowing someone else to control your happiness. Something or someone has judged you as bad when you are happy. You have been shamed into thinking that being your spiritual self is bad. You are afraid to let go of that shame-based person, being, or belief and just be yourself.

Distorted Sensory Feeling: Cynicism
You have decided that it is too scary to become happy ever again. After all, happiness might go away, and so you decide to chase it away before it can.

Spiritual Feeling: Fear
You need to move forward or move backward—do something! This is not working.

Distorted Sensory Feeling: Terror
You do not trust the Divine or your own spirit. You don't think you have the energy, power, or right to be safe and happy.

Distorted Sensory Feeling: Fright
You are giving away your power to circumstances instead of following your inner knowing. By judging an event or a person on only externals, you are disconnecting with yourself.

Distorted Sensory Feeling: Abandonment
You are failing to recognize your connection with the Divine and all things good. You are abandoning yourself and blaming someone else.

Distorted Sensory Feeling: Guilt (an aspect of disgust toward self)
You have moved off your spiritual path and need to move back

on. Your actions, thoughts, or relationships need to better reflect the spiritual principles you are designed to follow.

Distorted Sensory Feeling: Self-hatred
You are angry. Your boundaries have been violated. To spare someone you love or to earn the love of another, you internalize your anger and hurt. While the other person should feel guilty, not you, you feel their guilt for them as a way to either keep them close or to keep yourself from being rejected.

Spiritual Feeling: Disgust
Something or someone is really bad for you, and you need to get rid of it or them immediately. It, he, or she will make you ill.

Distorted Sensory Feeling: Shame
You believe there is something wrong with you as a person, and therefore, you do not deserve unconditional love. Because you are too scared to reject what or who is bad for you, or because you are unable to do so, you internalize your disgust and apply it to yourself.

Distorted Sensory Feeling: Blame
You feel worthless and bad about yourself and don't like this feeling, so you project it on others or on situations outside of yourself.

If. . .

a means of psychic opening

a psychic message

a psychic source

a person

an activity
a psychic impression
an action resulting from a psychic communication
a comment about your psychic gifts
a psychic message you want to send
a method for obtaining psychic information
a process involving psychic sensitivities

. . . makes you feel any of the distorted feelings or results in an obvious warning from your spirit:

stop what you are doing,
get guidance from a trusted spiritual advisor,
close down your psychic capacity temporarily,
pray or meditate,
read a well-informed spiritual passage or verse,
express yourself creatively,
discern before you go further, for your integrity is at stake,
perform the ground-center-affirm protection sequence from exercise 2,
reestablish your psychic boundaries, as done in exercise 3,
get a gatekeeper, as exercise 5 will instruct you to do,
and ask the Divine to help.

Universal Law: Rules of Spirit

The first healing class I ever took was held in the basement of a bed-and-breakfast. As I learned the basics of therapeutic-touch healing, now called Healing Touch, I became accustomed to this phrase: "Spirits have to follow universal law."

I didn't understand the significance of that phrase until I was studying healing in other countries. Most of the indigenous healers I met used the same type of phrase, though in different languages and words, of course. Don Francisco and Don Augustine of Peru separated "good spirits" from "negative spirits" based on "Sachamama's law." Pacos, a Belizean plant shaman, insisted that all plants have healing properties, even the poisonous ones. The critical issue is whether or not the healer comes from "God's intention" or "bad intention." A Moroccan white witch insisted that she worked with only spirits that could show that they followed "universal principles," while a psychic medium in England taught me how to see if a presenting entity was "of the light" or not.

There are universal spiritual laws. I don't know how they come to be, but I know that they are real and that it's our right to call upon them. I imagine when the universe came into being, these laws were imbedded in the Genesis Field, or Zero Point Field, a field composed of photons straight from the Creator's consciousness, that continues to flow with the light of unconditional love that motivated the Creator to create, and through which all of reality, on a quantum level or sublevel, is based. These laws are also written in our hearts during conception. These laws apply to the living and the dead, the seen and the unseen, the physical and the ethereal. We can't force someone to follow these ideals, which are based on the rule of love, but we can uphold them ourselves and use them as barometers of who or what we want in our presence. "Good" entities will follow universal law, which reduces to loving motivation and behavior. "Bad" or rebellious entities don't or won't. If asked to do so, a presenting entity must prove that it follows universal law. But you have to ask.

In my understanding, the universal laws include:

> ***Law of the innocent.*** No one has the right to manipulate, hurt, or take advantage of the innocent.

Law of redemption. No matter how "great the sin," all beings can receive forgiveness and healing from the Divine.

Law of truth. When asked to tell the truth, a disincarnate being cannot lie. (This doesn't mean it has to tell the truth. Most misleading beings disappear rather than state the truth.)

Law of "the light." When asked, a being must relate the name or nature of what it serves, which basically comes down to either "the light" (or the Divine) or something perverse.

Law of free will. All beings have the right to choose who or what to follow, what to believe or do, and how to respond to situations. They also have to respect your right to determine who or what you want in your presence.

These are great laws, and we'd all live happy lives if everything and everyone followed them. But the truth is that entities are similar to people. Some follow the rules, and some don't. Some respect and honor the innocent, and others take advantage of them. However, the Divine will enforce these rules upon request. If you ask an entity to tell you whom it serves, it cannot lie. It cannot say "God" if it doesn't serve the Divine. If it doesn't want to share any information, you can assume it has something to hide. By itself, it might disappear in a puff of smoke. If it doesn't, command it away, drawing on the law of free will.

If a demonic force is plaguing you, order it to leave. If an abusive character, dead or alive, is hanging out, you have a right to get rid of it. If it doesn't leave, the reason isn't an error in universal law; the reason is your own perception of the law. Most probably, you don't believe you deserve to be safe or that you have that much power. Review universal law. Know your own strength, and those around you will respect it.

I test every spirit that comes into my presence, even those that enter with my clients. I take shortcuts. Before working, I prepare my space with a general prayer, asking that the Divine clear it of anything that doesn't follow him/her. That takes care of 99 percent of all intruders. If I'm in doubt, I ask a being if it's of the light. If it doesn't answer, it goes.

Even if a being states that it's of the Divine, I don't necessarily enter a relationship with it. I meet a lot of people, but I don't make friends with them all. It's like dating: you meet a lot of potentials, but few probables. If I can't figure out if the being is helpful or necessary to my life, I tell it to prove its importance. And if I still can't decide, I tell the Divine to prove it to me. Remember, you get to decide if you want to know a certain being or not. You get to decide if you want it around at a given time or not. You get to decide if you want to enter, engage in, renew, transform, or end a relationship with any being, whether it's of the Divine or not.

My work with Agnes illustrates my point. Agnes was a four-year-old girl who was nightly visited by spirits. She couldn't sleep for the noise and her own fear. Some spirits would talk with her; others would rustle about the room. Yet others would sing songs or play music. She was terrified. I told her that she could ask if they were of the light or not, which she did. On her next session, she reported that one of them spoke to her, telling her that they were of the light, but that they wouldn't "go to the light." They were lovely beings, but they didn't want to be dead. I told her that she could go home and tell them that they had to go to the light (as in the heavenly light), or leave her house forever. Agnes came back to the next and last session ecstatic.

"Cyndi," she said. "An enormous angel came and swept them up into the sky!"

Her room has been quiet since then.

A few years ago, I learned that the same spooky activity had been plaguing my youngest son, but only after I spent a few nights sleeping in his room. Gabe liked sleeping with Mom, in Mom's bed. For weeks, he had crawled into my bed, complaining that it was "too loud to sleep." The problem was that Gabe snored, kicked, and talked all night long. In desperation, I started slipping into his room after he entered mine.

It didn't take long to figure out why he couldn't sleep. If there was a toy that could talk, snort, walk, zip, or zap, it did. Evening after evening, I was bombarded with sounds. "I'm Buzz Lightyear!" "Roar!" "Choo choo, chug chug." After a few nights, I sat up and shouted, "Who is there?"

I psychically perceived an array of little children. My sense was that they had recently died, but didn't want to go to the "other side." Gabe, a loving soul, had probably given permission, at some level, for them to play in his room. And of course, we owned every noisy toy ever invented, so why wouldn't the children busily make themselves at home? No wonder Gabe couldn't sleep!

I knew about the law of free will and understood that I couldn't make these children "go to heaven," but I also knew that I didn't need to let them stay in my house. I called upon the Divine to send angels, who came immediately and took the children to the light or elsewhere for healing. The toys haven't talked since then.

I knew that I had the right to decide which entities could be in my presence and which couldn't, but Gabe didn't know he too had that right. It's always ethical to invoke universal law for a minor. It's also sometimes necessary to do this for our own inner children, the wounded selves that have been victimized by psychic intruders or the negative messages given us by our families or surrounding systems. If, as an adult, you invoke universal law against a harmful being and receive no response, it's probably because your inner child doesn't believe he or she deserves to be rescued. Become your adult or God self. Act from your true self or inner spirit. Now self-parent. Be the adult taking care of the child within you. Eliminate cords, strongholds, and negative patterns. Take charge in a loving way, and you'll accomplish two goals. You'll heal from within, and you'll get rid of the negative presences.

Getting a Gatekeeper: The Best Defense, a Good Offense

The easiest way to gain control of the psychic and help yourself is to get a **gatekeeper,** a special being that will help you discern helpful from unhelpful entities, good from bad messages, and loving from non-loving behaviors. As noted earlier, a gatekeeper is sent from and appointed by the Divine to protect and guide you.

When I was first entering my own intuitive-development process, I was overwhelmed with the number and intensity of presenting psychic sources. It seemed that every night something "not real" would rap on my door and decide to chat, or intrude on my dream life. The daytimes weren't much better. I'd pick up an object at a friend's house, and an attached energy would decide that I could help it out. I'd travel and pass through land that carried trauma, only to have that trauma transferred into my body. I became convinced that there are both animate and inanimate psychic sources absolutely everywhere, and I longed only for the primacy of my own thoughts.

One night, I was ruminating on the subject in bed, and I had a visitation from an archangel. It was Archangel Gabriel. He told me that he had been appointed by God to be my gatekeeper until I was ready to screen energies and entities for myself. I felt safe with Gabriel and knew that I could trust him. For many years, I talked psychically with him alone.

Gabriel would filter energies from other people and their guides during my client sessions. He would tell me what healing or insight would assist my loved ones, my clients, or me. He established an energetic buffer around my physical self, so that I could actually go to bed in silence and sleep well. He served as my sole source of psychic and spiritual guidance.

Over time, he introduced me to other guides. Some, like the wolf, jaguar, or eagle, were of the natural world. Others were energetic and showed me how to work with the chakras, auric layers, and in the energy planes. At one point, Gabriel turned my training over to a master, a deceased shaman who loved to plague me with new and sometimes confusing ways to learn. Gradually, I developed my own set of ethics and the psychic muscles needed to enforce those ethics for myself.

Since working with Gabriel, I have helped hundreds, if not thousands, of people establish a gatekeeper for themselves. A gatekeeper might be an angel or a master, a soul guardian or a past-life friend. He or she could be a deceased and loving relative, a religious figurehead or icon, an archetype, or your own higher self. The key is that a gatekeeper guards your boundaries and psyche and invites in only that which is good for you.

To protect you, a gatekeeper undertakes any of the following:

- Regulating the flow of psychic information inside and outside of you
- Deciding which entities and spirits might communicate with you
- Selecting which personal prayers and questions should be directed to which external sources
- Helping you pay attention to necessary messages or energies from

both psychic and sensory sources
- Building your self-esteem and capabilities
- Helping you learn your lessons in a gentle way
- Attracting and summoning help from energies and entities
- Protecting you from harmful energies, information, and sources
- Overriding you if you might harm yourself or someone else
- Serving in the Divine's stead—and working only for the Divine

Over time, I have worked with many gatekeepers, although every time I go through a major life shift or psychic change, I renew my relationship with Gabriel. At many points, the Divine, in many forms, served as my gatekeeper. For a few years, I connected directly to the Mother, the name of the Divine used in Peru. She appeared like a big, bald, and bold African woman, covered with vines and flowers. She was soothing and strong and everything I needed at the time. At a different time, the Divine appeared as a flaming man, a version of the burning bush, at the foot of my bed when I was staying at a bed-and-breakfast in England. He actually shook the bed a couple of times in the middle of the night to get my notice. At first, I thought it was a ghost and began uttering unrepeatable comments in every language that I knew, only to finally shut up and ask, "Who are you?" The reply was, "God."

God as a flame followed me through England and Iceland and then home to the United States for a while. He was tangible. I could feel the heat off his body and hear him audibly. On the flight from England to Iceland, I wondered where he would sit, as I was placed in a seat, my son on my left and an East Indian gentleman on my right. Before takeoff, the flight attendant moved the gentleman. I looked over. The seat was flat. It then concaved. God had taken his seat.

When the Divine was my gatekeeper, I learned that spirits are concrete as well as ethereal. The spirit world is real and can impact physical reality. I have also learned that the most divinely inspired gatekeepers are real, not so-called imaginary friends. They love you and support you—and not only spiritually. The best guides are those that can impact physical reality. You are a material being, and some of the most important parts of life are concrete, such as relationships, house concerns, money, and health. Your gatekeeper should care about what matters to you.

I have also learned that gatekeepers can be trusted only if they come from the Divine. Gatekeepers can be any kind of being, from fairies, masters, the deceased, saints, and nature beings to entities from the most heavenly and holy of places. Always ask your potential gatekeeper: Are they committed to good? Are they committed to helping you help yourself and others create good lives? Do they accept you the way that you are, even though they want to help you become the best person that you can be? Are they loving rather than shaming? Again, remember: the Divine doesn't require perfection, just intention.

A gatekeeper can become an essential caretaker for the psychic sensitive. I heartily recommend that you consider forming such a relationship. The exercise at the end of this chapter will help you find your own gatekeeper.

Qualifying a Gatekeeper and Other Psychic Contacts

Sometimes we search for intuitive inspiration; other times, it simply comes to us. How can you tell which sources are worth paying attention to? Even more important, what sources are dangerous versus helpful?

The key is to qualify the source. You can figure out the validity of a potential gatekeeper or any psychic source by first analyzing it completely. This will tell you if you are compatible with it and vice versa. You can begin this analyzation process by asking your own spirit or the Divine these questions:

- What is the nature and origin of this source?
- Is this source internal or external (from inside or outside of me)?
- Is it animate or inanimate?
- Which level of reality does the input come from?
- What type of being or source is this revelation?
- Can this source show that it is "from the Divine?"

Ask any other questions that enable you to establish a sense of the source's personality, way of working, and origins. Then continue to ask questions that might reveal its credibility, ethics, and effectiveness, such as:

- What does this source want to show, tell, reveal, or become to me?
- Do I trust or believe its intention?
- Can I trust it in the short term, long term, or both?
- If I follow its advice, what might be the most likely outcomes?
- If the Divine were to show me the nature of this source, what would I perceive?
- Does this source meet the requirements as laid out in this chapter?

The Existence of Evil

One of the most common questions I receive from clients is about the nature of evil. Is there evil? Does being psychic invite evil or open you to being used by an evil being? My own father constantly questioned my decision to develop my psychic powers because he was so scared of evil. "Cyndi," he would say, "I trust you. But I don't trust all the bad things that could affect you." (He said the same thing about boys when I was a teenager, as I recollect.)

Evil is anticonsciousness. It is the absence of love. It is the end result of people or entities consciously choosing to thwart another's free will and attempting to destroy their own or others' recognition of truth. In the process, evil beings maliciously attempt to murder another's soul, spirit, mind, or body.

However, beings that turn to evil actions are not without conscience, or else they wouldn't be consciously refusing love! This means that at some level, they still carry and reflect the speck of light that we call the spirit, the eternal truth of the Divine and goodness that propels us toward helping others and ourselves. Therefore, I refuse to condemn someone or something as evil throughout, as they are essentially made of the same material of goodness and light as I am.

We are all capable of evil and have probably performed evil actions at one point or another. Let's be honest. Haven't you ever been motivated to hurt another, to exact revenge or show someone what you are made of? I'm sure that I'm not the only divorcée who has wanted her ex-husband to drop dead! And yet, I don't act on this impulse, physically or psychically. It's just plain not right.

There are many ways to enact evil. We can maliciously hurt others, but we also abuse ourselves. Addictions, food issues, self-denial, self-blame, self-criticism, self-hatred, and other dysfunctional patterns are all ways we do evil unto ourselves. Jesus said we are to love others *as ourselves*. Carrying out this commandment is contingent on treating ourselves with love and respect.

Many psychic practitioners and religious enthusiasts go out of their way to spot and confront evil, seeing a demon under every disease and badness in everyone's heart. My own work has proven that there are evil influences and that these can cause disease, mental illness, spiritual confusion, relationship ills, and financial difficulties. I recall a couple vivid demonstrations of negative influences. One involved a client who informed me that for two weeks, her house had been infested with hundreds of black flies. My immediate intuitive sense was that they were linked to a demonic influence that was attempting to scare her off her life path. As she was a committed Catholic (I usually work within the belief system of the client), we invoked Christ's power of grace and asked that guardian angels position themselves at every corner of her house. She went home and discovered that every fly was dead.

Yet another example involved a young boy who was playing with a Ouija board. His mother called me from Chicago crying, as he was levitating in the air screaming curses at her. I asked for spiritual protection, and he fell to the floor, sobbing, but back to normal.

Because negative influences do exist, I have designed many of the exercises in this book to offer protection. The ideal protection, however, is love. Love is not weak. It is not insipid. It is the activated power of grace, which insists that you deserve to be self-loving and intact even while you uphold the rights of others to be the same. If there is a consistent theme to evil, it is the tendency of evil-makers to deny others their rights to self-service.

Fearing evil, however, only feeds it. Fear is the food of evil. So is unrighteous anger. Feelings are energies. Feelings keep us moving. Evil entities steal others' emotions because they refuse to generate their own. Would you want to feel afraid, scared, joyous, or even angry if you were evil? No, because you might then expand your conscience to the point of feeling guilt and shame. And then you would feel even worse about yourself than you already do, because of all the bad things you've done to others! Not wanting to feel self-disgust, an evil entity or energy disconnects itself from the Divine—from the energy that provides us all with the love that literally runs our bodies. Devoid of energy, it thinks it has no choice but to steal energy from those of us still willingly connected to the Divine Source. And so it scares us into feeling strong feelings, such as fear or anger, which in turn, it steals and uses as fuel.

It's important to note that not everyone you might think to be evil actually is. Paranoia, the common mentality of just about any fundamentalist, whether the subject is religion, politics, diet technique, or an ideal, is a precursor to evil. Thinking others are evil just because they are different or ascribe to different values is mighty close to performing an evil and easily leads to evil acts, including prejudice, discrimination, or terrorism. Notice how most of these behaviors are done "in the name of God." If we can't sign our own name to them, we have no business ascribing them to the Divine. Love is always the best solution. It enables not only self-protection, but also clarity when looking at others.

One of the most frequent judgments I see is the one against individuals who work with magic, the New Age, alternative medicine, or sorcery. The Christian, Judaic, and Islamic scriptures are full of individuals called prophets and apostles who demonstrate the very same abilities and techniques as these groups do. A man I particularly respect actually calls himself a sorcerer, pointing out that the root of the word *sorcery* is *source*. As the Divine is the source of all, he is actually an instrument of the Divine. While he works with dark energy, we must remember that 70-plus percent of the universe is made of dark matter. Dark and light are simply vibrations of the same types of energy. Neither is good or bad. What matters is what we do with who we are.

The application of the psychic is mainly a matter of belief. Everything we do and become is a reflection of what we believe about others, the Divine, the universe, and ourselves. If you find yourself in the psychic victimization cycle very often, you might want to spend some serious time examining your beliefs. Your thoughts are what make you "you."

And of the Loneliness

Interestingly, having a gatekeeper resolves one of the paradoxes of being a psychic sensitive. Here you are, surrounded by voices, lights, images, sensations, and the plethora of psychic phenomenon that can drive you crazy. Yet as busy as your mind might be, you've probably also felt lonely.

Many psychic sensitives report feeling lonely, like a stranger in a strange land. One of the reasons is that most people simply don't perceive what you are feeling! This can leave you feeling sad, different, and alienated. You might courageously relate some of your psychic or spiritual experiences, only to have people misunderstand, ignore, or ridicule you. Some people might express care or interest, but that doesn't mean that they get it. Others might show concern, but of the variety that suggests that you are weird or that there is something wrong with you. Whether you keep your psychic impressions to yourself or share them, you might end up feeling very alone in them—and stuck within a world that no one else lives in.

Then there's the loneliness of having your companions be invisible or inaudible to others. We want friends that we can touch, call on the phone, and introduce to others. It's hard to bond with beings that aren't from your realm or time. Can a deceased relative from the seventeenth century really relate to your life, which is chock-full of mechanical and technological challenges? Something as simple as a microwave doesn't make sense to the dear departed.

My solution is to relate as often as possible to the Divine, which gets everything and everyone. My personal term for the Divine is *The Presence,* for that's exactly how I experience God. Though I often refer to the Divine as God (including in this book), the word *God* is too limiting for me. It doesn't reflect the complexity or the simplicity of the Being, the Consciousness, the Love, which we most frequently call *God.* I also experience the term *Divine* as cold. When sensing The Presence, I feel peaceful, held, accompanied, loved, accepted, befriended, guided, and accepted. I don't feel alone. Through my connection with The Presence, I ask to meet real people (clients, and friends) who "get" me. I'm lucky in that almost everyone I meet is kind and authentic. I can share some of my psychic self and be accepted.

Sensing the Divine as an always-present presence provides another benefit: safety. When you return to the Source, you are safe. As Larry Dossey says in his book *Be Careful What You Pray For. . .You Just Might Get It,* "There is an expert who knows the specific interventions needed in any complex situation—the Absolute." The Mundaka Upanishad, an ancient Indian text, says:

> *That which cannot be seen and is beyond thought*
> *which is without cause or parts,*
> *which neither perceives nor acts,*
> *which is unchanging, all-pervading, omnipresent,*
> *subtler than the subtlest,*

that is the eternal which the wise know to be
the source of all.

Ultimately, being connected to the greater presence presents you with the greatest gift of all: affirmation of your own presence.

Exercise 5
Finding a Gatekeeper

Connecting with a gatekeeper gives you a safe ally, a screen for unwanted intruders, and a teacher for your gifts. A gatekeeper also can help you move through confusing or painful experiences.

Whether we realize it or not, we all have invisible guides ready to assist. Universal laws about free will ensure that such guides are not able to interfere with our lives unbidden. We must invite them in and ask for their help. Once their help has been received, they do not leave us, but they do stop helping until we ask again.

Depending on your psychic style, you may be comfortable communicating with your guide visually, verbally, or through your physical senses. Choose one of these styles now.

Ground, center, and open using the techniques in exercise 2. In a meditative state, ask the Divine for a gatekeeper, specifying your reasons for wanting one and the parameters of the relationship, and ask that the gatekeeper communicate with you in the way that you have selected. Wait. If you don't immediately receive a message, don't be alarmed! Like when you send a letter sent in the mail, it may take a bit of time to receive a response. Go for a walk, browse a bookstore, take a bath, and continue with your daily plans. Throughout your day, periodically reaffirm your request and become mindful of any possible signs in your environment or any repetitive patterns that seem unusual. Is there a strange and colorful beetle on every doorstep you enter or exit? Is there a certain bird that keeps chirping at you? Do you keep seeing the same advertisement everywhere you go?

Pay attention to your dreams. Are there messages or patterns in them? Just plain pay attention! These types of signs will indicate that the Divine has heard you, but might also provide clues as to your gatekeeper's identity. A song such as "Angels Watching Over You" could be a message from the Divine, but also point to an angelic gatekeeper. The multicolored beetle that appears day after day might be the Divine in disguise and also representative of a beetle nature spirit that's come to instruct you.

Try to let go of any ideas about *how* the gatekeeper should look or act. One client of mine shared a good example of how her preconceived notions of gatekeepers got in her way. For many weeks after she requested a gatekeeper, she was bombarded with flashes of a creature with hooves, black wings, and a monstrous face. Frightened by his penetrating silent gaze, she commanded the image out of her mind and continued asking for a gatekeeper. The beast kept returning. Eventually she realized the creature wasn't harming her; it simply looked frightening. She began to talk with it and learned that it was an extremely powerful archangel who was there to teach her about neutralizing highly charged energies. She had received her gatekeeper and hadn't even realized it!

Keep opening to and getting to know your personal gatekeeper until you are clear and happy with the relationship you establish.

Chapter 6

Defining Your Gift Order: Making Your Life Real

> *Tanaquil, instead of throwing a roll at him, said, "You may be right. But what are they, the inner worlds? Dreams?"*
> *"Not at all. Places that might be. Places where we meet with ourselves."*
> *"But it was real."*
> *"Perhaps," said Jaive softly, "now you've made it real."*
> ~Tanith Lee, *Red Unicorn*

Your psychic gifts make you who and what you are. Despite any misgivings you might have about being "good at" being psychic, these inborn abilities explain your nature, personality, and your spiritual mission. The issue isn't whether they are positive or negative attributes; rather, it is how wisely you use them.

In the last chapter, you examined the many sides of discernment, from ethics to sourcing to selecting a gatekeeper. You have set the stage for a deeper understanding of your gifts. In this chapter, you will learn more about the three general types of psychic gifts, the eleven basic psychic abilities, and the chakras that house the psychic. The exercises provided at the end of this chapter are designed to help you assess and determine your gift order, the psychic abilities that are innate to you. This information will prepare you for Part III and the personalization of your intuitive process. Get ready to make your gifts real—and thereby realize your gifts in everyday life.

The Gift—and Genius—of the Psychic

Psychic gifts are more than a measurement of what you're good at. You might have a knack at cooking, a flair for design, or the ability to sell real estate. A gift, however, is a push from deep inside. It's born within you. It is a genius—your own unique form of genius.

Mozart was gifted in music. Virginia Woolf was talented at writing, and Vincent Van Gogh at painting. While these and other accomplished individuals worked hard to hone their arts, they didn't have much choice about it. Their gifts compelled expression.

Your psychic gifts may or may not have created a spectacular life for you. Your psychic gifts, however, are born within your spirit. When expressed in and through your body, they support your survival. When allowed to expand into spiritual gifts, they call dreams into reality. You are here on purpose, on a divine mission. In order to fulfill this mission, you must tap into the breadth and depth of your psychic abilities, for these ultimately hold the genius and power you need to accomplish your goals—and to be happy. They hold your genius, and the world is in need of it—and of you.

Stories of Psychic Styles

Alan remembers that he didn't want to get out of bed that long ago morning when his gut sense had been particularly strong. He was only four at the time and couldn't refuse to go to school, so he went in spite of his gut sense. His teacher had died of a stroke in front of the class.

Every time Julie is around her father these days, her heart

palpitates. She has seen a cardiologist, who just shook his head. "There's nothing wrong in there," he insisted. "Maybe you are just scaring yourself because your father has a heart condition."

Abdul is the matchmaker in the family. When his sister Fiona fell in love, he insisted that she was meant for someone else. He searched out this someone else and introduced him to his sister. Guess whom Fiona married?

Greg has a secret, but he can't say a word about it to anyone because he is a preacher and people might not understand. Greg doesn't prepare his sermons. He knows that as soon as he steps to the pulpit, the words will just enter his head. People love his preaching. The trouble occurs when words enter his head unbidden at other times—words from questionable sources. He can't even tell his wife about these.

Katie can see into everyone's past. Images float into her head. Most of the time, she doesn't mind—except for that one time she sat next to a stranger on the bus and grisly images entered her mind. She bolted, fearful for her life. Based on these pictures, she knew the man to be a murderer.

Each of these individuals is a psychic sensitive, a human prism of light. But each of these individuals has a different psychic style, a different way of being psychic.

- Alan is a physical kinesthetic. He is a mental sympathizer.
- Julie is also a physical kinesthetic. She is a physical sympathizer.
- Abdul is a spiritual kinesthetic. He is a relational sympathizer.
- Greg is verbal. He is a verbal sympathizer.
- Katie is visual. She is a visual sympathizer.

And you also are one—or more—of these types of psychic sensitives.

The Three Main Styles of Psychic Sensitivities
There are three main types of psychic sensitivities.

> **Kinesthetic:** receiving or sending psychic information of a sensory or feeling nature
> **Verbal:** receiving or sending messages through auditory means
> Visual: receiving or sending psychic information visually

All these styles involve interacting with the medium of life—light. They are all about translating and sharing streams of moving energy encoded with information, the building block of the universe and relationships. Each of these three main styles can be further subdivided to eleven categories. These categories relate to the first eleven chakras. (Each person's twelfth chakra is unique and personalized to the individual.)

Kinesthetic psychics register psychic information-energy through sensory means. There are several types of kinesthetics; Alan, Julie, and Abdul represent three of them. All forms of kinesthetic activity are body based. Kinesthetic psychics will receive and decipher psychic information as body-based messages.

There are nine specific kinesthetic gifts, but they can be divided into two main types: physical and spiritual. The **physical kinesthetic gifts** help you function in your body and in everyday reality. The **spiritual kinesthetic gifts** link you with the Divine and the world of spirits. Physical kinesthetic gifts are based in the chakras that emphasize the physical body and its senses. Spiritual kinesthetic gifts are housed in the chakras that highlight spiritual matters. Highly gifted physical kinesthetic psychics will be highly physical individuals. Their gifts may or may not need spiritual input to function. Individuals highly gifted in the spiritual area tend to be quite mystical. **Verbal psychics** will use psychic information tonally and through words. Greg is a natural verbal psychic. He hears spiritual guidance when at the pulpit. During his everyday life, his boundaries aren't as clear as they are on Sunday mornings, and he receives auditory input from more questionable entities and sources. His gifts can be called verbal sympathy.

Visual psychics receive and send psychic information through visual or pictorial means. Katie is a visual psychic. Her gift is functions one-way and involves seeing only into the past. Visual psychics might have a variety of specialties. They may psychically see medical conditions, the past, the potential future, the energy system, or others' current activities. All visual gifts can be labeled as visual sympathy.

These three divisions are similar to the basic learning styles discussed in education: kinesthetic, verbal, and visual. Psychic tendencies follow learning styles; most people communicate psychically the same primary way that they do through their senses. This means that if you are primarily a kinesthetic learner or communicator in life—someone who learns or communicates best by doing, by performing actions—you will probably be psychically kinesthetic; the same with verbal or visual. This isn't always true, however, which is why I have provided numerous psychic tests so that you can correctly identify your true psychic strengths.

As in everyday life, many individuals rely on all three basic ways of knowing, but usually in a certain order. I am mainly visual, secondarily kinesthetic, and verbal trots in at last place. My youngest son is off-the-chart kinesthetic, secondarily visual, and lastly verbal. Usually people are strongest in one category. Sometimes, though rarely, certain people are equally strong in all three categories.

Each psychic style is linked to particular chakras.

Type of Gift	Chakra(s)
Kinesthetic: Physical	1, 2, 3, 10
Kinesthetic: Spiritual	4, 7, 8, 9, 11
Verbal	5
Visual	6

Each type of psychic gift has a downside, however. This is because all psychic gifts are **sympathetic**. To sympathize means to feel something as if it's our own issue. When we sympathize, we merge with the other person or being. This is why being psychic can be so difficult. You can feel someone else's emotions, but you can't always distinguish them from your own. You can see someone's past, but you can't stop the filmstrip. You can hear voices, but you cannot turn off the soundtrack. Sympathizing can be a one-way ticket to the psychic victimization cycle.

The intuitive path involves transforming the psychic sympathetic gifts into **empathetic** gifts. To empathize means to register or mark that which others experience. While sympathizing blurs lines separating the self from others, empathizing allows compassion with separation. Traveling onto an intuitive-development path shifts psychic sympathies to intuitive empathies.

The Eleven Psychic Gifts

All three main psychic styles can be further divided into eleven main psychic gifts, each of which is housed in a particular chakra.

Chakra	Gift
First	Physical sympathy
Second	Feeling sympathy
Third	Mental sympathy

Fourth	Relational sympathy
Fifth	Verbal sympathy
Sixth	Visual sympathy
Seventh	Spiritual sympathy
Eighth	Shadow sympathy
Ninth	Soul sympathy
Tenth	Environmental sympathy
Eleventh	Force sympathy

As with psychic styles, you might have some very strong psychic gifts, others that are somewhat strong, and yet others that are barely there. You might have several strong gifts and one weaker one, or only one strong gift and many weaker ones. Your gift constellation will be unique to you and tailored to your spiritual destiny.

What does it mean to be a "first chakra physical sympathizer" or a "third chakra mental sympathizer?" You'll become more fully acquainted with all chakra gifts in Part III, but you might find it interesting to review each chakra and a brief description of the psychic gift housed within it. As you read through this list, pay attention to which gifts seem to best describe your psychic skills and keep them in mind when you do this chapter's exercises. A more complete description of each of these gifts and its corresponding chakra and auric layer is provided just after these synopses, so you can study the gifts that apply to you.

Chakra One Gift: Physical Sympathy

Style: Physical Kinesthetic

This is the ability to sense reality through your physical body. Physical sympathizers feel others' physical issues as if they were their own. If someone in front of you stubs his or her toe, your own toe may feel like it is broken! This gift is a dynamic expression of living in a physical world and knowing that world through the body.

Chakra Two Gift: Feeling Sympathy
Style: Physical Kinesthetic
Do you ever feel like an emotional sponge, as if everyone else's feelings are your own? Feeling sympathy is the ability to sympathize or register others' feelings. This psychic ability can attune you to the world a magical place of emotion, calling forth creativity and compassion—or cause you to be constantly overwhelmed with feelings to the point of being debilitated.

Chakra Three Gift: Mental Sympathy
Style: Physical Kinesthetic
Mental sympathizers are just plain smart in regard to information. You're able to perceive and sense information of all sorts, and since it comes in through your solar plexus, you also are usually in touch with your "gut"—for better or worse! Ideally, you can organize this information into neat packets, but if not, you can feel pretty overwhelmed by information you don't even want to know.

Chakra Four Gift: Relational Sympathy
Style: Spiritual Kinesthetic
When you attend a party, do you have an immediate sense of who is going out with whom, who wants to go out with someone, and who shouldn't be going out with his or her date? Relational sympathizers tune into information about just that—relationships! This can be a great trait unless you fail to screen out the information that's superfluous or if you take it all to heart.

Caretaking and codependency are two of the main deficits of being a relational sensitive.

Chakra Five Gift: Verbal Sympathy
Style: Verbal
Voices in the night, words in your head, tunes that never tone down—verbal sympathizers are just people who hear psychic information. This keen ability can provide invaluable insights and guided material, unless the sources are harmful, worthless, or just plain wrong. Verbal sympathizers must often contend with a plethora of psychic information that doesn't lead them anywhere but into the feeling of being crazy.

Chakra Six Gift: Visual Sympathy
Style: Visual
Do you see images or pictures—colors, filmstrips, or even written-out words—either in your mind's eye or with your actual eyes? Visual sympathizers receive just that—visual messages, sometimes in Technicolor, other times in shades of gray. It's a great gift, unless we're tuning into psychic data that's not for us or leaves us wondering about what it means. And there's nothing more annoying than closing your eyes at night and not getting a blank screen!

Chakra Seven Gift: Spiritual Sympathy
Style: Spiritual Kinesthetic
Have you always believed in a Higher Power? Felt a sense of destiny for yourself, others, and the world? Spiritual sympathizers are psychically aware of the Greater Spirit and the world of spirits. But not all that lingers in the spiritual realms are good. Because of this, the too-sensitive spiritual kinesthetic is often frightened

or depressed in relation to earthly matters. You might turn on the television only to feel dark and dreary because of the despairing nature of the news; you might sit on a bus only to feel sick because you sat next to someone you just knew was dishonest. This potentially awesome gift can be perceived as a curse in anyone who can't control it.

Chakra Eight Gift: Shadow Sympathy
Style: Spiritual Kinesthetic
For the shadow psychic, the world is a mysterious, magical place—and sometimes, so dark that it can seem that the light can't penetrate. The shadow sympathizer is really a shaman, someone who links heaven and earth and all the planes in between. You innately connect into and move between all five levels of reality. If you lack protection, ethics, or understanding, however, this can be a scary and dangerous endeavor. There really are not-so-good beings lurking in the shadows, as any shadow sympathizer can tell you.

Chakra Nine Gift: Soul Sympathy
Style: Spiritual Kinesthetic
Soul sympathizers know, deep in their hearts and souls, that we are all interconnected. They perceive the world as a community, and that's a good thing—except when they too-personally own the world's pain. No one can heal the world, but that won't keep soul sympathizers from trying, an endeavor that often drags them into the pits of depression and despair. While you might be able to sense what is happening in others' souls, you often can't do a thing about it, and that makes the world or certain groups seem frightening. It's difficult to perceive problems and not feel empowered to do anything about them. If this description fits, know that you are

actually psychically communicating to other beings through your soul, the aspect of self that stretches across all barriers to get to the truth, and so you *can* do something about the world's problems. Your soul is a vehicle for action, not only perception.

Chakra Ten Gift: Environmental Sympathy
Style: Physical Kinesthetic
Are you attuned to nature? To the waxing and waning of the moon, the call of the birds, the sound of the wind? Environmental sympathizers are highly sensitive to everything and anything in the environment and are in full relationship with all that is natural. This is a beautiful way of being, except that nature can be as grating as human beings are! Too-sensitive environmentalists often find themselves so affected by the natural—chemically, emotionally, energetically, and physically— that they can hardly function.

Chakra Eleven Gift: Force Sympathy
Style: Spiritual Kinesthetic
There are forces, both natural and supernatural, everywhere. Wind, fire, water, magic, powers, and ideas—all can be perceived and directed at will by the force sympathizer. Unfortunately, most in this psychic category haven't the least idea of their abilities, much less ways to manage them. Their moods and well-being, therefore, end up rising or falling with the barometer, as does their success. What might make you a leader often compels you to follow forces that control you, not the other way around.

Psychic Gift Descriptions in Depth
The following is a thorough description of each chakra and its related psychic gift, in addition to a brief overview of the corresponding auric layer.

Chakra One

Psychic Style: Physical Kinesthetic
Psychic Gift: Physical sympathy

Your first chakra is located in your pelvic area. It is frequently called the primal chakra because it is the entry point for your life-force energy, often pictured as a red flame.

Your first chakra is designed to continually renew your body by absorbing various types of elemental energy:

fire	stone
earth	wood
air	star
metal	ether
water	light

The first chakra is then able to connect and transfer these elements as life energy throughout the body, using the adrenal glands as the conversion organs.

To obtain the correct incoming energy, your first chakra emits frequency-based messages. These messages are psychically relayed from your external environment and others' bodies into your own body and then back again.

Activated from conception through the first six months of our life, this chakra makes a copy of your family-of-origin's beliefs about life to determine how it will direct life forces. In other words, the first chakra runs your physicality, using rules encoded from your family. If your family teaches you that you don't deserve to have your needs met, that message will control your perceptions about the physical aspects of life as well as your psychic boundaries.

You won't attract the physical abundance you need to be happy or thrive. Why would your body imprint such a negative program? Because survival in any family system depends upon following the rules. If your family sees success as negative, becoming successful would threaten your place in the family. Conversely, if your family teaches you that life is good, you will enjoy employing your life energy to meet your goals and needs. You will psychically attract the means to do so.

One of the ways psychic energy works in the first chakra is to communicate through the primary feelings of rage, joy, terror, shame, guilt, anger, and the like. You may feel any of the strong feelings if something or someone threatens your supply of life energy. Depending upon your family training, you may not believe that you can trust the Divine for nourishment. If you don't trust the Divine or believe that you are divine, you might steal energy from something or someone else, such as one or many addictive substances, including money, sex, alcohol, or other drugs, as a substitute for life energy. The false life energy from these substances closes off your energetic means of obtaining actual life energy, depleting your body of its personal energy reserves. Your psychic sense responds to the survival crisis by seeking even more energy, even to the point of taking on the diseases, sexual patterns, primal feelings, or survival issues of those around you. Your body desires homeostasis with the physical environment—even if obtaining this balance creates illness.

The negative uses of your first chakra's psychic gifts can be greatly alleviated if you can change your perception of life energy. Life energy is boundless since it comes from the Divine through the natural world. It runs through and around your body in tubules, subatomic vessels. The tubes feed the adrenals in particular. If the adrenals are stimulated by the appropriate energies from the higher chakras, especially the pineal gland, they actually carry a highly refined physical energy to the rest of the body. The key to this energizing process lies in accepting that your human and divine natures are actually identical.

Physical Sympathy. This chakra regulates your association with all peoples and objects important to your survival, including your birth family and, if applicable, your adopted and extended family. Later, you psychically connect to your own created family and sexual partners through this chakra. The psychic powers of this chakra also work to supply you with your bodily needs, including money, housing, air, food, touch, and clothing.

In order to assure your body's survival, this center may psychically pick up or notice diseases, others' issues or primal feelings, knowledge about money, or information about core physical needs. It will also emit information regarding these issues. If your life energy is low, this chakra will ideally drive you to obtain life energy straight from the Divine. Negative mental beliefs, however, will have this chakra looking to substitutes like addictive substances, sex, or cult sources of spiritual energies.

First Auric Layer. Located in and slightly above the skin, the first auric layer connects to your first chakra. Its primary psychic function is to prevent disease, strong negative emotions, and toxic thoughts or other toxins from entering your system. It also breathes bodily and emotional wastes into the atmosphere, eliminating them from your system. Your physical survival is highly dependent upon this auric layer, as it can actually transform higher energies into lower and vice versa.

Chakra Two

Psychic Style: Physical Kinesthetic
Psychic Gift: Feeling Sympathy

The second chakra, centered in the abdomen, focuses on feelings and creativity. In the Chinese system, this chakra holds and channels *chi,* or *expressive* life energy, which differs from the driving, fire-based life energy hosted by the first chakra. I often think of this chakra, as well as its partners, the tenth, fourth, sixth, and eighth chakras, as feminine centers, in contrast to first, third, fifth, seventh, and ninth chakras, with their descriptively masculine traits. I use the word *feminine* to reflect the receptive qualities of these chakras. They take in and absorb energy, while the so-called masculine chakras emit energy. Psychically, the feminine chakras read the psychic information-energy available, while the masculine chakras disseminate messages from us to the world.

You know that your second chakra is healthy when you're able to freely share your feelings with others. When balanced through your second chakra, you'll also be sensually open in that lovely, innocent way that children display. And you'll dazzle the world with your own creative force.

Signs of second chakra dysfunction include being overwhelmed with your own or others' feelings; feeling stuck, mired down, or in a boring reality; and being unable to show your special gifts to the world.

From a scientific viewpoint, your second chakra houses dozens of neurotransmitters. These chemical receptors emit hormonal building blocks that affect you in two ways:

- They help form or regulate hormones that run your bodily system.
- They serve as response mechanisms for emotions.

You have nearly as many neurotransmitters in your abdomen region as you do in your brain. Neurotransmitters create our feeling states. Like our feelings, they are affected by our hormones, but they also determine the health of our hormones. The major glands of the second chakra are the ovaries and the testes, our body's hormone producers. Biology underscores ancient wisdom, which has long testified to the second chakra as the key to emotional health.

Feelings are important for mental as well as emotional activity. Several brain researchers have shown that without emotion, we would be unable to lead normal lives. Without access to our feeling-based capacities, we can't reason, and small decisions become overwhelming. When your neurotransmitters are disconnected, you become either extremely myopic or completely unfocused, and either state incapacitates your ability to reason. The non-feeling person also lacks all creativity.

Developmentally, the second chakra is most highly charged during the ages of six months to two and a half years. This is when the second chakra initially opens. Programs locked in during this time period will affect your emotional and creative forces for the rest of your life. During these years, you learn about feelings from your parents and extended family. These are crucial years for having your feelings acknowledged and affirmed. If your feelings are stunted or judged during these years, they will remain frozen until you get therapy or other intervention as an adult. In fact, the emotional patterns engaged in during these years will repeat themselves in later relationships unless you create new patterns.

Your psychic programming will match your internalized emotional patterns. This is why so many of us keep experiencing the same emotional traumas over and over, or become afflicted with diseases that mirror the emotional pain suffered during childhood.

Physically, the second chakra is the area of your intestines and sexual organs, the kidneys, and the lower back. Conditions like irritable bowel syndrome (IBS), premenstrual syndrome (PMS), prostate cancer, and the like might be at least partially associated with psychic problems in the second chakra.

Feeling Sympathy. This chakra enables us to feel others' feelings and to allow ourselves and others access to our own feelings.

Second Auric Layer. This auric layer serves as a filter for emotional or feeling frequencies—those that you release and those you take in from outside of yourself. Its primary function is to maintain the emotional safety of your internal environment, releasing steam, if you will, when you become too emotional. This field will also open to external influences when you require energetic input. The second auric layer is located right outside of the tenth auric layer and is about one and one-half to two inches thick, except in areas that are drained, toxic, or overfull.

Chakra Three

Psychic Style: Physical Kinesthetic
Psychic Gift: Mental Sympathy

The third chakra is located in the solar plexus. It is often called the brain of the body because it rules your use of thoughts, thought forms, and consciousness waves. Because of its specialty, this chakra assists you with understanding the world in practical, data-based ways.

Sharing both sensory and psychic information with your brain, this chakra is responsible for forming beliefs, as well as mental strongholds. Through partnership with your second chakra, it also creates emotions and emotional strongholds. You may think that your beliefs or thinking patterns are rational and objective, but they are actually quite subjective. Most of us have adopted our beliefs unconsciously, and many of us are unaware of beliefs that inhibit our success. Rather than supporting love and a winning attitude, many beliefs create fear, hostility, and judgments—none of which are going to get you ahead in life.

Misperceptions and false beliefs often inhibit your personal power, the intrinsic belief in yourself that you need to succeed at anything, including your divine spiritual mission. If you don't have a sense of personal power, your self-esteem will be low. Self-esteem is a measurement of how well you like yourself. If you have low self-esteem, your self-confidence is probably also low. Self-confidence is the ability to put yourself into the world. When your self-confidence or relationship with the world is threatened, you'll either become highly anxious or overtly grandiose.

If you have personal power and high self-esteem, you'll project the self-confidence you need to become successful in the working world. But you won't be able to fake it. If you don't really like yourself, if you don't honestly believe in yourself, your third chakra will psychically tell the world. Others are psychic too, and they will sense that you aren't confident and think that maybe there is a reason for this. They will feel that you don't like yourself and wonder if it wouldn't be wise for them to dislike you, too.

If your third chakra beliefs are solid, your special gifts will be rewarded. You will feel good about work and how you deal with people. You'll be able to work in just about any organizational system. In fact, you will be able to establish and maintain information systems of any sort, whether they are administrative, procedural, or creative. A healthy third chakra can, therefore, help you fulfill your calling in practical and everyday ways.

This energy center develops when you are two and a half to four and a half years old. This time period is one of testing and checking out how the world responds to us. Based on the conclusions you drew from others' reactions during this time period, your third chakra will then:

1. Use the responses it received to form the basis of personal power, self-esteem, and self-confidence,
2. Lock in the beliefs underpinning your motivations for success,
3. Harness and direct the physical energy of the solar plexus organs to move you forward into the world,
4. Continue to gather and send psychic data that enables your physical energy to propel you forward, according to your preset beliefs.

Physiologically, the organs involved in helping us master success include the liver, stomach, pancreas, spleen, gall bladder, and aspects of the kidneys. The pancreas is the lead endocrine gland of this chakra, although the liver is highly important for full functioning. When your physical energy runs low, your psychic senses will attempt to adjust, perhaps by absorbing energy from others, overworking to build self-esteem, or compulsively craving stimulants.

Sometimes, if you've been overworking, your third chakra will make you sick to slow you down. You will psychically send out the message "illness needed," usually attracting the "tired viruses," like Epstein Barr, chronic fatigue syndrome, mononucleosis, or maybe just the common cold. All digestive disturbances not involving second-chakra organs are based in the third chakra.

Mental Sympathy. This chakra is the most active kinesthetic chakra involved in gathering and processing raw data or information. The type of data gathered is contingent upon your beliefs, especially those that relate to self-esteem (what you believe about yourself) and self-confidence (what you believe about your place in the world). The job of the psychic sensitivities in this chakra is to assure that your body has enough energy to run your digestive and absorption processes. These are the energizing functions that support you in achieving your goals in the world.

Third Auric Layer. Connected to your third chakra, the third auric layer is like a widespread fishing net, stretching into many dimensions. It serves as your conduit or connection point to places of information or knowledge. These information sources tap into all five levels of reality: the Spirit, the World of Spirits, the Energetic, the Antiworlds, and the Natural (see chapter 5). The purpose of this extensive outreach is to enable you to receive or send information necessary to achieve worldly success. As you might imagine, this netting can also broaden a current base of knowledge.

Chakra Four

Psychic Style: Spiritual Kinesthetic
Psychic Gift: Relational Sympathy

The fourth chakra, the heart center, is located in the chest cavity. Physically, this center's authority encompasses the physical organs of the heart and lungs.

The heart chakra manages the relationships that you need to survive. These relationships include the most obvious: your parents (birth and adopted, if applicable), your brothers and sisters, your extended family, and individuals that instruct you throughout life. The list also includes your relationship with other forms of life, the Spirit, other spirits, and, internally, the relationships between all aspects of the self. You will energetically attract, repel, and maintain the relationships you believe you need to survive and thrive.

The lungs, a particular facet of the heart chakra, serve love in a specific way. They take in and distribute oxygen, then release the breath's waste products. In the bigger picture, their function is about allowing the Spirit to bring you what you need and take away all that you don't need. In Greek, Hebrew, and Latin, the word for *breath* and the word *spirit* are the same, reflecting the fact that each breath is supposed to affirm your relationship with the Spirit of the Divine and your personal spirit.

Awakened between the ages of four and one-half and six and one-half, the heart center locks in your beliefs about love, relationship, and healing. From this point on, these core beliefs will control most of the aspects of your life concerning relationships—and just about everything else. Scientifically, research at centers such as the Institute of HeartMath in California are demonstrating that the heart might be the central endocrine gland in the body, regulating the conditions for brain function, hormones, oxygenation, nervous system function, and even certain forms of intuition. Energetically, the heart chakra is located in the middle of our in-body energy system, which might explain its physical importance. All lower and higher chakras flow into it; everything leads to the heart.

The heart has always been known as the center of love, which is really the center of life. If you don't give or receive love, your dreams won't come true and your true self cannot step forward. Lacking love, your heart will suffer and so will your relationships and life. A lackluster love life often leads to addictions; relationship and sugar addictions are common signs of a void in your love life. All cardiovascular problems relate to heart chakra issues as well; you can read more about this relationship in my book *Advanced Chakra Healing: Heart Disease.*

There is yet another layer to the heart chakra: dreaming. Your deepest desires lie like seeds within your heart. These include little dreams, like wanting strawberry ice cream cones, to big ones, like flying across the Atlantic. For some of us, the only time we pay attention to our dreams is when we sleep—or when daydreaming during a boring meeting! Paying attention to your dreams can tell you what is going on in your heart. If you know what's going on in your heart, you can figure out how to better live your life. Your nightly dream life also has a psychic dimension: when you are sleeping, your soul is able to connect your psychological and your spiritual selves to other people and places.

Relational Sympathy. This chakra is a convergent site for messages about love and relationships. It will emit signals based upon relationship beliefs in order to attract your heart's desires. Relationships, like the heart, are necessary for survival. When threatened, the body will shut down all other organs first and save the heart. Likewise, this chakra will psychically do anything it can to bring you relationships you perceive as necessary, even if they aren't good for you.

Fourth Auric Layer. The second auric layer connects us to others emotionally, as does the fourth auric layer. The fourth layer, however, connects us relationally as well.

This layer links you with the people, places, objects, and other beings that are, have been, or could become important to you. While the ideal connections are based on love or affection, many times the reasons we bond are based on fear, glamour, neediness, or even hatred. Even these seemingly bad relationships might be important from a survival point-of-view. The rationale for making relationship decisions is based upon the ancient need for security in a community. Your body and lower brain functions might perceive usefulness in negative relationships, even if your spirit does not.

This auric layer also serves as portal to the astral plane. The **astral plane** interlinks all dimensions, and you can find grace, as well as interfering characters, in it. When suddenly you become aware of a friend two thousand miles away, the reason might be the heartstrings interconnecting the two of you through the astral plane. If you dream about meeting your ideal mate and this event has not yet occurred, it is because the bonds might already be present on the astral, even though they have not yet manifested in sensory reality. Time is of no essence in the astral dimension. The astral dimension functions on magnetic or attraction energy, so it will draw all desired—or even seemingly undesirable—relationships to you.

Chakra Five

Psychic Style: Verbal
Psychic Gift: Verbal Sympathy

The fifth chakra, located in the throat, gives voice to your true desires, needs, and opinions. This chakra awakens during ages six and one-half to eight and one-half and is most potent during this stage of self-expression. Already brimming with feelings, beliefs, and knowledge about relationships, we begin to more fully express these internal states of being with definitive and clear statements:

"I want this."
"I need that."
"I will do this."
"I won't do that."

The reactions we experience to stating our needs shape the fifth chakra, setting the stage for later effectiveness in manifesting what we want. If others respected your statement of needs in childhood, you will now believe in your ability to manifest. You know that you can express your desires and obtain the support you need. If your attempts at individuation were thwarted, mocked, or ridiculed, you won't believe in yourself or in others. You'll either stifle your self-expression or overstate your needs. Others either won't be able to or won't want to help you.

The resulting frustration can cause problems. You might totally shut down, too scared to share your inner thoughts. You could become angry or volatile. Or you might mouth off and create constant trouble for yourself or others. On the extreme side, you could develop physical throat-area problems, such as thyroid, larynx, or ear difficulties. As the thyroid is the major endocrine gland in this chakra, many thyroid issues reveal undercurrents in the fifth chakra.

The most typical source of fifth-chakra problems is what I call old tapes. These are negative messages we heard when growing up, and they now work like a Memorex tape, repeating over and over in our head. Why do we hold onto these destructive thoughts? At some level, they are comforting. We think they keep us safe in an unsafe world.

Psychically, being shut down in the fifth chakra can cause you to tune out needed guidance or open to unnecessary or even harmful psychic sources. Psychic communication problems almost always stem from an inability to self-communicate. If you can't hear the song of your own soul, it's pretty difficult to hear the Divine. And if you mistrust the Divine, it's common to create energetic contracts with negative external sources. Discarnate entities hover on all five levels of reality. Many would like nothing better than to be heard, if only to feel more powerful. The trouble is that many of these entities have nothing worthwhile to share, and some have only bad things to say. Some of them like to plug into your **silver cord,** the linkage between your physical body and your soul body. This silver cord is located in the neck. Some harmful sources tug on this cord in order to keep your soul outside of your body, so that they can control either your soul or your body. If you are going to psychically open this chakra, you'd better be careful about how you screen for callers.

Verbal Sympathy. The throat center allows verbal communication for psychic as well as sensory sources. Depending on your gifts or your programming, it enables you to hear tones, noises, messages, words, languages, or other verbal communication from any and all psychic sources. Some types of sources can actually enter the body through the fifth chakra. This is usually a dangerous procedure, although inviting the angelic or healing sources can produce miracles. Psychically verbal messages don't always end in psychic communiqués. Fifth-chakra sensitives also include the world's best writers, the most sensitive composers, the most lyrical singers, heart-touching preachers, or favorite college teachers—all people who convert psychic to sensory messages through this chakra.

Fifth Auric Layer. The fifth auric layer, companion to the fifth chakra, is a medium for allowing in or communicating outside guidance from both live and spiritual sources. Information can also come from other aspects of your self, so you must be careful when interpreting the source of a message and its true meaning.

This auric layer stretches beyond the natural world into the four other levels of reality. Through it, you can communicate with just about anyone or anything, anywhere, at any time. In the past, this field served like a built-in cellular phone—a plus when a saber-tooth tiger was roaming just a few feet away, and you wanted to psychically tell your tribe about it. These days we have an entirely different set of dangers (which might actually include real cellular phones!).

I call this field the parallel auric layer because of how it works. The fifth auric layer transposes data upside down, and that data is then deciphered within the wheels of the fifth chakra. Listen with the outer wheel, and your programming might confuse the data. Hear with the inner wheel, and you'll interpret accurately. The word *parallel* also fits this chakra because this center serves as a portal to what are called the parallel universes (as does the eighth chakra). When you look back at your life, you can see the stepping stones that brought you into the here and now. Each of these steps, however, has another next to it. If you were to step onto one of these side stones, you would find yourself in a parallel reality (or attached reality), a life in which you took a different turn than the one that you actually took. These alternative realities might spin off for years' worth of experiences or for only one moment, but they are all available through the fifth auric layer. Through this chakra, you can then determine what might have been, as well as what might be.

Chakra Six

Psychic Style: Visual
Psychic Gift: Visual Sympathy

Known as the Third Eye, this energy center presents special sight or, you might say, *insight*. Through this chakra, you see beyond the sensory reality. You peer into the realms of the extrasensory.

Based in the pituitary gland, your sixth chakra helps regulate primary endocrine functions. Your endocrine hormones regulate your bodily systems, which means there is a strong correlation between how you see reality psychically and what you create physically. You will manifest what you can see—and believe—as possible.

Children are often born with "the sight," or the ability to see into different realities. Unfortunately, just when this chakra hits

its peak, cultural norms clamp down on the young daydreamers. This constraint usually occurs during the ages of eight and one-half to thirteen, when the Third Eye is most open. Though we are all able to see the world the Creator made, our culture usually forces its own worldview upon us. Because we want to be acceptable, we tend to reject visions that are good and interject the beliefs about men, women, power, and ourselves that are mirrored by the people around us.

The psychic system assures community cohesiveness. In primary or indigenous cultures, it is imperative to adapt to the clan. The chakra system still upholds these more primitive needs, and our Third Eye is a major force for integrating us within our culture. In more spiritual communities, however, it was important to help individuals see not only the truth of the larger community, but also truths about themselves, which included recognizing abilities, purpose, and importance. We no longer emphasize the unique and vital qualities of the individual; rather, the world insists in sublimating everyone to the same standard. This is one reason teenagers so often turn to addictive substances, gang membership, or problematic behavior. If no one sees you as you really are, how can you become what you are supposed to be? Rather than adapt to an inner template of truth, you'll adopt the norm, which isn't necessarily a good thing.

The ideas implanted during this chakra's opening create the picture of yourself that you carry into adulthood, as well as the template for endocrine health. Your body will evolve—or devolve—into the self-image forged during childhood. Adapt to negative images, and your hormones work against, rather than for, good health. Years of hormonal abnormalities can result in physical problems later in life. Weight issues, multiple sclerosis, adult-onset diabetes, migraines, vision problems, and secondary thyroid and heart problems are but a few of the potential issues stemming from negative sixth-chakra programming.

Your Third Eye also plays a critical role in the ability to envision your heart's desires. Potential life paths enter through the back side of this chakra. Let's say five bad, three medium, and one great path stream in. Your self-image, housed in the center of the pituitary, sees these potentials with X-ray clarity. What potential will it choose? What probable, if not a certain, future? The answer depends on your opinion of yourself! The selected path is projected through the front side of the chakra and transforms into a life goal. This vision or strategy of life will most likely be realized—we usually end up where we are headed. If you have assumed too many negative cultural norms, thus causing yourself to have a poor self-image, your goals will leave you falling short of your potential. Guess which type of objectives most of us pick?

Visual Sympathy. This chakra is often known as the center of clairvoyance, a word that means "to clearly see." You record psychic impressions as images, pictures, words, mental movie clips, dreams, or any other visual imagining. At baseline, this psychic ability clarifies perceived threats or opportunities so that you can make wise decisions. Reading the past, present, and the future, this center is critical for decision-making or for learning from past mistakes.

Sixth Auric Layer. Composed entirely of light, this auric layer receives or sends visual impressions. It also transfers particles and waves of light from this or other worlds into your body, where they can be used for healing—or for harm. Often called the celestial body, this field looks like a matrix of spun light filaments, vibrating at different levels around and beyond us. This is the origination point of many mystical experiences.

At the highest level, this auric layer enables our souls to work with higher truths and energies, like the powers or the shining ones (see chapter 5). When linked with higher consciousness or beings, you can perceive your true spiritual goals and decide how to meet them.

Chakra Seven

Psychic Style: Spiritual Kinesthetic
Psychic Gift: Spiritual Sympathy

In most cultures, the seventh chakra is known as the spiritual center. The color of this energy center, white, indicates what this chakra best represents: purity, purpose, the Divine, all things spiritual, and our own unique spirit. Through this chakra, you ideally connect to the Divine and divine messengers, as well as all beings in the world of spirits—good or bad. This is the energy center of your spiritual consciousness. It is also the center through which streams the higher energy required to serve others in a good way.

This energy center, which matures fully during the ages of thirteen to twenty-one, is also physically open during infancy through the fontanel, the soft spot of a baby's head. Its physical location is actually in the pineal gland, which sits in the middle of your head near the middle of your eyebrows. The pineal gland is a fascinating endocrine gland and not well understood.

Science knows that the pineal gland produces feel-good hormones, such as serotonin and melatonin, which help you sleep. Metaphysical history suggests this gland as the seed of spiritual awakenings. Recent scientific research, when blended with ancient knowledge of alchemy, reveal this organ as housing certain transitional metals, known as monatomic metals. When these metals are spun at certain frequencies, they actually decrease the weight of anything they are touching. When spun within bodily glands, these metals have produced amazing results in healing disease, raising consciousness, and reducing stress levels. My theory is that spiritual evolution stimulates hormone changes in the pineal, which initiates this metallic spin. Once the spin from the seventh chakra hits the first chakra and the adrenals housed there, a certain chemical—perhaps an enzyme—is activated in the heart. In turn, we are fully initiated on the divine pathway and can live life full of love and joy.

Because we're born with this and the first chakra already activated, we are born knowing the truth that the elemental and divine pathways are one and the same, that the body and the spirit are of equal matter—and even made of the same matter, which is love. When we're most vulnerable, these seemingly opposing energies commingle, thus symbolizing the two aspects of being human: the physical and the spiritual. We are embodied to follow our own will while living out divine will. When your pineal gland is functioning, you're able to link with your own spirit and spiritual truths. This connection assures harmony between your spirit and body, and you will feel fulfilled.

Prozac and other antidepressants act on the pineal gland, just as do spiritual energies and forces. Western civilization is currently undergoing a seventh-chakra crisis, as can be witnessed in the number of individuals on antidepressant or anti-anxiety medication. Western culture does almost nothing to help individuals uncover their personal, spiritual destinies, even though our history would invite us to do otherwise.

Before age fourteen, the chakras were focused on self-awareness and individuality. The seventh-chakra opening, from ages fourteen through twenty, marks a turning away from the self-centered "things of childhood" to the ways of greater humanity. We are called to live in community and to share our gifts with others. Almost all cultures, save Western white culture, recognize the need to help youngsters shift from an ego-based identity to community-based concerns. Many indigenous cultures perform rituals when this chakra awakens. By skipping these coming-of-age rites, usually called initiations or vision quests, we in the West are teaching kids to fear psychic sensitivities. But still they hear voices, and what are these voices supporting? Teen suicide, school absenteeism, delinquency, gangs, and school shootings. As discussed in the previous section on the sixth chakra, feeling important is contingent on having someone recognize your special qualities. When adults don't treat kids as unique or important, kids are vulnerable to less-than-savory authorities—including their own inner fears.

One of the reasons that the teen years are so confusing and complicated is that each of the seven years associated with the seventh-chakra development recycles earlier years. For instance, from age fourteen to fifteen, a young person functions in the newly awakening seventh chakra and the first chakra simultaneously. This period presents him or her with the opportunity to heal or transform long-standing security issues. The seventh chakra also triggers these security issues, which can be pretty overwhelming for the young person, as well as his or her loved ones. Having a better understanding of this process could help everyone benefit from these shifts.

During each of the seven years engaging this chakra, our emerging relationship with our own spirit invites analysis and change. These years provide the opportunity to reprocess the following issues.

End of thirteenth through the fourteenth year: Reprocesses first-chakra issues about security and survival, and psychic programming about material needs.

End of fourteenth through the fifteenth year: Reprocesses second-chakra issues about feelings and creativity, and psychic programming about caregiving and caretaking.

End of fifteenth through the sixteen year: Reprocesses third-chakra beliefs and thoughts, and psychic programming affecting worldly success.

End of sixteenth through the seventeenth year: Reprocesses fourth-chakra ideas about relationships and desires, and psychic programming about love and heart's desires.

End of seventeenth through the eighteenth year: Reprocesses fifth-chakra issues about communication, and psychic programming about sharing and receiving opinions and truths.

End of eighteenth through the nineteenth year: Reprocesses formative ideas creating vision, and psychic programming about self-image and life choices.

End of nineteenth through the twentieth year: Reprocesses all thoughts about spiritual purpose and unlocks psychic programming about our divine mission and role in community.

Spiritual Sympathy. The seventh chakra is attuned to psychic energy relating to spiritual matters, divine will, and your own spiritual calling. While the information is spiritual in nature, it is registered through the five senses and all other forms of psychic sensitivity. This means that the seventh-chakra data can be felt, sensed, smelled, known, seen, or heard.

There are many ways a spiritual message can be processed through the energy system. Entering through the seventh chakra, a divine knowing might be downloaded into the sixth chakra, where it is transformed into a vision. Perhaps your seventh chakra transfers the insight to the fifth chakra, which then turns it into words. Maybe your spiritual revelation is sent from the seventh to the third chakra, in which case you'll simply get a gut sense.

Spiritually inaccurate data or perceptions are frequently projections of personal will, childhood programs, or external manipulation. This manipulation can originate in several sources, including beings from any of the five levels of reality. Consciousness patterns can also affect your seventh chakra and, therefore, your psychic perceptions.

Seventh Auric Layer. Often perceived psychically as an egg-shaped skein about three and one-half feet around the body, this auric layer emits a thin but high frequency that guards against spiritual attacks, misperceptions, and negativity. If your seventh chakra is attuned to your spirit, the seventh auric layer will emanate a harmonic rhythm that broadcasts messages, needs, and healing energy to the rest of the world and magnetizes your desires to you.

This layer of the auric field could also be called an etheric field in that it opens to aspects of the universe and the Divine. As well, it connects to the **energy egg**, an energy body that links you to higher realms (see chapter 3).

Like all auric layers, the seventh serves basic survival functions. While it might seem difficult to relate spirituality with primal survival, a glance through history would prove otherwise. Without a sense of purpose, life would have no meaning. Lacking meaning, few of us want to be alive.

Chakra Eight

Psychic Style: Spiritual Kinesthetic
Psychic Gift: Shadow Sympathy

The eighth chakra invites the *heyoke* in us all. In the Lakota tradition, a heyoke is a person who brings balance to the norm by doing everything in reverse. He or she might spin backward during the native dances, speak in contradictions, find humor in the tragic, and see the world through black-tinted glasses. Other traditions use images like those of the coyote or fox to describe this paradoxical energy. Kokopelli and the Thunder Beings are other native North American figures for oppositional beings, as is the fairy character Puck in Shakespeare's *A Midsummer's Night Dream*. The eighth chakra is our connection to heyoke, which we might also call shadow energy.

Located just above the head, the structure of this chakra is heyoke in itself. The size of a mere pinprick, it paradoxically opens to all known time. Up here, you will find the personal records of everything that you have ever known, done, said, been, or thought. These recordings are called the Akashic Records in some traditions. Their placement in the eighth chakra marks this energy center as the center of time and space. Psychics often uncover their own and others' pasts by reading the Akashic Records.

Along with the fifth chakra, this center is an access point for current, potential, and alternative realities. One of the tools for viewing reality is the Book of Life, a set of records similar to the Akashic, but with one major difference. While the Akashic are exact renderings, the Book of Life reveals the best of what has been, is happening, or might occur. It puts everything in a good light and might just as well be called a book of light! Shamans, individuals with the ability to connect the various levels of realities and dimensions, often work with both records. When using their eighth-chakra gifts, shamans can also journey to parallel realities and universes, and to the Antiworlds.

There are many aspects of a person that can undertake such

travel: the soul; the soul's etheric body, which is the soul's personal auric field; and sub-aspects of the personality, including inner children, the higher self, and more. (These and other aspects of the personality are listed and described in *Advanced Chakra Healing*.) Depending on the mode they use, shamans can accomplish several tasks through eighth-chakra psychic travel. They can:

- Project their images so as to deliver messages or healing energies or to gather information.
- Enter a dream state and travel psychically to discover the real cause of a problem or to address it.
- Be in two places at the same time, thus sending psychic energy from the visited site directly back to their own or another's body.
- Send their consciousness fully into their personal travel vehicle. This way, they can manipulate people or events elsewhere as if they were present, move objects at will, or shapeshift into other forms.

In contemporary terms, such journeying is often called regression, hypnosis, futuring, visioning work, soul or astral travel, or, when done while sleeping, lucid dreaming.

Why would you do any of these things? A well-intentioned shaman wants to heal or help. A poor-intentioned shaman is gathering power for the sake of becoming powerful. The latter potential is one of the reasons that the eighth chakra is often known as a power center. Through it, you can download energy from about any source in any chakra—and for any purpose. That's power.

Physically, this chakra relates to the thymus, a gland located just above the heart and underneath the neck. The thymus has been little understood by the medical community, though it has been considered one of the two major immune-system regulators. Researchers and writers, including Richard Gerber, author of *Vibrational Medicine,* suggest that the thymus is a critical organ at every level, especially for overall health. Energetically, I believe it mediates between the Antiworlds and this world, transferring possibilities into concrete reality and vice versa. An intuitive shaman can regulate this transference; a psychic sensitive is often the victim of it. Hence, it is important to gain control of the shamanic gifts.

This chakra is primarily awakened during ages twenty-one to twenty-eight, and your first walk into this chakra is an invitation to address your karma. Don't be frightened of this word. *Karma* is simply a Sanskrit term for "issues." Your issues consist of tasks, challenges, responsibilities, and beliefs that you need to face if you are to meet your spiritual destiny. Karma can also include gifts you need to own and use.

The eighth chakra challenges us all to reexamine family-of-origin doctrines and to finish soul learning. Your path may include making amends for your own destructive behavior and relationship patterns. Many people would suggest that you also make reparation for what you did in past lives. Personally, I believe the real goal behind this time period is to figure out how to stop making the past more important than the present. We must learn to release, forgive, and move on. This is the message of Jesus Christ, a master shaman, as well as all other masters who follow the Divine. The real message of Christ on the cross is that our sins or karma are already erased. We aren't separate from the Spirit. We can live in our own spirits through the spirit of the Divine that unifies us all.

The key to this sacred power lies in understanding the nature of paradox. Sometimes the most tragic or painful circumstances of your life are the most critical and important. Sometimes that which you enjoy the most causes the greatest damage. The eighth chakra invites you to the understanding of paradox. It welcomes you into the heyoke dance. You must be willing to endure—and be—shadows in order to see the light.

Shadow Sympathy. The eighth chakra is the point for gathering and emitting psychic information regarding the past, present, and potential. Through the eighth chakra, you live in the seam between the worlds. The eighth chakra holds dark and light—and thus shadows. Here, a gifted mystic can journey to various places, lands, and experiences. Here a psychic sensitive can gather information, healing energies, and forces. Here lies the power of the past and the ability to direct the future with psychic means.

Here is the place you answer the question of why. Why do you seek power? Why do you want to be powerful? Traditionally, journeys conducted through this chakra are undertaken to conduct spiritual battle, to perform healing or divination, or to change physical reality through energetic means.

Eighth Auric Layer. The eighth auric layer, like its corresponding chakra, is complex and paradoxical. Occupying no space and all space simultaneously, this field could be compared to the scientific idea about time called string theory and an even more recent theory called causal dynamical triangulation (CDT). String theory asserts that all dimensions interweave like strings tied at different levels. From one string, you might jump from one dimension to another or one time period to another. CDT explains that these strings are actually part of a four-dimensional matrix of energy composed of tetrahedrons organized in triangular form. These combined theories illustrate a universe of interdimensional folds, in which the equipped or trained time technician can psychically visit or perceive what's happening in other worlds and along all dimensions. The eighth auric layer is created from the same type of material as this greater matrix, so this field can bring you to places real or not yet real through its webbing throughout all time, space, and dimensions.

Chakra Nine

> **Psychic Style:** Spiritual Kinesthetic
> **Psychic Gift:** Soul Sympathy

Key words for the ninth chakra are harmony, balance, truth, higher purpose, and love.

Your ninth chakra, located about an arm span over your head, could be called the seat of your soul. Picture it metaphorically as a cell containing genes. Actually, the templates and codes for your physical DNA begin as symbols and ideas located within the ninth chakra. What emerges in the body is first created in the soul, the origin of these etheric genes and programs. Look into your ninth chakra, and you'll find the blueprint for your soul traits, needs, issues, character, purpose, plans, and destiny steps.

Examining the ninth chakra begs a discussion on the main differences between your spirit and the soul; the ninth chakra is about soul, not spirit. Your spirit carries your overall mission, while your soul is invested with the powers needed to fulfill that mission in third-dimensional reality. Your soul will be more focused on what you're going to achieve and learn one lifetime at a time, while your spirit holds the big picture. The sum total of all soul experiences equals your spirit's divine destiny. Hence, the ninth chakra serves as not only the seed for this life's goals and purpose, but also as a channel for spiritual powers and truths. It also holds the records of all of the goals or missions undertaken by your soul throughout the past.

It could be said that to master this reality, you must live out your soul destiny. You must be self-accepting and self-loving enough to fully embrace and express all that is your soul. The difficulty most of us have is that our souls are not perfect. While the blueprint of your being is perfect and carried in your spirit, the imprint of experience is held in the soul. While your spiritual template remains constant and stellar perfect, your soul template is damaged and slightly off-key.

Your soul, the sum total of your upbringing, personality, needs, traits, desires, ego, reactions, and drives, requires healing and realignment with the divine plan. Healing is only possible if you accept what you've become, warts and all, and allow spiritual transformation, starting with forgiveness and self-acceptance. *As well, it helps to acknowledge that the plan changes as you go.* There's nothing written in the skies that says there's only one certain way to achieve your vital purpose; there is only support for the process of doing so.

When dancing in their ninth chakra, most people feel more blissful than they could ever imagine. This is because they are reconnecting with the self that they were programmed and designed to be. In the eyes of the Divine, we are entirely acceptable. Acceptability is not comparable to perfection or even perfectibility. Damage occurs because others haven't accepted us and we haven't accepted ourselves. When you internalize judgment, judge other people, or judge yourself, you are caught on this judgment loop. See yourself through God's eyes, and then God's eyes become your own.

The ninth chakra physically correlates with the diaphragm. Most Eastern traditions revere the breath as an imperative connection to the Divine. Through the breath, you connect your spirit with the Greater Spirit. Indigenous populations conduct sacred ceremonies with tobacco, smoke, and various medicines to use the power of breath in establishing divine-human relationships. Every time you breathe, you are linking your soul and spirit with your body. Between breaths, your soul and spirit are invited to program your body for higher ends. Our relationship with breath via the diaphragm often determines our overall health and welfare.

The ninth chakra is most active during two time periods. The first is during preconception. Working with the physical elements of the tenth chakra, the energy of the ninth chakra determines which egg, sperm, and particular genetic traits are needed for your body. The selection is made energetically, based on which characteristics will assist you in accomplishing your overall soul purpose. If it's imperative to have blue eyes, you'll have blue eyes; if it's imperative to be lame, you'll be lame. Between ages twenty-eight and thirty-five, this chakra reawakens, this time to alert you to the fact that you have a special purpose on this earth and it's time to live it.

As this chakra reblooms, you open to higher forces. You are now being entrusted with access to the spiritual forces set in motion eons ago. The ultimate energy, grace, is available to anyone through this chakra, should they choose to humble themselves enough to follow divine will. In doing so, you find out everyone is the same.

These great forces can be misused or misread, or they can be used for the higher good. It's your choice. By this time, you have experienced the lushness and dryness that life has to offer. You have opened to the need to help others, and you have stalked power. Toward what end are you going to use your skills, knowledge, and this power?

Soul Sympathy. This energy center screens and directs forces to create momentum for accomplishments. It also tunes into information-energy about your place in the larger world.

Ninth Auric Layer. If the Divine had skin, that skin would be similar to the ninth auric layer. The souls of everyone and everything that have ever existed are meshed together, at least energetically, within the skein of the ninth auric layer. Because this auric layer is both material and spiritual, you don't really need to leave your body to connect spiritually with another person. You only have to bring them closer psychically, and you will know what needs to be known.

Chakra Ten

Psychic Style: Physical Kinesthetic
Psychic Gift: Environmental Sympathy

The tenth chakra is also called the grounding chakra. Located about a foot and a half underneath the feet, this energy center houses your genealogical and spiritual legacies.

This chakra programs you with both the positive and challenging inherited traits that you are going to need to carry out your spiritual mission. It also establishes your connection to nature and the natural world, affecting your ability to adapt to various environments, the type of natural medicines or treatments that will work for you, your reactions to climactic changes and elemental forces, and your relationship to other organic life.

People highly energized by the power of this center can be very environmentally sensitive. They also tend to be sensitive to ancestral or genetically inherited issues. These connections are ultimately forged through the bones, the part of the body most connected to the tenth chakra. Bones are made of the same molecular pattern as silicon, the ingredient in crystals. Crystals are carriers and disseminators of information, as are your bones. Thus, your soul and ancestral issues are passed down, held, and determined by your bones.

Ancestral issues are potent; they can affect every area of your life. When aligned with the positive or clear aspects of your legacy or environs, you can achieve great things in life. You will tend to be practical and solid, even under pressure. When you are overly vulnerable to the negative influences of family-of-origin programming or your surroundings, you lose focus concerning your unique personal or spiritual powers. It's critical to consciously clear yourself of the inheritances that you don't want, so that you can use your natural and genetic resources to achieve your spiritual destiny.

This chakra is active during two extremely critical time periods. The first is during preconception. Working with your ninth chakra, the tenth chakra determines the physical genetics that will help you accomplish your life purpose and tasks. The soul, through the ninth chakra, acts like the director, while the tenth chakra focuses the material energy and matter involved in constructing your DNA. The tenth chakra again moves into active duty between the ages of thirty-five and forty-two. Through the assistance of the ninth-chakra data, you are now clearly called into your spiritual destiny. At age thirty-five, the tenth chakra activates to help you manifest your spiritual destiny in the material world. The tenth chakra is about the here and now. Its energy helps you ground your dreams in the day to day. Of major concern to the tenth chakra will be the type of home, companions, workplace, geographic site, and other practicalities that bring your spiritual destiny into the third dimension. Community becomes important, as does the question, what type of community? Who are your real relations? Just your blood relatives? The tenth chakra calls for pragmatic and practical decision-making, which itself is spiritual.

On the physical level, the tenth chakra regulates your ability to employ natural energies throughout your life. Issues specific to the tenth chakra include mineral, vitamin, and protein assimilation; environmental sensitivities and food allergies; bone function; foot, ankle, and leg functions; and your reactions to organic and natural foods, especially nuts, potatoes, and all other starchy vegetables.

Environmental Sympathy. This chakra regulates your relationship with your ancestors and the spirits associated with your heritage and the world of nature. People gifted in this area tend to be highly sensitive to any number of environmental stresses or occurrences, including:

- Geophysical or geothermal changes
- Climactic conditions
- Planetary or stellar movements
- Natural or human-caused environmental disturbances, including forest fires, roadwork, tide, or seasonal changes
- Alterations in or for plant or animal life
- Toxins, chemicals, or artificial substances
- Conditions on one's own land or personal living quarters

The environmentally sympathetic may react to or absorb any of these factors. As well, he or she can learn to psychically read the environment for information and to change the environment through psychic means.

Tenth Auric Layer. The tenth auric layer is also called the middle energetic layer, the black body, or body double, but the most well-known term in metaphysical circles is the **etheric body**. The etheric body looks like a shadow of your own body. It is, in fact, found immediately around your first auric layer and so really does earn the label of the body double.

This energy body primarily serves as a filter system and a template. By holding negative energies and diseases, it will prevent them from downloading into your physical body. If the "tank" becomes too full, these toxins—physical, emotional, mental, or otherwise—will be dumped into your body, often causing sudden illness or trauma. Conversely, this energy body will also absorb positive information-energy and distribute it evenly throughout your system. In the same vein, it seeks to retain positive information-energy and anything else that contributes to your well-being.

Connected to the tenth chakra, this auric layer is programmed by ancestral records and beliefs, which will affect its functioning.

Shamans often perform soul, astral, spiritual, or psychic travel through the etheric body, which enables them to stay linked with their physical body while visiting other realms. In this way, they can appear in two places at the same time. They are then able to translate information-energy from one locale to another. This auric layer is highly malleable and yet strong, as you can see by its various functions.

The Etheric Mirror

In addition to the tenth auric layer, a second etheric body surrounds the body. This second etheric body can be called the **etheric mirror** or the Christ body. This body double operates around your entire physical body, connecting in the energy egg, the final walls of your energy-based self. The effect is similar to that of your twelfth auric layer, which surrounds your entire aura and locks into secondary chakra points in the body, such as your knees and elbows. The difference is that your twelfth auric layer is programmed from your soul, while the etheric mirror is modeled from your spirit. As such, it contains the key codes of your spiritual destiny. If your etheric mirror were totally activated, over time, it would transform your physical body into ideal form for carrying out your spiritual destiny. Unfortunately, few of us activate this mirror for a variety of reasons, usually involving dysfunctional strongholds. Quite simply, we don't think we deserve to achieve our full potential.

The reason I call this energetic body the Christ body is that like Christ, it represents the full marriage of your human and divine selves. When awakened, the front side of this layer attracts spiritual forces through spiral movements. When active, the back side of the Christ body funnels powers, fueling your spirit through your body to make significant changes.

Chakra Eleven

Psychic Style: Spiritual Kinesthetic
Psychic Gift: Force Sympathy

Whenever I think of Jesus calming the raging waters, a yogi levitating, or a shaman changing the weather, I think of the eleventh chakra.

Probably the least well known of all the chakras, the eleventh chakra is simultaneously located, like a bubble, around your hands and feet and dispersed around your system. Through it, your energy system is able to convert or transmute negative energy into positive or neutral energy and vice versa. For instance, if someone is yelling at you, this energy center can neutralize the rage response lodged in your second chakra, so you can deal with the abuser in a strong and calm way. Through the eleventh chakra, you can sit through a family dinner at which you're being ignored and energetically transmute your family's shaming attitudes into pure physical sustenance. You could actually leave such a dinner recharged!

The eleventh chakra is most highly linked to your connective tissues. These tissues, including your muscles and fascia, represent your relationship with outside forces, ideas, and energies. Do you connect through negative programming or a belief in your own weakness? You won't get very far in life—or in healing personal illness—with this program in place. Do you connect through spiritual truths and a knowing of your own strength? The world will respond accordingly, as will the healing properties within your own body.

An activated eleventh chakra allows you to perform laying-on-of-hands healing without absorbing sickness. It will simply transmute the illness into a harmless substance. If honed, these eleventh-chakra abilities can enable you to maintain composure and be safe and secure no matter the circumstances.

This chakra activates between the ages of forty-two and forty-nine. Some people consider these the "pumpkin years," when men hit a second adolescence and women become dissatisfied with their bodies or lives. Force sympathizers will tend to take these years harder than other people, as their already-sensitive areas become even more stimulated. Just about anything and everything might seem to become bigger than life. On the other hand, the force empathizer or trained sensitive can use the increased link with natural and supernatural forces to assert leadership in his or her chosen professional field or toward desired personal ends.

As you might imagine, this energy center could be a dynamic protection organ for the psychically sensitive. It can also cause great trauma and tribulation if it fails to function. People who absorb negativity, who are drained dry in difficult times, or who are perceived as negative by everyone else might have an eleventh-chakra affliction. Better regulating and psychically managing this chakra can assist sensitivities in just about any area of life, from environmental to emotional.

Force Sympathy. This energy center is a vital protection and conversion center. It perceives all types of psychic data along the continuum of negative, neutral, or positive energies and can change one to another. Overstimulation or underperformance will cause too much information-energy, usually negative, to be dumped into your system. In turn, this extra energy can throw all other systems off balance. Anything from the seemingly spiritual movement of objects around a room to heart palpitations could be caused from an underfunctioning eleventh chakra.

Eleventh Auric Layer. The eleventh auric layer looks like ribbon candy—reams and reams of waving material wrapping in between the various dimensions. This neutral field is designed so that negative and positive energies are treated equally. A warped, twisted, or poorly programmed eleventh auric layer will taint what we receive and send.

Defining Your Psychic Gifts

It's time to further define your abilities so you can transform psychic sensitivities into intuitive abilities and, in the process, transform your life.

To truly develop your psychic abilities, you need to distinguish your strongest chakra gifts. Though you are working with only eleven basic psychic gifts (and therefore eleven chakras), your own personal psychic profile will be different than that of others. Most people have a certain gift that stands out stronger than all the others, though some people have several strong gifts. Following your strongest gifts, which will score highest on your tests, are secondary and weaker gifts. The complete analysis, strongest to weakest, of your psychic gifts is your chakra or psychic gift order. Armed with this information, you will be prepared for Part III, which will show you how to strategically move from being psychically sensitive to intuitively astute. Depending upon your psychic gifts, you can customize your discernment principles, sourcing practices, and psychic needs.

You can determine your gift order by figuring out which chakras are your strongest and which are your weakest, which are your most dependable and important, and which are less vital or necessary. For example, someone's chakra gift order might reveal that he is strongest in the fifth, first, and eighth chakras, in that order. Each of these chakras runs on frequencies that work with a certain spectrum of psychic energy. As you will come to see, someone with this gift order would have strong abilities in verbal communication, manifesting, and mysticism.

The real point of figuring out your psychic gift order is that it provides clues to your spiritual destiny. Why do you have a certain set of psychic gifts, whereas your siblings or friends have others? Each of us is here on earth on a unique spiritual mission. To accomplish your goals, you need the aptitudes and brilliance provided by certain chakra gifts. Your psychic gift order, therefore, indicates your spiritual destiny—and your genius self.

Let's say, for instance, that your divine mission involves expressing truths, perhaps through the medium of writing and speaking. One of the chakras, the fifth, in fact, houses the verbal psychic gift. This ability is fundamental to speaking, listening, and writing. If you're here to be a great author, chances are you'll be strong in this area. If you're writing about nature, your tenth chakra, devoted to the environment, might also be potent. If you're sharing messages of the spiritual nature, your seventh chakra, which reflects spiritual matters, will outshine your tenth chakra.

I can often tell peoples' chakra or psychic gift order by their personalities. I have a friend, for instance, who is the perfect tenth-chakra person. Devoted to nature, she grows her own organic food, wears Birkenstocks, and owns ten cats and dogs. On the other hand, I'm rather impartial to the tenth chakra; hence, I'm commonly found sporting high heels and buying food at the to-go market. Personalities reflect someone's inborn gifts, thereby making it easier to determine what these gifts are and, therefore, what a person's spiritual mission is.

Exercise 6

Chakra Gift Order: A Return to the Quiz

Look back at the Psychic Sensitivity Quiz you took in exercise 1. We're now going to use it to determine your psychic gift order and your most defined chakras.

The quiz's questions are structured and organized according to chakra type. They divide this way:

- 1–6: First chakra issues, physical kinesthetic, physical sympathy
- 7–12: Second chakra issues, physical kinesthetic, feeling sympathy
- 13–18: Third chakra issues, physical kinesthetic, mental sympathy
- 19–24: Fourth chakra issues, spiritual kinesthetic, relational sympathy
- 25–31: Fifth chakra issues, verbal, verbal sympathy
- 32–36: Sixth chakra issues, visual, visual sympathy
- 37–42: Seventh chakra issues, spiritual kinesthetic, spiritual sympathy
- 43–48: Eighth chakra issues, spiritual kinesthetic, shadow sympathy
- 49–54: Ninth chakra issues, spiritual kinesthetic, soul sympathy

55–61: Tenth chakra issues, physical kinesthetic, environmental sympathy
62–67: Eleventh chakra issues, spiritual kinesthetic, energetic sympathy

Calculate your scores within each of these eleven categories. Any category in which you score more than fifteen out of thirty qualifies you as gifted psychically in this area. Any marked twenty or above shows you as highly gifted, if not exposed and vulnerable, in this area.

Compare your scores. Is there one that jumps out in front of the others? A couple of them? Are there any that drop off the chart, as if you seemingly have no gifts in this area?

Line up your test results strongest to weakest. You now have an outline of your chakra and psychic gift order.

Exercise 7
Assessing Your Gifts Through a Pendulum

One fun and easy way to assess the development of a particular psychic gift is to assess the health of its corresponding chakra using a pendulum. A healthy chakra is likely to host a defined and healthy psychic gift. A pendulum is a weighted object on a chain or a string. There's nothing magical about a pendulum; it simply swings in relation to the shape and flow of a chakra's energy. Basically, the more circular and well formed a chakra's energy flow, the healthier the chakra and the correlated gift.

For this exercise, you will need a partner and a pendulum. One person will hold the pendulum while the other lays on his or her back.

Begin as the "patient." Lie on a sofa, bed, or the floor and breathe deeply. Ask your partner to stand over you and hold the pendulum, object down, about six inches to a foot over a chakra center. Then have your partner recite this passage:

> *You are happier than you have ever been. You are living the life that you are designed to live. Your body, mind, and soul are balanced through your own eternal spirit. Your energy system now reflects your innate and natural gifts. Each chakra is now open as wide as it needs to be to carry out your spiritual destiny. Your strongest and most important chakra is open and circling the widest.*

Your partner, using the pendulum, will now test the strength and health of your chakric swings. When you are face up, your partner is assessing the flow of the front side of your chakras, which reveal the status of your conscious, everyday life functioning. You can also reverse and test the back sides of your chakras, which regulate the spiritual and unconscious aspects of life.

In general, a healthy chakra swings in a large, clockwise, and circular fashion. A stopped flow indicates the chakra's energy is blocked, while a reverse, counterclockwise flow usually indicates it is clearing itself of something, holding a repressed feeling, or resisting healing. The bigger a stable swing in a clockwise direction, the stronger the chakra, and the stronger the gift. Make note of the biggest and healthiest swings on the front and back sides.

You may find a big difference in the size of the pendulum swing in the front side of a chakra versus the back. Your front-side chakra system will reflect which chakras need to be strongest to deal with the world around you in the present. Your back-side chakra system will show which chakras were originally, at birth, the strongest. Life hands us unexpected situations. Our innate gifts enable us to meet our higher spiritual purpose, but don't always assist us in fully coping with life's traumas, problems, or tragedies. Dramatic situations might force the development of an otherwise "less important" ability, leading to a gift that is stronger in the front than in the back. Other challenges might subdue our basic gifts. Perhaps our parents weren't accepting of our true personality, or in school we were shamed for being our true selves. In these cases, back-side gifts might appear stronger than the front side, as inherent gifts are still potent, but repressed in the everyday world.

Eighth- and eleventh-chakra individuals often won't show their full strengths on the front side of the chakra system; this is because the eighth- and eleventh-chakra gifts involve working with forces and realities other than the everyday, physical world. The Western world doesn't affirm the unusual, supernatural, or paranormal, and so these individuals often fail to even recognize that they have the shamanic or commander gifts. Testing with the pendulum, however, will reveal the occult, and we can then decide whether to develop a gift or not.

Part III

Putting the Psychic Gifts into Practice

Chapter 7

The Kinesthetic Psychic Sensitive

> *Why have the masters written nothing? Jesus was a rabbi, Siddhartha a prince. Both literate and famously well-spoken teachers wrote nothing.*
> *Why?*
> *Because they were spell-breakers, not spellbinders.*
> ~A. A. Attanasio, *The Serpent and the Grail*

Read this chapter if:

- You tested as a high kinesthetic in exercise 1, the Psychic Sensitivity Quiz.
- You ranked high in any of the kinesthetic gifts, located in chakras one, two, three, four, seven, eight, nine, ten, or eleven, when doing exercise 6, the chakra gift order exercise.
- You know the world through sensing, feeling, knowing, a gut sense, or any of the other kinesthetic means of perception.

Are You a Kinesthetic?

Do your best ideas come when you're daydreaming? Moving around? Walking? Playing football? Figuring out how you feel? Creating? Praying? Guessing what's going on inside or around you? Have you ever figured out how you know what you know?

Are you one of those people who live by your "gut sense," "feelings," or "senses" of things? Then you are probably a **kinesthetic psychic.** You are one of those people that kinesthetically receives or sends psychic information that is *sensory* or *feeling* in nature.

Your understanding of the world is body or sensation based. In school, you probably really hated to sit still. You'd rather have been playing soccer or dolls or anything other than performing rote math. Your learning style is one of active participation. Even now you would probably prefer to learn about a computer program by punching away on the keyboard rather than reading through a manual. You would rather select a perfume or aftershave by smelling it than looking at the bottle, and you keep a budget using cash rather than a credit system.

For better or worse, you're probably still learning life lessons the physical, and sometimes hard, way. Your psychic gifts work the same way. You know truth because you have a physical reaction. You select test answers because they *seem* right rather than making sense cognitively. You will decide whether to trust someone you've just met based on a gut sense. You may consider it more valid to buy a house based on the way its interior smells than on its layout.

And because of your kinesthetic sensitivity, you have blurry boundaries. The health of your marriage will affect your work. Your concept of time will change as you change your environment. When touching an antique, you might suddenly feel like you are in old Victorian England. When standing in a museum, you'll think that the armored knight's sword is going right through you. Your sense of right and wrong will be sensory based. Are you a champion for the underdog? That's because you can sense what the defeated are going through and why.

Being kinesthetic is a good way to be. Look at a few leaders: Jesus, Gandhi, Andrew Carnegie, and Mother Teresa. They touched to create. Unfortunately, being highly kinesthetic engenders difficulties in today's world. I think of one client who doesn't go to long movies because she won't use the theater bathrooms; she insists that she can sense all the people who have ever sat on the toilet. I know another client who smells smoke whenever someone thinks a negative thought, and yet another who feels tired if he sits next to someone who didn't get enough sleep the previous evening.

How do you explain knowing the world this way? You feel different and out of place, if not constantly out of sorts. For your part, being a kinesthetically psychic sensitive might leave you feeling constantly like you are in culture shock, regardless of what culture you are physically trying to live within.

The first way to cope with—and benefit from—being a kinesthetic psychic is to know exactly which type of kinesthetic you are. Let's review so you can better pinpoint your style and psychic type.

Types of Kinesthetic Psychic Sensitivity

As noted in the last chapter, all nine types of kinesthetic psychics fit in two basic styles: physical kinesthetic or spiritual kinesthetic.

Physically based kinesthetic people will sense or know reality through their five senses. A physically based kinesthetic registers the various psychic phenomena as a feeling, touch, knowing, taste, smell, or sense. Your psyche will highlight information about practical and tangible reality, like people's concrete needs or the state of the weather. You are the person who, as a child, knew you weren't going to like Grandma's meal because you could taste those awful peas and the stringy stew before you were served—in fact, before you even knew what was for dinner!

Spiritually based kinesthetic people will perceive psychic information about the paranormal and supernatural. You might still understand psychic energies through your senses, but the sources of data will definitely be from the other realms. Your primary psychic skill involves translating information from the spiritual into everyday understanding. If you operate on this level, you probably get gut instincts about a room, person, situation, book, politician—anything—that tell you about the integrity and ethics of that subject. Regarding a person, you might find yourself saying something like, "I don't trust him because he has shifty eyes," knowing full well that your impression has little to do with the man's eyes! Rather, you have a sense of mistrust and have to search for a rational explanation. Conversely you might just "feel" you have to do something because it "seems right," but then you have no logical way to explain that decision. Can you really say that you can tell something because of a feeling from an invisible presence?

You might be both a physical and a spiritual kinesthetic, depending on the strength of certain chakras. Each chakra houses a psychic gift, and your strongest psychic gifts lie within your strongest chakras.

Chakra	Type of Psychic Sensitivity	Type of Kinesthetic
First	Physical sympathy	Physical
Second	Feeling sympathy	Physical
Third	Mental sympathy	Physical
Fourth	Relational sympathy	Spiritual
Seventh	Spiritual sympathy	Spiritual
Eighth	Shadow sympathy	Spiritual
Ninth	Soul sympathy	Spiritual
Tenth	Environmental sympathy	Physical
Eleventh	Force sympathy	Spiritual

You can have two or even three equally strong chakras and, therefore, the psychic gifts inherent in them. I find, for instance, that individuals with a strong first chakra are often also highly evolved in their tenth and second chakras. This means that they will be physically, emotionally, and environmentally psychic. They can sense what other people are going through in their own bodies, feel others' feelings, and are attuned to nature. These are all strong physical kinesthetic gifts, making their owners extraordinarily sensitive to the world around them. On the other hand, someone might be sensitive in the third and the seventh chakras, which highlight mental processing and spiritual sensitivity. He or she will be good at spiritually sensing divine concepts through the seventh chakra, then using the third chakra to form a practical, concrete plan for using these ideas in the everyday world. This pairing of gifts demonstrates how spiritual and physical kinesthetic gifts can work together.

Breaking the Spells

If you are kinesthetically sensitive and are experiencing the downside of this gift, you must be willing to break the spells binding you. To be **spellbound** means to be chained by cords, beliefs, or restrictions that keep you from enjoying your genius-level psychic gifts and expressing your soul freely. We are all wrapped in spells or programs, which originate in our family-of-origin, religion, or culture. We also carry our own negative ideas into the world and live from them, to our own detriment. We are all challenged to break the "spells that bind," the self- and other-destructive beliefs that keep us unhappy and promote evil in the world. Kinesthetic sensitives also have the rather unusual task of breaking through their mind's fantasies and the world's illusions through trust alone. If you can't see or hear a problem, you are left with trusting your inner guidance.

There have been many kinesthetic spell breakers, all of which sliced through prejudice, lies, and delusions in order to change the world for the better. If you are highly kinesthetic, you could consider these your mentors:

- René Descartes, who fashioned the tenets of empirical science following a series of revelatory dreams. He was a fourth chakra relational sympathizer.
- Albert Einstein, whose intuitions formed while he napped. He was a third chakra mental sympathizer.
- Teresa d'Ávila, a Christian mystic who could feel Christ's presence in her own body. She was both a first chakra physical sympathizer and a seventh chakra spiritual sympathizer.

As a kinesthetic psychic, you have the same potential as these famous great people. You have been gifted with your psychic abilities for a reason—a divine reason! If your gifts are an asset, keep on using them. If you are comfortable with your current level of psychic expression, offer a prayer of gratitude. Unfortunately, kinesthetic psychic sensitivity is the most difficult to control. The psychic information involved is so sensory, it can seem elusive. Because it's so elusive, it's hard to substantiate or prove. Kinesthetic psychics, more than any other type of psychics, have a difficult time justifying their gifts or knowledge, and frequently have difficulty with verbal expression. All of these troubles indicate an oversensitive kinesthetic gift and a lack of psychic boundaries.

Red Flags for the Kinesthetic Psychic

Many of the psychic problems already described in this book relate to kinesthetic sensitives. These problems include:

Physical Sympathy

- Taking on others' illnesses or diseases
- Replacing your own primary needs, desires, or motivations with those of others
- Money and prosperity problems
- Sexual fears or phobias
- Difficulties separating your own physical conditions from others
- Food issues involving lactose (milk sugar), meat, or sugar
- Anorexia and excess weight
- Addictions to substances such as alcohol, cocaine, or crack
- Money addictions, such as gambling or excessive shopping

Feeling Sympathy

- Taking on others' feelings or emotions
- Emotionalism
- Emotional strongholds that inhibit growth, sensuality, and creative expression
- Physical difficulties in the abdominal area and organs because of psychic overstimulation
- Emotionally related illnesses, like arthritis, diverticulitis, and bulimia
- Food allergies involving gluten, cheese, ice cream, and lactose

Mental Sympathy

- Overstimulated thoughts or thinking; hyperactive mental activity
- Mental strongholds inhibiting success at work
- Difficulties in organizing or systematizing data
- Control issues—overcontrolling others or allowing others to overcontrol you
- Physical issues involving digestive organs, viruses such as Epstein-Barr, and other fatigue-related illnesses—all stemming from

psychic overload

- Food allergies involving corn, caffeine, diet sodas, and beer

Relational Sympathy

- Fear of intimacy or intimate relationships
- Exhaustion from taking care of everyone else all the time
- Nightmares or bad dreams
- Physical problems with the heart, lungs, breasts, and circulation—all related to psychic overflow
- Food allergies related to wine and sugar
- Compulsive eating and craving patterns
- Relationship and love addictions—you *have* to be in a relationship
- Codependency and caretaking patterns

Spiritual Sympathy

- Oversensitivity and vulnerability to spiritual interference from negative entities from the World of Spirits, such as demons, extraterrestrials, and negative ghosts
- Complete inability to connect with the Divine
- Anxiety, insomnia, depression, or other pineal-gland-related problems
- Spiritual fundamentalism or fanaticism
- Higher learning issues—including some cases of attention-deficit disorder (ADD), attention-deficit/hyperactivity disorder (ADHD), autism, and schizophrenia—due to psychic interference or repression

Shadow Sympathy

- Inability to be in present time
- Loneliness from feeling or being different or contrary to others
- Food allergies including sugar, tobacco, or family-karmic foods (those to which the family is highly allergic or addicted to)

- Psychic-overload-based addictions to psychotropic drugs, hallucinogens, and the like
- Physical problems involving the thymus
- Physical problems carried over from other lives or experiences or assumed from others

Environmental Sympathy

- Not being grounded or being too grounded
- Interference from ancestral spirits or nature-based spirits
- Sensitivity to conditions in your living space; your house or living space can also display symptoms of your issues.
- Physical problems involving the feet, legs, bones, or hips due to psychic overload, which is usually generational in nature
- Allergies to nuts and root vegetables
- Allergies to natural elements like flowers or animals

Force Sympathy

- Unexpected movement of forces, natural elements, or physical objects
- History of hurting, using, or manipulating others through ability to move energy
- History of being hurt, used, or manipulated by others who seem to overpower you
- Physical issues with the connective tissue, feet, or hands because of an overload of forces

There are many causes for the symptoms just listed. If you believe that some of your challenges are psychic in nature, you need to develop psychic boundaries. You need to stop being spellbound and move forward spell free. You are here to create positive change, and changing yourself is the place to start.

Moving Forward Spell Free

If you are a kinesthetic psychic, ask yourself whether your tendency has been to allow others to victimize you through your gifts or if you have perhaps used these gifts against others. Unless we do as Jesus did, which is to love our neighbor as ourselves, but first love the self as the neighbor, we will fail to develop our psychic abilities harmoniously or ethically.

The Divine intended that your kinesthetic psychic gifts would serve as conduits for creativity and channels for transformation. These are holy endeavors. If you have been imbalanced, there is a reason. It's important to understand just how and why your abilities became warped. The key to shifting from being psychic to being intuitive, from having no boundaries to having boundaries, is to shift the reasons you access your psychic gifts. By believing in yourself, the Divine, others, and the goodness of the world, you heal yourself from past wounds and convert your survival-oriented psychic abilities into transformative intuitive skills. Try trust! Deal with the negativity of your past and decide to trust your intuition to help you negotiate the land mines of reality. Cultivate self-love, thus giving you reason to trust yourself. With faith and trust as your companions, you can establish the basis necessary to open your seventh sense, the uplifting use of the psychic for spiritual endeavors.

You may have concluded that the root of your difficulties lies in any of the following areas:

- **Family-of-origin beliefs or messages.** All families live by a code. We learned as children that we couldn't survive unless we upheld this code. (And by the way, rebelling against the code doesn't solve the problem—the opposite of something is the same as that something.) This code very seldom mirrors higher spiritual truths and principles.

- **Childhood experiences in the family home or at school.** We internalize experiences and our own reactions to them, creating strongholds—mental and emotional patterns—which we regurgitate the rest of our lives. Just because we ran away from the first bee that stung us doesn't mean we need to run away every time we see a bee.
- **Abuse (sexual, physical, emotional, or mental) or neglect.** There are severe traumas that leave us feeling bad about ourselves. Usually therapy is necessary to regain our sense of innocence and break free from the spell of being a victim. If we feel bad about ourselves, we will be unable to trust our inner knowing.
- **Destructive personal-relationship experiences as an adult.** Not all tragedies occur in childhood. We are affected by everything that we go through, no matter what our age. Focusing on the realities of your current relationships and not projecting past relationship dramas onto them will keep you from creating new wounds and help you remain openhearted—and these are the keys to accessing your intuition.
- **Destructive experiences as an adult in work-related settings.** Work distresses affect our ability to open to prosperity. Don't personalize problems—solve them instead. Your intuition will help you do this.

In and of themselves, intuitive-development procedures are not going to change deep-rooted beliefs or patterns, nor will they heal the boundary violations that may have created your fear-based responses to life. Intuitive development is not a substitute for the cleansing and healing necessary to repair ego and self-worth issues. The intuitive-development techniques or principles described in this chapter can alleviate some of the psychic symptoms that may be preventing you from getting to your core wounds, but they will not heal the wounds themselves.

The major barriers to healthy psychic boundaries are fear and shame. We may fear that we are unlovable or unworthy or evil or stupid. We may fear for our safety. We might think we are bad or don't deserve boundaries; after all, don't other people count more than ourselves? Some of us have experienced such severe abuse or neglect that we would benefit from professional assistance when working through our issues. Being accompanied on your journey inward can change your outward life. The word *therapist* actually means "witness." We all want our lives witnessed, the good and the bad. If you have been severely traumatized during your life or treated poorly, you deserve to have a loving and trained professional guide you through the recovery process.

If you are ready to proceed with intuitive development, know that some of these techniques might work for you and others might not. You are an individual person with your own unique set of beliefs and personality traits. I encourage you to alter any of the processes to suit your own needs or work with an intuitive trainer who can better customize a process for you.

On Being an Intuitive Kinesthetic

Making the switch from kinesthetic psychic to kinesthetic intuitive involves moving from psychic sympathy to intuitive empathy. The most obvious differences between the kinesthetic psychic and kinesthetic empath are:

1. The ability to control the type of data received
2. The ability to control when you receive desired data
3. The power to decide what to do with the psychic energy and when
4. The ability to choose whether or not to use your psychic ability
5. Accepting responsibility for the ethical use of your gift

Here is how your specific gifts change in the intuitive-development process.

Chakra	Psychic Sympathy	Intuitive Empathy
One	***Physical Sympathy:*** Hold others' physical issues.	***Physical Empathy:*** Transform others' physical issues, as well as your own, through your energy system.
Two	***Feeling sympathy:*** Feel others' feelings.	***Feeling empathy:*** Feel others' feelings and your own feelings.
Three	***Mental sympathy:*** Absorb psychic data.	***Mental empathy:*** Organize psychic data into useful systems and categories, to be used when needed.
Four	***Relational sympathy:*** Absorb relationship issues.	***Relational empathy:*** Sense your own and others' relationship needs, drives, desires, and dreams, and serve as a conduit for healing energy to help all concerned receive their heart's desires.
Seven	***Spiritual sympathy:*** Assume spiritual energies.	***Spiritual empathy:*** Sort through spiritual sources to find highest insights and signs of spiritual destiny for yourself or others.

Chakra	Psychic Sympathy	Intuitive Empathy
Eight	***Shadow sympathy:*** Attract psychic data from all worlds.	***Shadow empathy:*** Screen information from all worlds, synthesizing it to help others heal or for divination purposes.
Nine	***Soul sympathy:*** Read psychic data about soul needs and drives.	***Soul empathy:*** Glean psychic information about soul purposes and soul ideals, then help yourself and others achieve those soul purposes.
Ten	***Environmental sympathy:*** Read energy in nature and the genealogy of yourself or others; can hold these energies in your own body.	***Environmental empathy:*** Interpret natural occurrences and use natural forces to make changes in creation.
Eleven	***Force sympathy:*** Attract both spiritual and natural energetic forces.	***Force empathy:*** Summon and command spiritual and natural energetic forces for your own or higher will.

What's in a Name? Kinesthetic Subtypes

Within most of the major kinesthetic gifts are several subtypes. As you think about your kinesthetic gifts, pay attention to which of these might best describe your abilities.

Physical Sympathy

Telekinesis, or deforming objects with psychic powers.

Psychokinesis, or moving objects with mental powers; in this case, application of thought through the first chakra.

Psychometry, or sensing the energy in objects.

Psychic surgery, or using the hands as surgical tools in such a way that hands actually pass through, remove, or shape tissue.

Feeling Sympathy

Creative ideation, or originating creative ideas that impact solid reality.

Feeling transmutation, or changing one feeling into another.

Mental Sympathy

Clairsentience, or clear sensing.

Relational Sympathy

Healing, or assisting people with change. Common types of healing that are often intuitive or conscious in nature include:

- Reiki, a Japanese healing method.
- Energy healing, the application of energy for healing.
- Energy medicine, energy healing, but also using specific spiritual forces for healing.
- Hands-on healing, or healing involving energy channeled through the heart.
- Mari-El, a hands-on healing method using Mother Mary energy.
- Healing touch, a hands-on healing method used often by nurses.
- Faith healing, a Christian-based healing using energy of the Holy Spirit.

Astral projection, in which the soul leaves the body to visit other places, specifically through the astral plane.
Remote viewing, in which the soul either leaves the body or remains within it and employs the gifts of the sixth chakra or visual sight to psychically envision someone, something, or a situation in the past, present, or the future.
Lucid dreaming, being fully conscious when dreaming.
Journeying, in which the soul or an aspect of the consciousness visits other places when the body is awake.
Dreamwalking, in which the soul visits other places during dreams.
Dreamstalking, seeking power or healing via a dream.

Spiritual Sympathy
Spirit sensitivity, or the ability to sense the presence of entities, positive or negative.
Fate sensitivity, the ability to determine what is or is not destined to happen; when sensing intuitive or spiritual destiny, this gift transforms into prophecy.

Shadow Sympathy
Shamanism, walking between the five levels of reality and Antiworlds.
Healing, assisting people with making changes.
Regressing, in which the soul, mind, or an aspect of consciousness moves backward through time to see or experience the past.
Futuring, in which the soul, mind, or an aspect of consciousness moves forward through time to see potential futures; can also involve the spirit "showing" possible futures to the current self.
Astral projection, *remote viewing*, *lucid dreaming*, *journeying*,

dreamwalking, and *dreamstalking*. See definitions under "Relational Sympathy."

Soul Sympathy
World sensitivity, or sensing of the world's needs, issues, or problems in your own body.
Soul sensitivity, or sensing of another's soul wounds, needs, story, or feelings in your own body.

Environmental Sympathy
Shamanism, walking between the world of nature and the other four realities.
Naturopathic medicine, using organic or natural substances for healing.
Herbalism, a form of naturopathic medicine using herbs and plants.
Homeopathy, vibrational medicine in which a patient is given minute doses of natural drugs or drugs that in larger doses would produce the disease itself, thereby stimulating the immune system to respond.
Nature-based healing, using the energies of nature for healing.
Medicine healing, use of natural substances and compounds in nature to produce medicines that invoke visions; communion along the five levels or reality; or healing. Unlike drugs, medicines are considered living, organic, and conscious.
Spirit medicine, invoking spirits of the natural for healing.
Animal medicine, invoking spirits of animals for healing.

Force Sympathy
Weather shamanism, the ability to perceive possible climactic changes, or to alter the weather at will.

Consciousness shamanism, the ability to perceive group consciousness patterns, such as those occurring within a group heart, group spirit, group mind, group feelings, or other ways that groups share ideas and feelings; some consciousness shamans are able to shape and impact these collective consciousnesses.

Power shamanism, the ability to sense and direct the energetic forces at will. (More information on the power pathway is available in *Advanced Chakra Healing*.)

The Kinesthetic Intuitive Healing Process

Before exercising your psychic ability at all, you need to work internally. The following healing process is designed to help the kinesthetic psychic move into an intuitive-development process. This process will take you from psychic sympathy to intuitive empathy and prepare you for the responsibilities of being an empath. The transformation will always involve, and often necessitates, a healing process. What a great opportunity to heal old wounds and free your spirit! The following step-by-step process can assist you.

Step One: Introduce Yourself to Your Chakras

As a kinesthetic person, it is imperative that you learn how to separate and categorize the types of information-energy you perceive. The best way to do this is to physically distinguish the different types of psychic information. By figuring out where your kinesthetic chakras are in your own body and sensing the psychic information-energy in each one, you can begin to manage your psychic processes.

Many of your kinesthetic chakras are in your body. The tenth chakra, however, is underneath your feet. The eighth and ninth are above your head, and the eleventh chakra is strongest around your hands and feet.

Here are two good methods for sensing your chakras and the energy flow within them.

1. Become quiet. Asking for Divine help, breathe into each of your chakras. By working with your breath, you receive divine care and protection. As you bring your conscious focus to each chakra site, pay attention to the physical sensations in each area. When you are finished, reaffirm divine protection and closeness.
2. For one day, give permission to the Divine or your gatekeeper to show you the various ways that you register information-energy in your kinesthetic chakras. Throughout the day, deliberately monitor how you perceive information-energy. When you sense a pain in your gut, ask yourself what is causing this sensation. Are you noticing psychic data? If your heart suddenly becomes heavy, ask for guidance to explain why.

At the end of the day, review your findings. Were there one or two chakras that seemed primary, or did you register information all over? Did you feel comfortable with all of the psychic stimulations or not? Those areas of discomfort are probably those in which you are overly sensitive and might be the ones where you most need to establish boundaries.

Step Two: Seek Out Energetic Cords and Life Threads

As described in chapter 4, cords, the energetic connections between ourselves and other people, situations, or objects, keep us locked into a certain time and space and spellbound to old patterns. Kinesthetic people can often sense or feel these energetic contracts simply by asking their bodies to create sensation where the cords exist. **Life threads** are like cords except that they split your life energy into two points on the time-space continuum. If you have a life thread, it's as if your life energy is flowing to two different versions of "you." The current self will lack energy, vim, and vigor. Fourth- and eighth-chakra kinesthetics—those whose gifts involve parts of themselves actually traveling to other times and dimensions (instead of just seeing into those places)—are especially susceptible to life threads. They are energetically living in two time periods, often this one and a past life. (There are many other types of energetic problems and attachments, all of which are covered in my book *Advanced Chakra Healing*. Please read that book for further information. The steps described here will help you with any of these energetic problems.)

One way to determine if you have a cord or life thread is to use the method covered in exercise 2, from grounding to closing, or to ask the Divine or your gatekeeper for feedback. If your questioning produces a physical discomfort, a memory or flashback, a dream or—through your visual or verbal psychic gifts—a revelation or a word from spiritual guidance, you might be dealing with a cord or a life thread. Ask yourself to whom or what you are still connected and why. Ask if this contract *is meeting* or *did meet* a need for you. Ask if there is a different way that you can meet this need. When you are satisfied with the responses, ask the Divine or your gatekeeper to take away the cord or thread and to heal the entry point. Ask your guidance to open the correct energy in the now-empty space, while simultaneously creating within you a new, healthy neurological and energetic pattern. Ask that the Divine bless and assist anyone else who has been affected by this cord contract or life-thread link. You must break these spells of the past in order to move freely into the future.

In general, cords and life threads are negative and harmful. There are circumstances, however, in which they serve a higher purpose. A mother and child are corded for the first three years of the child's life. This cord helps the mother sense a child's needs and fills the child with mother's love, learning, and guidance. Of course, this cord might be damaging as well as supportive, as noted in chapter 4. A short-term cord or life thread can also save someone's life. Healers, physicians, and even loved ones often inadvertently establish a life-saving bond with the ill or injured. These types of cords or threads work like a life-support system, providing life energy from the sender to the recipient. Usually, these links fall away as soon as the recipient recovers or dies, but sometimes they remain in place, to the detriment of both parties. The sender often loses his or her life energy, which can result in exhaustion, illness, or death. The recipient could also be overwhelmed by the psychic energies flowing in from the sender.

I once established a short-term cord between a client and myself. She had attended a two-week workshop on shamanism that I led in the jungles of Peru. Before coming on the trip, my client was afflicted with a severe neck problem. She was scheduled for surgery upon our return. Over the two weeks, her neck completely healed. She was mobile, happy, and pain free. On the day we were leaving, she walked into the roof of the bus that was taking the group to the airport, and she fell over, as if dead. I immediately stuck a life-giving cord onto her and prayed that God would keep her alive. Two others on the trip, both healers, psychically envisioned her soul, which was floating away. They caught it and forced it back into her body. My coleader took the wounded woman to the hospital; somehow, they both made our plane home. My client? Her neck was back to status quo, exactly the same as when we left for the trip. She had surgery upon return.

This example shows a positive use for cords; however, I made sure to disengage from my client as soon as she was breathing again. I didn't want to be responsible for her life-and-death choice nor become tied up in her drama. The story also reveals the challenges of healing. We're all guilty of holding on to our traumas and dramas, and even if we receive healing, we don't always let it stick. Who knows? Maybe we're constantly in a state of health, but we keep undoing it! One of my spiritual guides said something very wise to me once. "You can instantly heal, but not always see the healing instantly. Sometimes, it takes time to accept the healing."

Step Three: Release Energy That Is Not Yours

Feelings, physical energy or illnesses, relationship desires, truths, or spiritual messages that are not yours only hurt you and never help. You can't heal an issue, benefit from a feeling, or address a belief that's not yours, no matter how hard you try. To have real peace and achieve your destiny, you must release any and all energies belonging to or sourcing from someone or something else.

Second-chakra kinesthetics are famous for holding onto others' feelings. I'll give you an example. In my family, anger was considered a bad emotion. Like any emotion, anger is an actual substance with its own vibration. My dad could only repress his rage and anger so long. Pretty soon it would begin to float around the house. Being corded with my father, I learned to *pick it up* and *act it out*. I was angry on my father's behalf. A black cloud would descend about me and within moments, I would be pouting, crying, or freaking out and would be sent to my room as punishment. Consequently, I became the family scapegoat, the one always yelled at when the family would become tense. I was lucid of this pattern throughout my childhood, but didn't know how to stop it. I was too scared. I assumed that if my father were to act upon anger, I would be slapped or hit.

Because the anger wasn't my own feeling, I couldn't process it. As an adult, I pounded pillows in therapy, screaming out angrily until, thousands of dollars poorer and much hoarser, I gave up. I was still angry. I was only able to free myself from this excessive anger when I decided to energetically shift the anger over to God and, if God thought best, to return it to my father. And then I released the idea that because I changed, my father would. Just because we change doesn't mean anyone else will.

If you are kinesthetic, chances are you are holding onto some energy that didn't originate in you. As stated, the key to releasing any held energy is to figure out why you are holding onto it and find a different way to meet this perceived need. Once you've established your intention, you can ask the Divine to take the unnatural energy and/or to return it to the other person's higher self.

A caveat on this advice: I've learned to never directly send energy back to its original recipient. If he or she couldn't handle it in the first place, how do I know that person can now? I learned this the hard way. Early in my career as an intuitive healer, I worked with a woman named Louise, who was suicidal. Together, we determined that she was holding her father's depression. She returned the depression energy to her father, who killed himself the next day. Was she guilty of killing her father? No. If she hadn't been holding his energy, he probably would have committed suicide years earlier. She had ruined much of her own life by energetically taking care of her father, and she deserved to be set free. If we had sent the depression to the Divine, to her father's higher self, or to his gatekeeper, however, we might have rewritten the ending of the story. Perhaps her father would have more gradually accepted his own pain and trauma and slowly learned to process it. Then again, perhaps the outcome would have been the same. I've learned it's always better to be compassionate rather than impassioned when doing any energy work involving other people.

Step Four: Learn and Practice a New Pattern

Lifelong issues, including those originating in the psychic realm, create patterns. We all have patterns that must be broken. For example, we kinesthetic sensitives must watch out for thinking we know it all. That's more challenging than it might sound, because we do know a lot (usually a lot more than we want to). The easiest way to break our old patterns is to switch from being sympathetic to empathetic. This shift automatically frees us from our old beliefs, opinions, and strongholds. The act of separating energies defeats the psychic victimization cycle and forces us to examine our own beliefs and behaviors.

Kinesthetics usually ask me how they are supposed to sense psychic information if they don't sympathize. I remember one client saying, "I don't know who I'll be if I don't feel everyone else's pain. How can I remain psychic, but safe?" The key to doing so sounds simple, but it takes a lot of practice. You must *register* others' energies without *absorbing* them.

To **register** someone else's energy is to kinesthetically sense it while simultaneously retaining our sense of self. When we **absorb,** we completely exchange someone (or something) else's energy for our own. In my practice, I register clients' energies all the time, even over the phone. I can sense their pain, feelings, needs, experiences, and even reactions to me. All the while, I am still fully aware of my own situation. As soon as I sense or register the others' energy, I release it—with a blessing. I always ask that energy, once witnessed, be blessed by divine love. That way I am delivering a healing even if I'm only providing information or feedback.

Tips for Registering Instead of Absorbing

There are hundreds of methods for registering, but not absorbing, psychic information. Finding a way that works for you can be a confusing, convoluted, and perhaps long process. You have to discover what works for *you*, not someone else. In general, however, all of the kinesthetic gifts lend themselves to the following types of protection techniques, which will help keep you grounded, safe, and in integrity.

Use the elements. Select stones, crystals, feathers, and other natural objects that strike you as helpful or aligned with your personal energy. Set them in your environment, ring your bed with them, or carry them in your pocket. Allow them to energetically protect and stabilize you. There are many books and Internet sites that describe the energetic meaning of these objects.

Consider tinctures, potions, and energetic medicines. There are many vibrational medicines that provide healing and help to the kinesthetic. Consider homeopathy, supplements, Bach flower remedies, or making your own energetic medicines.

Set wards. Wards are protective barriers, fashioned from physical or psychic means, to keep out danger. Put crystals in the corners of your room or around the four corners of your house. Burn sage or lemongrass to cleanse a space. Ask the Divine to bless oil or water and use it to make the sign of a cross (or any other protective symbol) over a door or window frames. Or invoke a guide or gatekeeper to establish angels or other protective beings at four corners of a room or your lawn.

Detoxify. The kinesthetic is particularly susceptible to picking up others' physical and psychic energies, which can then transform into physical toxins. Work with a holistic specialist to periodically detoxify yourself and your energy system. Dietary changes and colonics are just two means of detoxifying. Bathing in Epsom salt pulls others' energy from your body.

Perform ceremony. Throughout the ages, kinesthetics have participated in spiritual ritual or ceremonies to discern information, cleanse, purify, or heal. Look to your own spiritual tradition to find a method that fits for you.

Bless the physical. Do not underestimate the power of blessing, which is the invoking of the Divine to transform a physical object or substance for spiritual purposes. You can bless your food so it fortifies you on all levels, bless your bedding so you can sleep, and bless the sun so you feel happy all day. Creating your own blessings attracts more blessings to you.

Empower talismans. You can bless talismans or spiritual instruments for a particular use, such as blessing a wand to help in healing, a rock to attract abundance, or a stick to with which to dowse for water.

Enjoy nature. All kinesthetics are purified and fortified by nature. Get outside.

Change your environment. If you want to change your life, change your surroundings. Feng shui is one of many ancient arts that suggest that you can alter your moods, thoughts, feelings, and life by altering your environment. Learn some of these techniques or hire a consultant and get to work. The basics will include decluttering, the proper use of color, or the placement of objects to match your desires.

Watch what you wear. If you're kinesthetic, your moods, emotions, thoughts, and actions are often affected by the clothing you wear. Pay attention to the color, texture, feeling, and message of your clothing. For instance, if you require courage, wear red, the color of boldness and passion. If you want to remain calm, wear blue.

Take care of your body. A kinesthetic processes everything through his or her body, which means there's a lot of wear and tear. Eat healthy. Sleep. Exercise. For particular techniques that work with your chakra type, read my book *Attracting Your Perfect Body through the Chakras*.

Psychic Kinesthetics Who Became Intuitive: Case Studies

Let's look at a few kinesthetics who made the switch from psychic and sympathetic to intuitive and empathetic.

Chakra Two: From Feeling Sympathy to Feeling Empathy

Dr. Cooke, a Brooklyn-born colon specialist, was a feeling sympathizer. His patients loved him. They often spent up to an hour with him discussing their life difficulties, not just their intestines. Dr. Cooke reported, however, that these long days left him totally drained and lethargic.

"It's as if I just keep absorbing all my patients' feelings," he complained to me.

He was. The only way that Dr. Cooke was able to deal with this slush of feelings was to overeat carbohydrates and sweets, a vain effort to simultaneously calm himself and raise his blood sugar. Despite being diagnosed with adult-onset diabetes, he couldn't seem to control his diet. "My muffins are the only thing providing me comfort," he swore. "I just can't give them up."

Dr. Cooke needed to stop soaking up his patients' feelings. Before he could do that, he spent quite a few sessions with me, as well as a therapist, to figure out why he thought he needed to sacrifice himself for others' needs. He dated this pattern back to his early relationship with his mother, who had used him as a surrogate spouse. Finally, at age fifty-two, he decided that he deserved his own psychic space. We worked to help him break a cord between himself and his mother and to claim his own feelings. He practiced registering instead of absorbing others' energies. Now he eats carrots instead of muffins and uses his abilities to empathize with others' feelings.

One of Dr. Cooke's fears was that he would lose patients if he stopped caretaking their feelings. The opposite happened. First, he was more precise in his diagnosis. While he was still caring, he didn't get bogged down in the emotional pain of his clients. This pleased his patients and freed up more time for him to see more people! Since becoming less psychically codependent, Dr. Cooke has taken on two new partners in a year. Because others' energies are no longer weighing him down, his own energy and feelings have reasserted themselves, and the result is a newfound creativity. He recently started taking a series of art classes to put this creative energy to use.

Chakra Seven: From Spiritual Sympathy to Spiritual Empathy

Martha's eyes spun in her head as she discussed her New Age beliefs, which included the idea that if she could only channel angelic beings she could ascend, or leave the earth without dying. These beliefs were based on an intense experience with a religious commune.

Martha had narrowly escaped a cult that had indoctrinated her to believe that the leader was the returned Jesus Christ. I considered Martha to be clearly susceptible to many types of extreme spiritual beliefs. But what was the root of her spiritual sympathy?

Further probing revealed that Martha's family had been extremely strict Christian fundamentalists who had judged just about *everything* to be evil, from dancing to card playing to women wearing pants. Even though she thought she was evading her strict upbringing, Martha wasn't escaping fanaticism. Her new beliefs were as imprisoning as the ones she had renounced.

Because of Martha's depression, I sent her to be evaluated by a psychiatrist. He put her on drugs for obsessive-compulsive disorder and used regression techniques to help her probe her past. Gradually, Martha began to gain a sense of her self and to acknowledge the right to choose her own beliefs. Over two years, her life changed. Before she had dressed drably, hung her head when speaking, and shied away from conflict. All that altered. She began wearing brighter colors, sharing her opinions, and challenging others when necessary. Eventually, she sorted through her spiritual beliefs and found a church that felt more uplifting. During our last conversation, she expressed the relief that God wasn't the dictator she'd been led to believe; in fact, maybe "She" was more interested in happiness than rules!

Chakra Nine: From Soul Sympathy to Soul Empathy

Jason was a typical ninth-chakra psychic. His true longing was to be a retro-sixties hippie and live in a world of causes. The problem was that he was only sixteen, and the issues of the times just didn't do it for him.

His body pierced in dozens of places, his hair greased like that of a swamp man, and sporting a vampire cloak, Jason began to collect knives. He figured that if he built his own private arsenal that someday a cause would present itself. He began to hear voices: "You want to free me. You want to free the world." Visions of violence accompanied these voices. When his parents found the knife stash, they were obviously concerned. Jason was hauled in to see a guidance counselor, as well as me.

The voices spoke through his fifth chakra, but his sensitive spot was the ninth. The ninth chakra hosts the innate desire for idealism. Jason was a ninth-chakra gem with strong ideals, but no overall guiding purpose.

Jason's shift was from a world of untruths to a desire to perpetuate world peace. He agreed to finish high school so that he would have the basic life skills for creating positive change. It took months, but Jason was eventually able to forge a relationship with a cause worthy of his efforts. Last I saw him, he had shut down the voices and was entering the Peace Corps. He decided that after returning from his two years of volunteer work, he would attend college and major in theology and pre-med, with the long-term goal of doing mission work.

Chakra Ten: From Environmental Sympathy to Environmental Empathy

Every time Julie had a problem in her life, her house mirrored her inner frustrations. The last time she had a bladder infection, her sewer pipes backed up, and she woke to two inches of water in the bathroom. Not a plumber in the world could correct the situation until Julie examined why she herself had her bladder infection. Eventually she concluded she had been holding anger at her ex-husband for over a decade. Know which plumber was able to fix her toilet? The one who arrived the day she forgave her ex-husband.

Julie didn't actually completely shift from being a tenth-chakra sympathizer to a tenth-chakra empathizer. Despite the success with her toilet, she felt resentful about "owning" her part of the dynamics in her house. Deciding that her house was the real problem, she sold it and moved to a new one. She now has the same set of problems in her new situation. Our patterns follow us.

Being environmentally sympathetic caused (and continues to cause) Julie a lot of money in household expenses. I've met other environmental sympathizers who can't sleep at night if lightning strikes a tree nearby or forgive themselves if they accidentally kill a flower—that is how deeply they feel the awareness of the Natural. I've met others who can't function anytime there's a full moon or a tide or the planet Mercury shifts, and still others who can't move on the anniversary of an ancestor's death. Others can't cope with any artificial products of any sort; one woman I know had to build a completely organic house in the woods, or she couldn't breathe. Still others are plagued with the voices of nature, animals and trees, or the insistent demands of ancestral spirits. Once an environmental sensitive becomes empathetic instead of sympathetic, he or she is much better able to see to personal needs first and nature's changes second. Those who can own their environmental sensitivities and work with, not against, their immediate environments have successfully shifted to being empathizers. They love their houses, yards, and nature in general. In turn, the natural world provides them signs, messages, and the gift of mirroring needs and issues.

The Challenge of Change

As you gain control of your kinesthetic psychic sensitivity, you will find that many people happily support you. But an equivalent number of people will prefer the status quo. Do the rulers of a dysfunctional family dynasty want to be challenged by a child who insists that something doesn't seem right? How many patriarchal institutions want to value the kinesthetic who points out the ageism in their system? Would a pastor, priest, or rabbi want to be confronted by the sexism that a feeling empath may sense in a congregation? Regardless of whether the systems are emotional, mental, spiritual, familial, cultural, or financial, people stuck in them don't like change. They and other sorts of psychic sources will resist anything or anyone that wants change.

Remember the psychic awareness that you had as a child? You *knew* it was wrong for your father to yell at your mother. You *sensed* that the teacher was presenting false information in class. You *knew* that the Divine didn't approve of only boys, not girls, lighting candles on the altar. You *felt* the wisdom of the wind and its contrast to what you learned in school. Even now, you probably are troubled by senses, feelings, knowledge, or physical signs that challenge the established order. When you were young, people tried to shut you down because *they* didn't want to change. You were the casualty. But by inferring that you needed to submit to the status quo, others were submitting you to agony. Agony occurs when we don't get to be our real selves.

When my clients begin to gain control over their psychic sensitivity, I tell them to expect resistance. We are mirrors for each other. Your new self-honesty compels others to be honest with themselves. Your refusal to be a storage space for other energies, whether these sources are alive or dead, ancestral or natural, feelings or thoughts, will disturb those now forced to find other ways to meet their needs. Remember to assume divine protection. Remember that your spirit is stronger than anything physical and that through the Divine Spirit, all the support, guidance, and safety you need accompanies you on your journey. Remember too that this is just a journey, and as with any travels, sometimes the path is easy and sometimes it is hard. In the end, all you have is your own integrity.

Exercise 8

The Kinesthetic Gifts: Assessing Your Gifts and Needs

Return to the gift-order scores you tabulated in exercise 6. You will now work with your kinesthetic gifts, which reside in every chakra but chakras five and six.

First, consider if you are more physically or more spiritually kinesthetic. Add your scores according to this division:

Physical kinesthetic chakras		**Spiritual kinesthetic chakras**	
Chakra	**Score**	**Chakra**	**Score**
One		Four	
Two		Seven	
Three		Eight	
Ten		Nine	
		Eleven	
Total		**Total**	

Is your total higher for either the physical or the spiritual chakras? If there is a difference, what does this tell you about your gifts or your way of receiving, interpreting, or sending psychic information? How does your gift type make you psychically vulnerable? What great capabilities lie latent within you?

Now go through each of the kinesthetic chakras to determine how best to shift from psychic to intuitive. Look at each chakra and assess them with these questions.

1. Is this chakra strong, weak, or midrange?
2. This chakra has created the following psychic vulnerabilities:
3. This chakra has provided me the following strengths and assets:
4. To better manage the information, psychic and sensory, that flows through this chakra, I must do the following:
    - Establish this protection:
    - Heal these issues:
    - Forgive the following people (may include yourself):
    - Use this gatekeeper in this way:
    - Enjoy my gift in these ways:
5. I can enfold the gift inherent in this chakra in these ways:
    - In my personal life, I can . . .

- In my relationships, I can . . .
- In my professional life, I can . . .
- In my health, I can . . .
- In these additional ways, I can . . .

6. In summation, this chakra provides me the opportunity to do or become the following:

Chapter 8

The Verbal Psychic Sensitive

> *An angel of the Lord came and sat down under an oak tree, and began speaking with Gideon, who was threshing wheat. When the angel of the Lord appeared to Gideon, he said, "The Lord is with you, mighty warrior."*
>
> *Gideon had his doubts; all the troubles that his people, the Israelites, were undergoing made him think that the Lord had abandoned them. Understanding this, the Lord turned to him and said, "Go in the strength you have and save Israel out of Midian's hand. Am I not sending you?"*
>
> *Gideon, awed but still doubtful, replied. "If now I have found favor in your eyes, give me a sign that it is really you talking to me. Please do not go away until I come back and bring my offering and set it before you." And the Lord said, "I will wait until you return."*
> *~Judges 6: 1–17*

This snapshot from the life of Gideon, a hero of the biblical Old Testament, illustrates verbal psychic sensitivities. It shows Gideon:

- Hearing what is not audible to other people,
- Thinking that he knows who is speaking, but not being sure,

- Hoping for the best—that the speaker is whom he thinks it is,
- Deciding to test the voice to be on the safe side.

Being a verbal psychic can be a harrowing experience. If we're dedicated to being ethical, we're constantly faced with a dilemma. Either the messenger is divine or good and we're receiving valid information, or the messenger isn't and we're being fooled. There are so many pitfalls for those of us who are verbally sensitive. Which of us with this gift hasn't suspiciously wondered:

- Am I hearing anything at all?
- Am I hearing the message correctly, or is it garbled?
- Is the source of these words (or tones, sounds, noises, music) godly and good, or not?
- Could it just be my imagination or a fantasy?
- Am I hearing only what I want to hear?
- If I follow the advice, will I be led astray?
- Will I be leading others astray?
- How can I authenticate the message or the messenger?
- Am I just crazy?

Wired for Sound

As with any gift, some of us have more talent for receiving sound than others. The site for the psychic verbal gift is the fifth chakra, which is located in the throat area. Through this chakra you receive, process, and send verbal psychic information.

Psychic energy is received through the back of the fifth chakra, which is connected to the auditory system, the thyroid, and the thymus. These bodily organs or systems are the ones most affected by the type of psychic data you attract and send. Based on your fifth-chakra programs, you attract the type of verbal psychic data that you think you need. Your chakra, linked with your brain, interprets the data and then sends out a response. Some of your reactions will actually involve the front of the fifth chakra, through which you speak. Others will involve your other primary senses or other chakras.

The classic mode of verbal psychic sensitivity is that you hear a message, figure out exactly what it means, and then decide what to do with it. This is a practical process to solve a complex problem: survival. The survival of the fledgling human race might have depended upon receiving psychic words and information. Imagine one hunter telepathically telling another that the caribou herd is entering his tribe's territory; a runner might have taken three days to communicate the message in person.

The very recording of history is dependent on our verbal abilities. We speak and say, sing and compose the stories of our personal and communal lives. The making of history, however, has been tied to verbal psychic sensitivity, to the sources of inaudible words, tones, and sounds that encouraged the following:

- The voice of God and angels that spoke so frequently in the Old and New Testament
- The wisdom that helped Black Elk guide the Lakota people
- The inspirational words that came to Billy Graham, Martin Luther King, Jr., Susan B. Anthony, Mohandas Gandhi, Sai Baba, Confucius, and other preachers, teachers, and leaders
- The higher wisdom (or truth or ideas) that inspired Socrates's teachings and advice
- The muse that infused Ernest Hemingway, Virginia Woolf, Emily Dickinson, and countless other writers
- The messages received by John Edward and James Van Praagh, who psychically connect with the dead

These well-known figures were and are clearly using their verbal gifts to write and speak their messages to the world. But this gift center extends beyond the use of human language. Beethoven and Mozart, for example, tapped into it in a way that incorporated sound frequencies beyond words. A dolphin trainer or sound technician may also be highly developed in the throat chakra.

Types of Verbal Psychic Sensitivity

Let's look at several of the terms used most frequently and directly to describe different aspects of verbal psychic sensitivity and explore how each type of sensitivity works. You might see some of your own ability in these descriptions.

Telepathy is the ability to hear the thoughts of others.

Channeling is when spirits or consciousness use you as a vessel or channel to communicate through. It is also called **transmediumship**, because you, the receiver of the verbal information, are serving as a medium or a connection to the other side. There are many levels of this ability, such as:

- **Clear channeling** (**full transmediumship**), when the receiver's body is fully occupied by the source of the message. When this occurs, the soul of the receiver usually departs temporarily. After the communication, the channeler usually cannot remember that which has taken place.
- **Partial channeling** (**partial transmediumship**), when the receiver is present within his or her body at the same time the communicating entity is also occupying it. Receivers usually remember some of the communication.
- **Translational channeling** (**mediumship**), when the receiver is simply presented with information. The receiver's body is not

occupied, though sometimes the receiver is called upon to translate the information so that listeners can understand it.

Automatic writing involves communication with the spirit world through writing. Usually the recipient steps aside, and the spiritual messenger partially or fully enters the recipient's body. The messenger then takes over the recipient's writing function. When done, the visiting communicator leaves. Typically, the recipient is unaware of what has been written in his or her absence.

For **guided writing**, the recipient remains present as the invisible communicator writes through him or her, often in reply to verbal or written questions. There remains the sense that something outside of the recipient is communicating the message, but the recipient is usually aware of the process.

Telepathy, channeling, and transmediumship rely almost totally upon the fifth chakra. Automatic and guided writing also make use of the heart chakra, which is the chakra connecting to the arms and hands. Information-energy is sent from the receiving chakras through the fifth chakra and then into the heart, which, in turn, transfers this information through our hands and onto the paper, or in some cases through a musical instrument, such as a piano.

There is one more major form of verbal psychic sensitivity: **kinesthetic audition**. The external message is first received by a kinesthetic chakra and then relayed to the throat. As a kinesthetic auditor, you might get a gut sense in your third chakra, but not understand the meaning until you open your mouth and begin to talk. You surprise yourself with the information. Or you might perceive that someone else is sad through your second chakra, but again, you may not be clear about your sense until the data is transferred to your fifth chakra. You begin to talk and find yourself speaking words of comfort.

In this same way, your first chakra might send you red-alert signals, but until you suddenly open your mouth and begin screaming, you don't realize that there is an intruder downstairs. Many, many psychic people are kinesthetically gifted, but need to verbalize their perceptions in order to understand the type of information-energy that they are receiving. We've all heard of people who "put their foot in their mouths" when talking, but sometimes it's a matter of putting your stomach—or feelings or thoughts—in your mouth!

While the idea of hearing psychic guidance sounds great, being a verbal psychic poses its own set of challenges. Let's look at the downsides of verbal psychic sensitivity.

The Red Flags of Verbal Psychic Sensitivity

In the Christian New Testament, the verbal psychic gift would fall under the description of "speaking in tongues" or "interpreting tongues." These terms basically portray what it is to be verbally psychic. It's as if an alien being suddenly starts speaking in your ear or in your head, and it's your job to try to figure out what's being communicated. If you are gifted in this capacity, be of good cheer. While kinesthetic input can be confusing, verbal psychic sensitivity is the clearest medium for receiving spiritual guidance. Unless the verbal messages are extraordinarily cryptic, they usually provide more clarity than the other psychic means.

The most fundamental problem with verbal psychic sensitivity is the difficulty in sourcing the message. There are millions of channels to tune into and millions more beings that might want to communicate with us. Unless you're well rehearsed at operating the telephone lines, you can potentially:

- Hear yourself instead of a desirable external source.

- Fail to discern a helpful from an interfering, evil, neutral, or misleading source.
- Garble the message you are hearing and completely misinterpret the information.
- Confuse verbal psychic sensitivity with a psychological issue.
- Give more power to the invisible messengers than to your own common sense, your own spirit, or to the Divine.
- Misunderstand a perfectly acceptable message and think it's bad.
- Over rely on verbal psychic sensitivity, to the point of not thinking for yourself.

There are additional problems associated with the gift. Many verbal psychics question if they should reveal the source of their knowledge. No one wants to be accused of working for the devil, being crazy, or thinking too much of themselves. It's also scary to be given a lot of power by others who think of you as their conduit to the celestial. You don't want to run others' lives!

Many religions believe that unless you follow their dogma, your source of information is the devil or something equally nasty. For centuries, people hearing voices have been accused of being crazy or satanic. Equally problematic is the tendency to indiscriminately revere outside sources and give elevated status to channelers of any kind. Too often, verbal psychics are considered expert problem solvers because of their ability to channel or speak for an entity. Many people consider otherworldly data more valid than that offered by live human beings. But who is to say a dead person knows more than the living? Unfortunately, there are always individuals wanting to rid themselves of self-responsibility. Verbal psychics are prone to attract these types of followers.

Added to these potential problems are the very real physical side effects that strike so many verbal psychics. Two of the most significant problems are weight gain or hormonal problems. In order for your body to let in or channel an external source, it often bulks up to remain safe or becomes altered biochemically. There are several reasons for this.

First of all, when you allow a foreign soul or energy into your body, you take on this external source's vibration. We all run on our own harmonic, or set of frequencies. If your frequencies aren't running at top intensity, you are susceptible to invasion or control by sources stronger than you. Energies from outside of you can overwhelm and change your soul capabilities, energetic bodies, brain waves, neurological programs, and intracellular functions.

Your most susceptible physical systems are the lymph and endocrine functions. The lymph system processes both physical and psychic wastes. When you exercise your verbal psychic sensitivity, your physical system, through your energy bodies, is infused with alien psychic particles. It can be hard for your lymph system to keep up with cleansing the psychic information-energy swirling around your own body. Eventually, the buildup in the lymph system encourages the storage of toxic deposits in your fatty tissues.

Verbal psychic sensitivity can also affect your entire endocrine system, or certain hormone glands, through your energy bodies. As described in chapter 3, every chakra is linked to a different endocrine gland or other body part.

Chakra	Endocrine Gland or Other Body Part
First	Adrenals
Second	Ovaries and testes
Third	Pancreas
Fourth	Heart
Fifth	Thyroid

Sixth	Pituitary
Seventh	Pineal
Eighth	Thymus
Ninth	Diaphragm
Tenth	Bones
Eleventh	Connective tissue
Twelfth	Secondary endocrine glands

When you physically incorporate another entity, soul, or consciousness, their energetics takes over your chakras, at least temporarily. Through your chakras, these foreign energetics translate into your endocrine glands' organs. Your weakest glands will be the most affected, usually adversely. The only exception involves infusion of the Divine or your own spirit, which will actually heal your endocrine glands.

When your endocrine system or any particular endocrine gland is disturbed, you can experience annoying to dangerous physical problems. Here are a few of the body-based signs that could signify a verbal psychic victimization cycle.

Immediate Symptoms

These body experiences could indicate you are dealing with an interfering source when using your verbal psychic gift. During the actual psychic connection, you might experience:

- Rapid or arrhythmic heartbeat
- Sweating
- Intense numbness or cold
- Feeling faint
- Tingling or prickly feelings, usually where the entity is entering your body or chakra system

- Reddened or flushed skin
- Rushing sounds or noises
- Blackouts
- A sense of being taken or forced out of your body or into a small area of your own body
- Muscular weakness
- Skin sensitivity

Long-Term Symptoms

Immediately to months after an interfering verbal experience, you might have the following:

- Continued physical weakness
- Bouts of emotions, as if you are processing the external entity's feelings
- Waves of nausea
- Changes in eating or sleeping patterns
- Memories or thoughts that aren't your own
- Overwhelming sense of being toxic, full, heavy, or dirtied
- A loss of appetite or overwhelming cravings
- Changes in menstruation or sexual function
- Weight gain

Obviously, many mental or physical conditions can also result in the above symptoms. If you are performing verbal psychic functions, however, and experience any of the above, immediately stop channeling and see a doctor.

So Many Sources!

The various sources, entities, energies, or consciousnesses you verbally connect with depend upon:

- Physical genetic influences
- Soul experiences
- Destined spiritual needs
- Spiritual genetics
- Family-of-origin teachings
- Cultural standards and beliefs
- Religious beliefs
- Your own experiences
- Divine intervention

As you've learned, verbal messages can be received from beings or consciousnesses on any of the five levels of reality. A verbally gifted psychic can potentially tune into sources from the Natural, including that of the faery realm, plants, animals, power animals and totems, ancestors, the deceased, and demons. On the human level, all peoples from all time periods are available. This group includes sub-personalities of the self, of others, as well as individuals' higher selves, the aspect of each of us that understands what's really going on. The level of the Energetic contains beings and masters from the various energy realms and dimensions, and some would add extraterrestrials and other life-forms. There are the Antiworlds, in which everything that did or didn't, could or won't ever happen, is currently happening. The World of Spirits is vast and busy, containing messengers that might include demons, angels, allies, guiding beings, and the like. Then there is the level of the Divine Spirit, the highest domain of all.

Though I've tried to outline this list of potential psychic speakers, it's really an interminable undertaking. There is no end to the beings— dead or alive, organic or otherwise—that can and want to make themselves known!

While we are all equipped with the capacity to be verbally psychic, it doesn't mean that we are supposed to be communicating with everything floating around. To communicate implies being open to communion. Do you really want to be conjoined with an ax murderer or the demon that's been plaguing your family for centuries?

I had one client come into my office exhausted. She had been awake for months channeling a group of beings from the Pleiades, a planetary system far from earth. She was enraged when I suggested that she didn't *have* to undertake this job or, if she wanted to, at least she could establish her own working hours, say before midnight. She left in a huff. The truth is that being preyed upon by these beings made her feel special.

If we're stuck in a psychic victimization cycle, we nearly always have to figure out why we have bought in the sources and messages we receive. Typically, we don't know we have rights, but sometimes, we like the sense of being different. Being open to psychic words, sounds, or noises isn't any great feat. In fact, such vulnerability can be rather foolish or, at times, just plain wrong.

Moving from Psychic to Intuitive

Here is how your verbal gifts change in the intuitive-development process.

Gift	Psychic Sympathy	Intuitive Empathy
Telepathy	Hearing what others are thinking, whether beneficial or not.	Hearing what others are thinking in a way and at times that are helpful for yourself and others.

Gift	Psychic Sympathy	Intuitive Empathy
Clear channeling	Being fully occupied by the soul and energy of something or someone else, with no control over the process or its effects.	Being occupied with the soul and energy of something or someone else in a way that only benefits both yourself and others.
Partial channeling	Being partially occupied by the soul and energy of something or someone else, with no control over the process or its effects.	Being partially occupied by the soul and energy of something or someone else in a way that only benefits both yourself and others.
Translational channeling	Receiving psychic information-energy from outside sources, with no control over the process or its effects.	Receiving psychic information-energy from outside sources in a way that only benefits both yourself and others.
Automatic writing	Removing your own consciousness to enable another consciousness to physically enter your body and write what it wants to write, regardless of cost to yourself.	Removing your own consciousness to enable another consciousness to physically enter your body and write what it wants to write; in the process, the self receives healing, inspiration, or assistance.

Gift	Psychic Sympathy	Intuitive Empathy
Guided writing	Opening yourself to written guidance from another consciousness, with no control over the process or the outcome.	Opening yourself to written guidance from another consciousness in a way and manner that benefits both yourself and others.
Kinesthetic audition	Simultaneously receiving psychic information-energy through kinesthetic and verbal means, with no control of outcome or its effects.	Simultaneously receiving information-energy through kinesthetic and verbal means, with benefits for all involved.

Protection techniques are only as effective as the individual using them. Before any intuitive boundaries will work for you, you must be willing to move from being psychic to being intuitive, which means moving from maintaining the status quo to managing your developmental process.

Intuitive boundaries assure that we psychologically progress. Paradoxically, to hold solid intuitive boundaries, we must progress psychologically. There are four major reasons that we might have penetrable psychic verbal boundaries:

1. We haven't learned that we are in charge of our verbal gift.
2. Our psychological development, or lack of, inhibits the correct use of these gifts.
3. We don't know how to discern between verbal sources.
4. We have not yet brought our gifts into the Divine's domain.

Let's look at these points, beginning with numbers one through three. We'll discuss number four, ways to bring your gifts under the Divine's umbrella, at the end of the chapter.

1. Being in Charge

While lack of knowledge isn't grounds for condemnation, ignorance didn't save Little Red Riding Hood from the wolf. Eventually, we must realize that any audition that isn't helping us is hurting us and must immediately be stopped. When you're standing in the middle of a television show room with each TV tuned into a different station, you're not going to catch any one plotline. The Old Testament book of Job says that God speaks, which implies that you won't be hearing much from God if you're lost in surround sound. If you find yourself constantly deluged by noise, simply close down until you've learned how to discern. The Divine or your gatekeeper will find a way to get through, if necessary.

2. Developing Psychologically

Healing Negative Beliefs and Mental Strongholds

Often, family-of-origin programming is the reason that verbal sensitives are too open. The negative scenarios that I find most frequently are:

- If your family was chaotic, you have learned to be comfortable with chaos. It will seem strange or maybe even wrong to think of tuning out the noise.
- If your family was too controlled or enmeshed, you might attract messages or messengers that seek to control you. Again, this will feel comfortable. It might be uncomfortable to seize authority for yourself.

Various mental strongholds can drastically affect the types of beings you attract to you. For instance:

- Believing yourself to be *inadequate,* or "less than," you may attract messengers that will convince you to not take risks or move forward in the world.
- Believing yourself to be *unworthy* of love, you may attract messengers that reinforce your fear of love or that advise you to select unavailable partners.
- Believing yourself to be *undeserving*, you may fail to hear the messages that create success. Instead, you will tune into messages that keep you stuck and frustrated.
- Believing yourself to be *bad*, you'll attract evil sources that want to make you feel worse about yourself. Your shame is their food.
- Believing yourself *powerless*, you'll magnetize entities (and people) that will victimize you. They will feed off your fear.
- Believing yourself *unlovable*, you'll connect with entities and energies that will reinforce your unlovableness. They want to keep you for themselves.

Want to alter the types of messages or messengers inhabiting your space, intruding on your life, and occupying your mind? Change your beliefs. Do the hard work you need to do to get rid of those old programs from your parents, your family, or your culture. Get rid of the ideas that detract from your life and expose you to negative influences, whether they stem from the concrete world or are otherworldly. The following are a couple of energetic methods for healing issues that might be creating a psychic victimization cycle.

The first thing you can do is check for cords. Ask your gatekeeper to help you pinpoint the source of messages that are keeping you stuck in the past. Who or what is feeding your consciousness, probably through your unconscious or subconscious? Is there a string of cords or old messages still attached from Mom, Dad, family, school, or the religion in which you were raised? The types of cords affecting our verbal psychic gifts usually enter through the back of our neck or our heart. I suggest that you work with a spiritual or holistic therapist to plug in a new set of messages so that these old ones can fall away. You can always ask to hear only divine truths. The less dependent we are on old, limiting beliefs, the more likely we are to hear what's good for us.

Another way to heal your negative beliefs is to decide to hear only the Divine or a divinely appointed gatekeeper. You may not know how to hear the Divine. You may not know exactly who "God" is to you, or what form you want to perceive this being or consciousness. But making the decision to allow only the Divine or its gatekeeper to speak with you puts the Divine in charge of your psychic process. The Divine can now not only teach you, but also protect you.

Healing Stuck and Distorted Feelings

Old, crusty, or triggered emotions can also keep you vulnerable to psychic overload. The feelings alone don't cause you problems; we become verbally sensitive only when we've failed to deal with or express our feelings. Feelings are energies, and they each operate on a different frequency. Having a feeling stuck in your throat alters the vibrational frequency of your throat and attracts entities that match this out-of-tune vibration. Distortion of the verbal psychic gift leads to distorted feelings.

Distorted anger. Warped, non-spirit-based anger prohibits hearing messages about love and forgiveness, exposing you to messages that increase judgment or criticism of self or others.

Distorted sadness. Distorted sadness blocks the flow of power or messages that will bolster your self-confidence, opening you to information-energy that causes further despair, hopelessness, or sorrow.

Distorted fear. Warped fear leads you toward evil or interfering sources, attracting manipulative forces or entities seeking to use you as a tool or a reservoir of energy.

Distorted pain. Hurt might attract beings that want to help and heal, but not always in a healthy way. Some sources of information-energy are "super caregivers" that seem understanding, but are invested in keeping you victimized.

Distorted guilt. Warped guilt usually ends up drowning you in your already low self-esteem. When sitting in a self-pity cave, it's frightfully hard to hear anything but your own breathing or beings that want to keep you inhibited. You need to own when, why, or where you've moved off base and get back on the road.

Shame. Shame coats us with self-loathing. Energetically, this gray, pasty-looking energy keeps you glued to the past and too scared to move forward. It also keeps your unexpressed feelings blanketed and stuck. Feelings are also prayers, and shame holds them inside.

When you release feelings to the Divine, you receive in return spiritual energy that reprograms your limbic system, the center of your feelings, beliefs, and physical reactions. This is an actual technique for healing feelings. It is also the natural result of dealing with your feelings using therapeutic means. Feeling our feelings heals us and brings us closer to the Divine. Interfering entities desire to keep you in shame and these other distorted emotions, in order to hide you from divine light—your own light! As long as these entities can keep you in these emotions, they can steal your energy and prevent you from carrying out your spiritual destiny. This keeps them in control (and prevents them from feeling their own shame and guilt).

This is not a therapy book. I am not going to cover all the wonderful and amazing therapeutic processes that can free you from these constraining emotions. I can only encourage you to seek out and work with a trusted person, even before you continue learning about your psychic gift. To determine the level of assistance you might need, track the types of messages or beings that frequent you most often. If any of them seem to produce the same negative feelings repetitively, you might be stuck in an emotional state that is keeping out the good stuff and holding in the bad. Find someone to help you dig deep. You don't want to be at the constant mercy of old parental programs, your own denigrating messages, or external, negative influences. After all, if you're going to use your verbal psychic gift to your own advantage, you want to do more than just hear yourself think or receive the same messages over and over. You want to hear *truth*.

3. Discerning Between Voices

Once you are on track and clearing out old programs, you are ready to begin discerning between your own inner voice and voices from outside of yourself, as well as negative and positive sources of information-energy. Briefly, you can differentiate between your own voice and that of another because:

- The timbre or quality of an external voice is usually different from yours.

- Your own voice will tend to reinforce what you already think or believe about a topic.
- An external voice will have a clear reason for speaking.

Frequently, my clients report that their introduction to hearing external sources began with hearing knocks, ringing in their ears, sounds, or the calling of their name. My own verbal opening process started with a voice calling in the night. I heard "Cyndi!" three nights in a row. I got tired of answering and hearing no response, so I finally asked whatever it was to come clean. It turned out that the voice belonged to a new, divinely sent spiritual teacher, who began visiting me in my dreams to train me in shamanism.

Have you not yet received a calling? Ask for one. Ask for the Divine to call you. You will be heard, and you will hear.

What if you don't know if you are hearing a good or a bad source? Refer back to chapter 5 on discernment and go through the points listed there. Remember that a divinely inspired messenger will always wait until you are sure that they are of the light. Helpful sources will never coerce, force, or arm-wrestle you. You can say, "Prove yourself," and they must. Know also that you can always wait for a sign, as discussed in chapter 5. You will receive one.

Remember also that you can always use praise as a tool. As did Gideon, praise or pray to the one in which you believe. Do you think that "God" really cares what name you use—or that you worship Him/Her/It? No! The Divine knows that if you seek only the Divine, you automatically establish a channel of light that keeps the darkness from entering. When you are focused on the Divine, it's much easier to perceive what is not of the Divine.

Intuitive Boundaries for the Verbally Gifted

It is wise for verbally gifted psychics to set up intuitive boundaries.

This way, negative energy is unable to leak through and cause confusion. There are two main ways to ensure healthy verbal boundaries. The first is setting up a good defense. The second is running a good offense.

Intuitive defensiveness involves establishing parameters that make it unfeasible for anything harmful to reach you. You need good defenses under any conditions, but they are extremely important if you are prone to uninvited messengers or if you are going through a good deal of change. You wouldn't unlock your front door just because someone wants to come into your home, especially if he gives his name as Cat Burglar.

Major transitions include recovering from life-changing stresses; grieving a loss; experiencing a tremendous physical, emotional, psychological, or spiritual growth spurt; or undergoing a significant spiritual alteration. During these times, the defenses that might have once worked may no longer work. Malicious forces and people often take advantage of this new vulnerability to scare you into regressing. Your destiny is a curse to them; if you're unavailable to interference, you deplete their power sources.

Guidelines for Screening Incoming Calls: Your Defensive Maneuvers

These are some ideas for establishing safe parameters for incoming sources.

- State aloud exactly who or what you will allow to speak with you (such as the Divine, messengers of the Divine, or your gatekeeper).
- Set intentions or needs through conscious prayer, writing them down when possible.
- Employ kinesthetic techniques—like blessing or warding negative energies away from your bed, car, and other areas of special

vulnerability—against invisible marauders. You can ward off negativity by picturing a white light surrounding the exposed area or yourself, using sage or incense that has been blessed for protection, using oil to trace a cross within a circle around the window sills and doorways, writing words of protection on the wall before painting them, or asking the Divine to establish guardian angels on the exposed parameters.

- Refrain from using techniques that could open you to interfering sources. The lower the frequency you use to make a verbal connection, the higher the likelihood you will attract interference. Ouija boards, violent tarot cards, séances, and full channeling or transmediumship sessions are all practices that can open the door too wide to malignant influences.
- Be vigilant regarding your internal thoughts or questions. You might believe, for instance, that you would like to know when your mother or father might die, but do you really want to know this? Be sure before you ask.
- Decide that all incoming messengers must appear in your mind's eye as they really are, if you are visually oriented. You can state this decree out loud, or simply decide it internally. The key factor is the intensity with which you make the decision. The more forceful you are, the more alert sources are to the need to follow suit to be acknowledged and accepted by you.
- Create a ritual for incoming messages. For instance, you could decide that you will only hear God's messengers in the morning when your hands are on the Bible, the Torah, the Koran, or some other holy book. Or you could decide that you will only listen to voices that introduce themselves a certain way. Or state that you will only pay attention to suggestions that you receive at the church or a home altar or synagogue or out in nature. And always use your spiritual gatekeeper.

- Select a partner to help you screen messages for source or validity. For women, it can be vital to share your senses or received words with a man friend, husband, or any other extremely rational and ethical person. Men have a different angle and are usually highly kinesthetic. They get an immediate body sense regarding accurate versus misleading information. Men would serve themselves by asking women for guidance and insight and allowing women several days to provide it. A dream, a sense, a phrase in a book—women will psychically attract the information a man might need in a way that he can't.
- Keep a daily journal of information-energy received and review it monthly for signs of psychological or spiritual growth. You can also go over parts of this journal with a trusted and ethical spiritual or mental-health counselor. Be willing to be held accountable for the information that you act upon.
- Decide whether it is right for you to seek others to provide verbal psychic sensitivity for you or not. As Morton Kelsey suggests, "It is one thing to receive spontaneous experiences . . . it is another to seek out those who can provide these for us."[1] No one is infallible; if you tend to give your power away to others rather than follow your own common sense or sense of the Divine, you might want to deliberately avoid getting psychic input from others.
- Choose to tune out all auditory messages. You might be one of the people who are just plain too vulnerable to negative entities. That's okay. Know your limits, and if you need to completely abstain, do so.

Guidelines for Contacting Verbal Sources: Running a Good Offense

While the defensive measures can help you identify messages and messengers that come to you, there are times that you should proactively attempt to seek divine spiritual guidance. I frequently do so on behalf of both my clients and myself. To assure safety and validity, I have developed a protocol that challenges me to open only to guidance that is "F.D.A." approved—Fully Delivered from Above.

Here are ideas for safely contacting verbal sources.

- Follow a strict ritual before opening to guidance. I ground, center, assume divine love and protection, open, and then pray directly to the Creator for information. Experiment with procedures that will work for you.
- Pray directly to the Divine in order to create a beam of energy between you and it. The Divine can send its messengers up and down this tractor beam while screening out would-be infiltrators.
- Meditate. Besides calming you, meditating can open you to your own and others' higher selves.
- Contemplate. We don't always need an answer. Sometimes it's better to simply bask in the presence of the Divine. Once we're in a more holy, or whole, state, we'll naturally screen out negative influences.
- Seek out others who have proven themselves able to receive godly guidance.
- State specifically which messengers or sources of information you would like to hear from or are willing to entertain.
- Develop code words for good and evil and ask the presenting spirit or messenger which side it's from. Many people use comparative words like *light* versus *dark, God* versus *evil, good* versus *bad*. When you ask, beings must answer—it's a universal law. If you're doing automatic or guided writing, write your code question and refuse to continue with your communication until you get a response.
- Invoke universal law, as covered in chapter 5, to make a source reveal its allegiance.

- Demand that all presenting messengers tell you if they are the primary source of the information. Sometimes, there's a being behind the being.
- Ask for a sign, as covered in chapter 5. A helpful being can take its time getting to know you and helping you get to know it. Consider how much time God gave Gideon in the passage at the beginning of this chapter!
- If you have kinesthetic psychic gifts in addition to the verbal, use these to confirm the veracity of messages you receive. Check to see how the source psychically smells. (Really!) Kinesthetics often report that bad beings have a bad smell. Center in your second, feeling-based chakra. How would you feel spending time with this being? Happy or scared? Believe your kinesthetics.

A Verbal Psychic Who Became Intuitive: A Case Study

Let's look at one verbal psychic who made the switch from psychic and sympathetic to being intuitive and empathetic.

Max was a forty-nine-year-old mechanic who was tired of the noise—not machine noises, but the noises that no one else could hear. All day long, some invisible being talked in his head, telling him where to put the wrench, bolts, and tires. If his unseen assistant was correct once in a while, Max might have put up with the inconvenience of being constantly distracted and unable to hear the "living." As it was, "Mr. X" was not only loud, but also gave bad fix-it advice. Every so often, Max would shake his head and absolutely refuse to listen to Mr. X. He would pretend that he had cotton in his ears, hum loudly inside his brain, or talk as often as he could to bystanders. Mr. X would punish him.

In Max's words, "If I ignore him, he just jumps into my skin! Then it's like I can't even think, his voice is so loud—and worse, it's in my head. It drives me crazy, and I itch like mad when he leaps back out."

Max was clearly a verbal psychic. Most of the time, his gift operated in a garden-variety version of translational channeling, hearing messages from outside of self. When Mr. X was unhappy, though, he was able to enter Max's body. Max remained consciousness; therefore, he was a partial rather than full medium. Max wasn't happy about it.

In our first session, I informed Max that he had the right to decide just whom he wanted to listen to or not. He shook his head, not believing me—and little wonder. Mr. X was in charge. To help Max gain his own personal power, I had him "invite" Mr. X into the room with us. I enforced the invitation by employing the Law of the Innocent, as outlined in chapter 5. Mr. X was victimizing Max, and now he had to answer for himself.

We ordered Mr. X to sit in the chair in front of Max. I then had Max converse with him, Max listening through his verbal psychism. Over the course of the session, we uncovered Mr. X's story. He had once lived in a house that had burned down in that area, and he had perceived Max's gift. Wanting someone to speak with, he attached himself to Max and proceeded to do just that—speak.

By the end of the session, Max felt powerful enough to dismiss Mr. X. We called an angel to take Mr. X to the light, or wherever else he should be taken. From that day on, Max never heard from Mr. X again.

Even though Mr. X was gone, Max was still shaken. His experience with Mr. X had uncorked an intense psychic gift, one that could switch on again at any moment. We spent several sessions honing this ability until he felt like he could control it, not the other way around. He decided only to use it to contact his gatekeeper, and he selected a gatekeeper that was—guess what?—good at mechanics! Max insisted that his gatekeeper operate in a translational nature rather than through occupation. Because this gatekeeper was "of the light," it respected Max's boundaries.

Remember, it is *your right* to test voices. It is also your right to command for right. This is a universal principle. To enforce this right takes confidence in your right to remain inviolate. As illustrated by shaman Ultima in the book *Bless Me, Ultima*, we all have the right to command for good. Says her young charge, Antonio:

> *The terrifying end was near. Then I heard a voice speak above the sound of the storm. I looked up and saw Ultima. "Cease!" she cried to the raging powers, and the power from the heavens and the earth obeyed her. The storm abated. "Stand, Antonio," she commanded, and I stood.*

How do we peer into the universe so as to distinguish right from wrong? To figure out what we should command versus that which we should let be? We must be willing to be a disciple. We must be walking the walk of a disciple, of one devoted and disciplined to divine will. We must employ our verbal gifts in ways that move beyond us and into the greater all. We must decide that we want to first hear the voice of the Divine, for truly that is our own primary voice.

Exercise 9

The Verbal Gift: Assessing Your Gift and Needs

Return to the scores you tabulated for exercise 6. Now look at the specific questions that you answered in exercise 1, the Psychic Sensitivity Quiz, and review your highest scores. Ask yourself these questions:

- What are my verbal vulnerabilities?
- When do they mainly strike—at a particular time of day or

evening, when I'm feeling certain feelings, when I'm around certain individuals, or at other particular times?

- What are the main sources that create interference or a psychic victimization cycle?
- What makes me feel powerless in regard to these sources?
- Is my current gatekeeper capable of helping me screen interference and opening me to positive sources? If it is, ask this gatekeeper to provide you with a plan for safety and intuitive development. If you don't think the gatekeeper is sufficient, ask the Divine to appoint you a gatekeeper that is, or ask the Divine itself to assume the role.

At this point, conduct your normal life for a while and keep adjusting your needs until you feel safe in your life. You can then continue to evolve your psychic verbal gift through daily prayer, meditation, and contemplation.

Chapter 9

The Visual Psychic Sensitive

"I'm to tell you to watch out," he said. "There's danger at the crossroads."
"You can't mean traffic, it's so quiet around here?"
"I can't mean traffic, young human sir—but you are to use the eye of clarity when you get to the spot. There's deluderings at the crossroads, such as would confound Geography and Cartography, such as would make Pandora's Box into a tuppeny lucky bag," the old angler said earnestly.
~Pat O'Shea, *The Hounds of the Morrigan*

Eyes of Clarity. The Sight. The Vision. Creative visualization. Foresight. The Gift. Viewing. The Evil Eye. The Knowing. Inner Sight. Dream Eyes. Scrying. The Third Eye. Almost every culture has a term for and knowledge of visual psychic sensitivity.

Connotations of the Sight have populated countless tracts of religious documents, mystical tracts, and popular fiction. Wars have been won or lost, foes have been foreseen or forgotten, great loves have been promised and never delivered on basis of the famous predictive values assigned the psychic sense of vision. The oracles of Delphi, Greece—women who would enter trance states to answer questions—always insisted that their visions were correct. Any difficulties were attributed to the failure of their listeners to interpret the cryptic messages correctly. But we visual sensitives wonder. It seems that one of the innate traits of the visionary sense is to confound. Viewing with the visual sense is popularly considered more acceptable than the other psychic senses. Compared to the other two psychic senses, verbal and kinesthetic, however, the visual one can be fraught with interpretation difficulties.

The Sight of the Sight

The psychic sense of vision has been vital to the human condition for eons. The visual information necessary to the primal human included:

- Warnings
- Foretelling
- Explanations
- Reality checks

Wouldn't you, as a caveman, have wanted to be warned of the impending hurricane? (There were no Doppler weather machines in prehistoric days.)

Wouldn't you, a warrior going off to battle, like to know in advance where the enemy is hiding?

Wouldn't you, a woman about to give birth in a stark, cold cave during the winter, want to foresee any potential difficulties, so you could prepare for them?

The basic purposes of the innate psychic visual sense, both in the past and now, are twofold:

1. To enhance our physical survival by illuminating facts about the past and the present

2. To give us greater control over the present by providing insights to the potential future

As we learned in previous chapters, the means for gathering and depicting information-energy visually is the sixth chakra, based in the pituitary gland. Often called the Third Eye, this seemingly magical equipment actually involves a biochemical process, as does normal vision. When light hits the physical eye, it stimulates a complex set of enzymatic, hormonal, and additional chemical reactions that enable the mind to perceive the object being viewed, access memory, and add interpretation. Psychic visioning works much the same way, except the Third Eye is able to perceive both ultraviolet and infrared frequencies that are outside of the visual light spectrum. Add the fact that information-energy can come from past, present, or future, and we must wonder why the entire world doesn't better cultivate the visual psychic gift. Think of how much more we could see!

Information-energy can enter physically or psychically through the normal eyes or the Third Eye, and be converted to psychic pictures. It can also be received by any or all chakras then sent to the sixth chakra, which will then transform the gathered data into pictures. There are two primary ways that this information is registered visually:

1. Through the inner eye
2. With the external eye

How Visual Psychic Sensitivity Looks When Internal

Visual images can appear on a mind screen, seen only by you. They can present as:

- True-life images that appear as a slideshow, one photo at a time
- True-life images that run together in a film-like fashion

- Symbols, metaphors, or representations, such as stories or fairy tales, that convey messages
- Written words, which may actually appear like handwritten or typed notes
- Apparitions or ghostly forms, such as those seen on the astral plane
- Energetic equivalencies—shapes, colors, chakras or auric layers, grid patterns or the like—depicting what is going on energetically or underneath sensory reality
- Thought forms, strands, or layers of lines that show the cause of a situation
- Hallucinatory images, such as those experienced in a trance state, guided meditation, or medicine ceremony, which involves the use of sacred plants and ritual to invoke a spiritual process
- Spiritual equivalencies, which show what something looks like in the world of the Spirit. You might see the Great White Light or omnipresent love force, or you might see shades of dark, gray, or white that depict consciousness.

How Visual Psychic Sensitivity Looks When External

We usually perceive psychic images through our inner rather than our sensory eyes. In fact, ancient lore purported that mystics needed to be physically blind in order to have the "true sight." However, there are many records of external psychic visual sensitivity, such as:

- Seeing, with your physical eyes, flashes of what has happened, is happening elsewhere, or will happen. Versus with the inner eye, these images will be as distinct as anything else in the physical environment or be incorporated into the setting you're seeing with your outer sense.

- Blurred sensory vision, followed by the formation of a single image. This blurring can alter sensory images to metaphorically reveal emotional states, transmute the scene into another time period, present an alternative way to view a situation, or highlight a future possibility.
- Seeing guides, angels, or demons, either in true form or as colors, shadows, lights, or shapes. Many people see these entities or spirits as flashes of colors. Some psychics call them "orbs," and these orbs sometimes appear in photographs, as well.
- Seeing deceased relatives or other spirits, either in true or altered (apparition) form.
- Viewing energy or energetic patterns, such as images of the auric field or a particular chakra. Children commonly see the aura, but usually only one or two colors at a time.
- Having an aggravated sense of visual reality, such as when in a trance or a ceremonially induced state.
- Seeing pictures or projections of potential pursuits, such as the art piece you are going to create.
- Full-body experiences. In these, your consciousness or soul is drawn into another realm, and you fully experience that which is occurring elsewhere.

Basically, all visual renderings help us survive. Seeing your just-passed mother, now happy and blessed, in your mind's eye might help you stop grieving. Dreaming about a demon might warn of a psychic attack. The same demonic picture may warn of a problem with a negative neighbor.

If, at some level, these various pictures and visuals are valid, we must wonder why different visual psychics seem to get different visions about the same subject. The answer to this question lies within the mechanics of visioning.

The Mechanics of Visioning

The fundamental structure for visual and all other sensory communication is the nervous system. Some embryologists, scientists who study what life is like in the uterus, have observed that the various senses develop at different stages or time periods before birth. These different senses, from smell to touch to vision, aren't separate. They are joined together at junctions along the nervous system. These junctions, the places where different nerves come together, are called ganglia. At the ganglia, our various senses associate with each other.

For instance, certain smells may trigger a visual picture because the physical sense of smell was developing at the same time as physical vision; these two different senses share some of the same nerve cells. Likewise, a particular sentence may invoke an emotional reaction; a sunset may always cue the remembrance of a touch, for example, because memory is laid down not only in the brain, but also in the body.

Understanding this process can help you better figure out how psychic visioning works. When you see a lamp, whether it is in your mind's eye, your imagination, or your office, your nervous system might trigger all sorts of reactions. If a lamp has been a consistently positive object, you might smile and turn on the lamp, musing how nice it is to have the light penetrate darkness. If you were raised in a cave, however, and your only association with a light was its blaring explosion into your quiet dark, you might become scared and shove the lamp off the table.

The point is that different visual images trigger different reactions in different people. Francis Crick, one of the two noted scientists whose paper on DNA rocked the world, has explored this idea at length. In his book, *The Astonishing Hypothesis: The Scientific Search for the Soul*, Crick asserts that the issue of what we pay attention to may be one of consciousness. Each of us is programmed with a unique set of ideas, and our consciousness will recognize and accept visual cues about these ideas. Our history, along with other factors, will determine our interpretation of the visual data.[1]

Memory assists us in recognizing visuals. For instance, we associate the back of someone's head with his or her unseen face. When we see an object, a set of neurons fires. Different neurons from various areas bind together, either strongly or weakly, possibly by relying on memory, so that we may recognize the object or pay attention to it. Hence, other points of sensory reference—taste, smell, touch, words, sounds, feelings—can be caught up or registered simultaneously.

This is why our psychic visual senses differ from person to person, time to time. It's a matter of impression, perspective, memory, and purpose. The visual process is complicated and personal.

Let's add our knowledge of the chakras to this. Each chakra is organized around different neurological ganglia. For example, the first chakra will perceive information-energy about our physical world; the second will recognize data about feelings. These centers can access not only physically measurable stimuli, but nonsensory or psychic information as well. So each chakra can feed our nervous system with data that can be transformed into a picture. The vision center, or sixth chakra, can also see through the auric layers into our mind field, the morphogenetic fields, the soul, and our physical eyes. The emerging psychic image, whether perceived internally or externally, will be a composite of energy from any or all of the chakras.

Our psychic perceptions also depend upon the initial source of the information and our feelings and beliefs about this source.

To track our internal views, we have to explore the complex relationship between our reptilian, mammalian, and higher learning systems. Bottom line, our psychic vision will add, subtract, change, alter, or encapsulate reality, not to confound us, but *to encourage us to react.*

Types of Visual Psychic Sensitivity

Over the centuries, many terms have been assigned to the various visual psychic senses. One term is ***clairvoyance,*** which literally means "clear seeing." Many people gifted with visual psychic sensitivity are called *clairvoyants*.

While your two sensory eyes see the everyday world, the **Third Eye**—your sixth chakra, located in your forehead—sees into the unknown. Several ancient mythologies describe this eye, attributing its great powers of extrasensory sight.

Futuring is the ability to see or see into possible futures. With futuring, you can see into not only your own potential future, but also that of others and even the world in general. These possibilities are screened by your pituitary gland, which holds your self-image—and also the Divine's picture of you—and determines which potential future is best for you. The middle of your pituitary holds your psychically based self-image. The back of the pituitary receives life choices, which filter through your self-concept and are then projected through the front of the pituitary as a selected path. Ideally, information-energy about your spiritual destiny, your karmic gifts, and your current life tasks downloads into your sixth chakra from the top three chakras to assist you in making the best choices about the future. All other chakras then link under the auspices of the sixth chakra and work to turn the chosen vision of the future into reality. Other words for futuring include *foresight*, *foreseeing*, *predicting*, or *visioning*.

Viewing is the ability to see what is taking place elsewhere. Most scenes appear as if you were present in them. There are many types of viewing. **Remote viewing** involves watching a situation like an outsider, either from inside of your body or through the projection of your soul or etheric body. In **full viewing**, you can actually play a part in the drama, either energetically or in your mind.

Scrying is a divination process that usually involves a bowl with water or a crystal stone. Typically, the visual psychic looks into the object to forecast the future or to check on a present event.

Five Types of Psychic Visions

Accurately defining the type of vision you're receiving is the key to working with visual psychic sensitivity. There are five types of psychic visions:

1. When you're using your **full sight**, you are seeing a situation with utmost clarity. For instance, you might be reviewing a time in history just as it actually happened.
2. **Half sight** implies that you are receiving half of the potential full image. A half-sight image might be a blurry image or difficult to interpret. It might disappear before you can fully understand it. A half-sight image isn't necessarily bad or a mistake. Sometimes we're only meant to see partially and not fully into a situation. But half-sight imaging is always frustrating.
3. **Hindsight** involves seeing into the past, typically from a vantage point that provides more information or a greater clarity as to the causes of a particular situation than was available initially.
4. When in **current sight**, you are receiving pictorial illustrations of concurrent or possible available choices.
5. **Foresight** is a generic term for seeing the range of future possibilities.

Often the image of most likely possibility comes in the strongest or clearest and invokes an emotional reaction.

The Red Flags of Visual Psychic Sensitivity

There are many problems inherent in visual sensitivity. These are the most common:

- Inability to distinguish between what is really there (physically present) and what is only psychically present.
- Confusion about the nature of a source. We commonly assume that a bright, light, or angelic-looking source is good or of the light, and that darker shapes, colors, or beings are bad. This isn't always the case, and it's easy to follow a misleading source.
- Distraction from daily life due to overwhelming images, pictures, colors, or shapes from the psychic realm.
- Difficulties in sorting fantasy, hallucinations, or make-believe from true vision and psychic activity.
- Susceptibility to eye problems, headaches, migraines, and memory problems.
- The sense of "being different" and the feeling of loneliness that incurs.
- Self-image and body image issues and the resulting problems, including anorexia, bulimia, and weight issues. The Third Eye stores our self-image, which is often programmed in during our later childhood and early teenage years. If these programs don't match our inner self's opinion, we will develop self-image issues.
- In some communities, the sense of "being used." People come to you with their problems, seeking solutions and insight on the future. You become your gift, not someone with a gift.
- Problems distinguishing between real, probable, and possible events.

- Over-responsibility. If you can see an impending problem, why can't you change it?

The Intuition of Vision

The most important first step in changing from psychic to intuitive visioning is to get distance and gain perspective. So what if you can envision purple around someone's body, view tomorrow's relationship sagas, or check out what happened in 1984? What's important is that this information means something to you. You may receive valid psychic visuals, but find that they might lead you nowhere. Visual sensitives have probably experienced this many times. Great Uncle Andrew appears to you in your dream life, but all he does in sensory reality is sit in his chair and snore. Not much of a message, is there? You want to be able to screen the psychic phenomena that are useless, prohibit those that are harmful, and encourage those that are beneficial.

There are a few key steps that greatly enhance your use of the psychic visualization process for healing and even manifesting. When working with vision, it is nearly impossible to not work spiritually. The higher we work in the chakra system, the more apparent and necessary it is to enlist the Divine in the process. These are a few of the consciousness-based steps and processes that will help you become more intuitive; some of them incorporate sourcing of the Spirit.

Step One: Taking Command of Your Visionary Ability

Psychic information can visually present itself in many forms. To move from psychic to intuitive, you must understand that you have authority over the physical appearance, as well as the occurrence of the vision itself. Controlling vision begins with knowing that you get to command your visionary ability. You are in charge. If you want clean and pure visions, you must understand this point. Know that:

You get to ask questions. In fact, the key to understanding your visions lies in asking questions. If a picture doesn't make sense, ask the Divine to show you another image. You can do this over and over until you can grasp the message of the vision.

You are in charge of the psychic process. You have the right to command the process. If something doesn't feel right at any point, at any stage, ask the Divine for protection and quit your psychic imaging. *Tell* the visions to dissolve and the apparition to leave. *Command* truth to appear. *Change* channels. *Close* down.

You control your relationship with the vision. You can experience a vision many ways. One of the most important techniques is to move from one point-of-view to another. Point-of-view refers to the perspective or way that you are seeing the presenting message. The visual points-of-view include:
First person: You are the center of the vision and are seeing it through your own "eyes."

Second person: You are watching yourself in the psychic vision. It's as if you are standing outside of yourself while watching yourself.

Third person limited: You are on the outside looking in, but can see only from the perspective of yourself. You can't tell what's going on inside of other people, though you can see or watch them.

Third person omniscient: You are on the outside looking in, but you can see into everything and everyone. Omniscience allows you to fully comprehend the motives, feelings, beliefs, and needs of all associated parts of or people in a vision. Basically, you are all-knowing and all-seeing.

If you're not getting enough information while in a visual state, you can switch perspectives. For instance, move from first to third person. If there is something you need to work through, switch from second to first person or into third person omniscient. You hold the camera. Practice with different angles!

Step Two: Seeking a Vision

Once you understand and exercise your right to command your visual ability, you can begin to actually seek out a psychic vision. In many ways, you follow the same control procedures when seeking or receiving a vision. You still have to remember your right to command and to manage the psychic process. You can still shift perspective and play with point of view. You can also use the techniques described in this section to encourage more visions to come, until you receive one that you fully understand. (If you receive a vision and can't alter it, you will skip this step and go right to step three: interpreting a vision.)

There are many ways to seek a vision. As with all the psychic senses, your best methods begin and end with the Divine and the three main ways of connecting with divine sources:

1. Prayer: reaching toward the Divine
2. Meditation: receiving from the Divine
3. Contemplation: enjoying the presence of the Divine.

In any of these states, you can safely request a vision or visual communication from a grace-filled source. By following the five steps you've already practiced in exercise 2, including grounding and centering, assuming protection, and opening and closing, you can securely open your visual sense.

Step Three: Interpreting a Vision

Interpreting visions is the key to being safe and benefiting from your innate visual sense. To interpret correctly, you must discern between the five types of visions (full sight, half sight, hindsight, current sight, and foresight). These questions can help you learn how to identify what type you've received:

- Is this vision about the past? (Hindsight.)
- Is it about something occurring right now? (Current sight.) If so, is there something you are supposed to do with this knowledge?
- Are you getting all the information right? (Full or half sight.) If not, is there more you need to see?
- Is this vision about the potential or probable future? (Foresight.)
- What is the truest form of the source of this vision? (Full sight.)

Step Four: Acting on the Vision

After interpreting a vision, it's important to decide how to act on it. Remember, non-action is an action, and is always a viable choice. Return to our discussion about integrity and altruism in chapter 5. What are the most obvious responses to the vision? What are some less-than-obvious reactions? Which fit your value system? Which lead to acts of integrity or altruism? As you discern appropriate from inappropriate responses, know that you can test an action and stop at any time.

Vision as a Tool for Personal Growth

One of the most satisfying ways to apply the visual psychic gift is for personal growth or to assist someone else. Let's look at some ways you can access vision intuitively for these purposes.

In order for a psychic vision to really qualify as intuitive, it must be personally helpful. It must lead to a new level of life-enhancing awareness. It must produce at least one of the following results—positively affecting one or more of the chakras—for yourself or someone else:

- It can improve your physical well-being (first chakra).
- It can free you from imprisoning feelings and emotions and move you toward joy (second chakra).
- It can unpin you from negative beliefs and move you toward higher self-esteem (third chakra).
- It can unbind you from harmful relationships or patterns and encourage more loving ones (fourth chakra).
- It allows you to share yourself powerfully and communicate lovingly by removing old tapes and increasing your ability to set respectful boundaries (fifth chakra).
- It can rid you of false impressions about yourself and allow you to see yourself and your potential more realistically (sixth chakra).
- It can help spiritually by enabling you to better understand divine love and accept the Divine's provisions (seventh chakra).
- It can help you work through the experiences of the past that are holding you back and help you claim the gifts you have yet to use (eighth chakra).
- It can remove the blocks to living your purpose (ninth chakra).
- It can lead you to take practical, concrete steps toward living a good and decent life (tenth chakra)
- It can discourage the selfish use of your energies and abilities while encouraging ethical applications of your personal and positional power (eleventh chakra).

Typically, an intuitive insight accomplishes these goals by:

- Bringing up psychological issues for clarification or healing.
- Highlighting actions or perspectives that, over time, lead to a closer relationship with the Divine and others.

The sixth chakra is ideally suited for this type of personal challenge and healing because it contains your conclusions about your place in the world.

The sixth chakra develops during your preteen years. Look at what's going on with kids today, and you'll have a pretty good idea about the type of beliefs that we've all taken into our systems. They add up to a communicable disease called meaninglessness. It seems that we're all prone to this infection, especially women and members of any non-mainstream groups. Too often our cultural beliefs result in depression, low self-esteem, and addictions. These symptoms speak to a culture that has programmed its peoples with perfectionist standards that lack a foundation in true spirituality.

Your body and physical health are affected by these demoralizing perceptions. The pituitary gland is one of the master endocrine organs. It connects with your hypothalamus to regulate basic body concerns, directing your reproductive glands, thyroid, and, indirectly, the adrenals. When you're constantly seeped in negative or limiting beliefs, even if only psychically, your hormones become imbalanced. Results can range from general anxiety to deep depression, lack of motivation to hyperdrive, low metabolism and weight issues, and stress-related conditions that include back problems, chronic fatigue, and even cancer.

You need to allow your psychic vision to provide you with the insights and perceptions needed to heal the issues and beliefs underlying these types of problems. To do that, you can turn to your toolbox of intuitive techniques for opening to vision. You can use any of these techniques for personal growth, to professionally assist others in their expansion, or to open to visual signs or information.

Your Intuitive Toolbox: Applications for Growth and Learning
Intuitive processes operate at a higher level than psychic ones in that they require more conscious involvement on your part. If I desire to receive a psychic vision, I always ask that the Divine send or invoke one. Let's say you've prayed for a vision and received one, or you received one without a specific request. Now ask for the following:

- To see this vision in its truest form.
- To have it erased by the Divine if the Divine is not its ultimate source.
- To have the Divine provide a new visual if the old one was not divine.
- To have the Divine protect you from this or other visions if they are not to be received by you at this point in your life.

While the above tips will work with any psychic visioning process, there are dozens of methods that enable a deeper use of the visual gift. Here's a condensed guide to these processes:

Guided Imagery
Guided imagery can help you with anything from problem solving to manifesting, from sourcing to interpreting visions. It's really a mental process for getting visual answers. It is easiest to conduct a guided meditation with an actual guide, a trusted friend, a spiritual counselor, or a therapist. As this person brings you into

a meditative state, he or she will assist you in walking through any presenting visions or visual dramas. To make sure that your concerns are covered, you may want to prepare a set of questions in advance. The process is complete when you feel resolved, when you have a better understanding of what a situation means in your life, or what you need to do about it. A few particularly popular applications include:

- *When dealing with a problem or an issue:* Visualize yourself in a safe place. See yourself in this place. Now ask the Divine to send you a helper. This helper holds a gift that, when unwrapped, helps you better understand your problem or provides you with a tool for dealing with it.
- *When experiencing body pain or illness:* Ask your gatekeeper to help you visualize the disease or stricken body part in symbolic form. Now hold a dialogue with this image. Allow the image to show or tell you the message it holds for you and what action you need to take to clear up the problem.
- *When trying to figure out if a difficult life challenge contains a lesson:* First, request a messenger to assist you in uncovering insight. Go right to the Divine and ask for a personal guide that can offer instruction and perhaps even, ongoing teaching. Fully picture your guide. Now relate with this guide. Remember, the key to all visual imaging is that if you don't understand the first picture, ask for another. Questions that can help you uncover the reasons for your life difficulty include:

    - What is the lesson to be learned from recent events?
    - What action do I need to take?
    - How will I look or what will my life look like when the learning is complete?

Guided Meditation

Guided meditation involves achieving a quiet state and following a thought-out process so that the Divine, a gatekeeper, or a good source can help you. Through guided meditation, you can reach a state of calm, recover from stress, open to ongoing answers or assistance, or simply bask in the Divine's presence. Guided meditation is a type of regular meditation, which involves awaiting answers from the Divine. In guided meditation, however, you pre-establish a process for a specific purpose. You might, for instance, imagine yourself walking down a path and meeting your gatekeeper in order to obtain an answer to a question. You might visualize yourself in a park, forest, jungle, or desert, opening to divine inspiration. The key to an effective guided meditation is deciding your goal and process in advance. A few mental images that can help you create a guided process include:

- Visualizing yourself in nature
- Imagining yourself in the past, at a time when you were happy and fulfilled
- Projecting yourself into a desired future and owning it as real
- Becoming a white light and surrendering to the Greater White Light of the Divine
- Imagining yourself in a special place at which you meet a guide
- Creating an evolving journey, such as walking down a path, traveling through space to a far-off planet, burrowing down in a tree to talk with elemental natural beings, flying in the sky to the heavens, time-traveling through a wormhole to find your answers

Experiential Sighting

Experiential sighting is equivalent to guided meditation only easier to do solo. It involves combining sixth and eighth chakra abilities.

Ground into your tenth chakra, center, and assume divine protection and guidance. Concentrate on the presenting situation, which could include an episode from the past, a current dilemma, or a possible future event. You are now linked to your eighth chakra. In a trance state, project yourself into this situation. Now ask to be told by your messenger what you need to know.

Typical questions to ask about the past include:

Why did this happen?
What was my responsibility for the events as they enfolded?
What was I supposed to learn from it?
How can I forgive or release others and myself?
What do I need to do to break any recurring patterns?

Questions about current dilemmas might include:

Why am I now in this situation?
Is there something I'm supposed to be learning?
Am I seeing the situation truthfully, or is there a higher perspective involved?
Is there a belief I'm to adopt that will heal the situation?

Queries concerning possible futures include:

What potential future would the Divine suggest is best for me?
What do I need to heal or change within myself to assure the best potential outcome? (This could be something such as changing a habit, adopting a new belief, seeking atonement for past behavior, or feeling certain feelings.)
What do I need to do immediately to create the best possible future?

You are searching for the answers or reflections about your situation. The Divine will see through all presenting problems to the essence or truth. If you can see truth, you can align with it and make it your reality.

Foreknowing

This intuitive process combines the third chakra gift with the sixth chakra to clarify and resolve issues. I use it when I feel blocked or when I'm resisting something that I know I should know. The process involves entering an interactive meditative state.

Ground and center, affirm spiritual protection, and then request to know what fears or blocks are preventing you from knowing what you need to know. One at a time, envision the various reasons for resistance and ask to see what has caused them. Once you can diagnose the reasons for any blocks, determine if you can release them yourself or if you need professional help. Once these blocks are cleared, you can employ other intuitive techniques to arrive at the answers you seek.

Foretelling

This intuitive process combines the fifth and the sixth chakras and will assist you in speaking or writing the truth. Start with a question and ask for a picture of the solution. Then either write or speak the meaning of this vision. Be careful here, for it can be easy to allow other sources of information to slip in and cloud your process. Remain true to the task by going slowly or having another person help you.

Foreseeing

Connecting the sixth and seventh chakras, this process allows you to scan the future for potential or probable events. This can be tricky, for who among us doesn't want to see what we want to see or to try to control an outcome? Protect yourself from your own ego or fears by limiting your use of this procedure. As well, always ask that you receive insights that uphold your spiritual purpose. There are lots of choices. Some of them lead in the right direction, and some don't. We all have personality aspects that will mislead us, either out of fear or resistance.

To tap into your foreseeing abilities, meditate on your question and any presenting vision through your seventh chakra. Ask the Divine to open your seventh chakra to the world's greater destiny and to specifically show you the role you are supposed to play. Continue to work with your images until you fully understand the answer and are at peace with it.

An interesting note about this process: We receive life-path choices in the back side of the sixth chakra and project them forward through the front side. This actually means that we are viewing the future from *behind us* not in *front of us.* Physically, an image reverses in the brain before it is registered right side up. Knowing about this inversion can help you get around blocks or resistance to the future. If you can't see what you think you ought to, imagine looking through the eyes "in back of your head" instead of in front!

Forewarning

Some senses or visions can be alarming. You might see or sense a threat and wonder if you're on target or not. Sometimes you might hope everything is going to be okay and just want to make sure.

There are many factors governing the validity of possible threats. First, there are things we are supposed to know and things we aren't supposed to know. Then there are internal psychological issues, such as your own paranoia, fears, and neediness, that make you think something bad might happen, but it won't. And, of course, there's the possibility of entity or other psychic influences. I have found that the best way to deal with forewarnings is to maintain a policy of not specifically looking or asking for one, but accepting it only if it's presented to me.

If you believe that you have received a valid vision or warning, you might conduct a process that links your first, fourth, sixth, and seventh chakras.

Form (visualize) a connection in your heart between your first and seventh chakras. I usually imagine a pink bubble. Ask that the Divine or your gatekeeper join you in the bubble. Now ask to see the meaning behind the threatening vision or the potential dangers in an upcoming situation. Keep asking questions until you are clear about the message and your own best response to it. Clear the bubble and commit to allowing the Divine to direct your actions.

Creative Visualization

Creative visualization hit it big with Shakti Gawain in the 1980s and has since been adapted to many mediums and career fields, including sports performers. Creative visualization connects your kinesthetic chakras, including your tenth, with your vision center so you can practice for a future performance. See yourself accomplishing your goals. Imagine yourself responding more lovingly to your mate in the future. Watch yourself hitting that tennis ball. Creative visualization is a prelude to manifestation. The key? Ask first that everything be carried out according to divine will, not just your own will. Allow the Divine to direct your visualization and see what happens!

Strategizing

Strategizing is a practical application of psychic visioning. Whether applied professionally or personally, the basics are the same. Your potential choices enter psychically through the back of the sixth chakra. Your programming, typically a mix of positive and harmful strongholds, operates like a screen. Your programs either prevent you from or allow you to perceive your best choices and propel you into a great future.

Because your programming may block you from seeing all available choices, request that the Divine or your gatekeeper help you visualize the paths now available to you. Ask to see the paths that should be available, and then ask to visualize any resistance you may have to attracting or making the most positive choice. Ask what you need to do in order to clear this resistance, and then, reviewing your options, ask the Divine to highlight the choice closest to your spiritual destiny.

Now project this selected path forward through the front of your sixth chakra. Then project your selected path into the rest of your chakras to reinforce your decision, as well as to bolster your auric field, which will in turn attract what you need to fully manifest your chosen future.

Mapping

Some of us are more left-brain than right-brain oriented, or more circular and experiential versus linear and progressive. Mapping is a great strategic-planning trick for anyone who is both visual and left-brain oriented.

Get a huge piece of paper and post it on the wall. Now get hundreds—yes, hundreds—of sticky notes. If you're a color person, get magic markers or crayons, though a pen will do in a pinch.

Divide this large paper into sections. You are going to label each section as you see fit. One suggestion is to categorize holistically, using divisions like physical (lifestyle, exercise, eating, clothing, housing, bill paying, and so on), mental (learning, changing beliefs, reading, schooling), emotional (fears, desires, joys), relational (important people, people causing you pain, coworkers, friends), and spiritual (relationship with the Divine, worship place, spiritual practice, community). Other divisions could be self, others, or the Divine, or you could use the five levels of reality as your sections.

If you want, you can also prioritize your categories by putting your most important ones near the center of the paper and less important ones farther out. However you label the divisions, within each category, add a subsection for blocks, another for attitudes, and another called action.

Then write goals for each section. Every morning, review your goals. Fixate them in your mind, affirming that you have already achieved them. Visualize yourself living your most desirable life and decide that today, *it's all true*.

Pack sticky notes to take with you as you leave the house. As the day goes on, pay attention to what you feel and think, and to what occurs that fits into your map categories. Do you become aware of an inner issue, tension, or emotion that might be preventing you from achieving a certain goal? Write your awareness on a sticky note, and when you're in front of your map, stick it in the section called "blocks." Is there an attitude that seems to be preventing you from believing in your dreams? Write it down, and stick the note under the "attitudes" section.

At the end of the day, look at these two sections. What actions will help you release your blocks to success? Which might help you switch your attitude? Actions can be internal or external. They might involve undergoing healing or performing a new behavior. Now visualize yourself taking these actions. See them succeed. Picture your ultimate success.

You will find that as you give form to your needs and desires, the blocks and attitudes sections will shrink, but you should continue filling in the "actions" section. Actions lead to achievement, and you will get there!

Opening to Signs and Guidance

There is yet another way to use intuitive vision, and that is in your everyday life.

Ask that the Divine show you through your daily life the images, words, books, people, or information that you need to help make a decision. I use a rule of three; if I see something three times within a short time period, then the Divine is sending me a message. If you're pondering where to go on vacation and in a single day, each time you turn on the television there is a special on Antarctica, it might be time to take out the parka. If you're wondering how you're going to get through a stressful meeting and three times in an hour you see a cardinal, you might want to consider what characteristics this bird presents and begin to act the same way. This is a fun and delightful way to bring the Divine and the rest of the world in on your intuitive process.

Pineal Gland Visioning

Structurally, one of the best ways to source is to focus your vision sense on the top of the seventh chakra, through which you can see the threads that run through the universe. These are **thought threads** or mental cords that show connections. Through this type of visioning, you can trace a vision to its origin or follow a vision to its conclusion.

By focusing through the pineal gland, you can see the real nature of something, usually in shades of black and white. A negative or dark vision that has penetrated your defenses cannot stand up to the eyes of truth. While a sixth-sense reading might visually reveal an angelic source, a seventh-chakra insight will illustrate the true nature of this being. Interference will appear black, fuzzy, or gray. Further visual examination will reveal the energy movements of your vision source. Interfering sources swirl like a tornadoes, and grace-filled ones are calm and imperturbable. Disturbed energy patterns indicate that the being behind the received vision is trying to use you as a source of power for itself.

Pituitary Gland Visioning

Typical psychic visioning is done through the pituitary gland. Sometimes a vision can be difficult to see or perceive, however, because it isn't completely locked into your sixth chakra. You will know when your vision is in full sight rather than half sight when you can envision a wonderland of color. Allow these colors and forms to settle until you can clearly picture your vision's source. If a picture doesn't make sense, ask for another, and keep asking until you understand the message.

The Visual Gift: Five Steps for Safe Visual Psychic Activity

Here are some common techniques that can help anyone with even the slightest bit of visual psychic sensitivity to use this gift safely. Included are several choices for each of the five steps.

1. Visual Techniques for Grounding and Centering

Here are several ways to ground and establish your center as a visual intuitive. You might choose one each time you work or try them all.

- Imagine that you are a tree, rooted deep in the ground. Your roots allow in only healthy and organic sustenance. Because you are safe, you are able to reach into the sky and accept all that the world has to offer. To maintain the balance between earth and heaven, picture the part of your body that is centered, that is equidistant between your deepest root and your highest branch. Place your conscious awareness in this space and breathe deeply. You will make all decisions from this space.

- Imagine a bright white light, straight from the Divine, entering your body through your ninth then eighth then seventh chakras. This white light is a healing and cleansing light, and it washes clear through your spine and legs, then through your tenth chakra and into the earth, keeping you grounded and connected to the Divine. Now ask yourself which chakra regulates the flow of this white light. This is your centering chakra. You will remain centered or located within this chakra for balance.
- Your spirit is fully in your body, and you can picture its colors, as well the flow of divine energy that continually emanates from it. As you connect with your spirit, notice which area of the body your spirit is strongest in. This is your center. In this space, you are most connected to the Divine. Expand from this center, allowing your spirit to combine with the Divine Spirit to fill and encompass you internally and externally. You are now grounded and centered spiritually, as well as physically.
- Gold energy represents magnetic and spiritual forces, while blue energy reflects electrical and physical. Look at each of your chakras to discover which one is composed of equal and balanced amounts of gold and blue energy. This is your center. Next, ask your spirit, with the Divine Spirit, to accept the spiritual energetic force of grace into your body from your top chakras. Picture this spiritual force as gold and allow it to fill your entire body. Then ask your spirit to accept the spiritual force of holiness. Holiness is a spiritual force that can easily be recognized and assimilated by the body electrically. Picture this force as blue and bring it in through your lower chakras. Allow these two energies to mix in

your center and to then be shared throughout your body and your auric field. You are now grounded and centered within the spiritual forces.

2. *Visual Techniques for Assuming Protection*

The following are different ways to accept divine protection as a visual intuitive:

- Imagine that you are a tree, rooted within a safe space in the natural world. Above you, the sun shines, bright and white. This white light flows from the sky into and around you, flowing through you into the ground. As it washes through you, it collects psychic and physical toxins, cleansing them from your body. You are now purified and harmonized with your environment.
- The earth is full of its own special energy—elements such as water, earth, stone, and metal. These and all the elements are necessary for your well-being and safety. As the white light cleanses your body and connects with the earth, it also activates these earthly elements. These now rise into and around your body, carried on earth energy. Energy is now flowing down and flowing up, renewing you and also surrounding you. This energy will continue to flow like a bright, protective waterfall in and through your auric field, keeping you bathed and protected. Constantly replenished by the Divine from above and cleansed by the earth from below, the energy will constantly replenish and cleanse you.
- Your spirit, with the Divine Spirit, is already in and throughout your system. Now ask that the Greater Spirit harmonize your spirit with your intentions, plans, and the rest of the world. Whatever you need is provided. Whatever you desire will be brought to you. Whatever image you require will be shared from Above. You will be in harmony, and you are secure.

3. Visual Techniques for Opening

Here are several ways to safely open yourself to visual information:

- Set an intention. State that you would like a vision (or insight, healing, daily support, revelation, or the Divine's presence made physical). Now see yourself as the tree, receiving what it needs from nature. Accept the gift and ask the Divine, your own spirit, or your gatekeeper to help you understand it.
- So much bright white light flows through you that you now understand yourself as light. Light can reflect any truth. In your center, imagine the intensity of your own light. This light now opens all your chakras and energy centers, so you can receive that which the Divine has to give.
- Your spirit through the Divine Spirit is connected to everywhere and everything in the universe. With this assurance, allow your spirit to open your energy system to that which the Divine provides for you.

4. Cross-Referencing with the Kinesthetic

Even if you are primarily a visual psychic, you can and should use your other psychic senses to crosscheck your visions. Your kinesthetic senses, for instance, can tell you if you're being fooled or fooling yourself with a vision. Your verbal sense can command a source to appear in its truest form, therefore offering an important protective element.

Your kinesthetic senses can confirm or deny the true source of a psychic vision, as well as the plausibility of your interpretations. For example, I frequently use my first-chakra senses to test the source of a vision. I might *smell* the presenting being or the pictures of the source. A good being will smell good; a bad being won't. I might psychically *touch* the vision's source. Is the source warm and inviting, or cold and clammy? Using your kinesthetic senses can tell you a lot about the nature of a vision's source.

The following questions, associated with the individual chakras, can help you access your various kinesthetic senses for help with a particular psychic vision.

- *First chakra:* Do you feel safe and secure when viewing the vision's source? Does the source or the message lead to a sense of health or of disease? You want to pay attention to only the life-affirming messengers.
- *Second chakra:* Does this vision enhance your feelings of joy or happiness? Can working with the vision potentially clear disturbing feelings and bring you into spiritual feelings, which are life enhancing? Can this vision show you the real meaning of a particular feeling?
- *Third chakra:* What do you intrinsically know to be true about this vision or the source of it? Do you trust this source or not? Is this vision providing accurate information or not? Is your interpretation of the vision accurate or not?
- *Fourth chakra:* If you pursue this path or believe this source, is there healing to be had? What is your relationship with any beings or entities in the vision? What is it supposed to be? Does the source of this vision wish you harm or help?
- *Seventh chakra:* Is this source from the Divine or not? If the Divine were to give you a vision about this particular topic, what might it be? How does this vision support your divine mission?
- *Eighth chakra:* What world or plane does this source come from? Is there another, more valid dimension or plane from which to receive an image? If you could receive a vision with the message opposite of this one, what would it be? If you could travel to the source of this vision, to a world changed by this vision, or to

the space showing the truth of this vision, what would you see?

- *Ninth chakra:* What does the soul of this source really look like? If this vision were to address a matter important to your soul, what might it be?
- *Tenth chakra:* What is the practical application of this image? Is the source from nature? Is it one of your ancestors? What is the motivation of that source? Will this message support your everyday, practical reality or not?
- *Eleventh chakra:* What percentage of this vision's source is negative versus positive? If you were to follow the wisdom of the vision, what outcome in negative or positive effects would be created?

A Visual Psychic Who Became Intuitive: A Case Study

Geri is a "recovered visual psychic," as she puts it. Her earliest memories are of seeing colors, pictures, and beings that others couldn't see. As a child, she would watch her dead grandmother walk around the house, drinking coffee and chiding her mother, who couldn't see what was going on. When older, Geri would see red splashes of color on others' bodies, only to later find out that these images revealed sites of developing illnesses. She would see orbs around people, indications of guides and ghosts, and at night, would be subjected to dreams about accidents, deaths, and mishaps that would, all too unfortunately, come true. Geri saw too much.

It took me quite a while to convince Geri that her visual sensitivity was a gift, not a curse. Her mother thought her ability was evil, misquoting the Bible in its statements against psychics and soothsayers. Her brothers and sisters used to make fun of her stories, calling her insane. She was constantly distracted by her daily and nightly visions, and wanted nothing more than to shut them off.

Geri and I conducted a past-life analysis, in which she remembered that she had once been a Delphi Oracle. The Oracles were priestesses in Greece who offered their visions to visiting questioners. That life had ended with Geri being killed for providing "inaccurate" information. (Most likely she had been correct, and some king had disliked her prediction of battle loss.) Geri had decided that her gift could give her only grief and pain, and her current life was proving the accuracy of this belief. Beliefs create reality. To change Geri's reality, we had to alter her beliefs.

We spent several sessions in which Geri worked through her past and present life beliefs, until she began to see the beauty of her ability. I taught her psychic control, until she could open and shut her visual gift at will. Then another gift opened! As Geri developed safe standards and uses for her visual gift, a heart-centered healing gift activated. She was then able to psychically see disease—as well as the means to help heal it. Geri began to take holistic healing classes. Last time we talked, she had just opened her own healing practice.

Exercise 10
The Visual Gift: Assessing Your Gifts and Needs

Return to the scores you tabulated for exercise 6. How high was your visual score? Scores between fifteen and thirty indicate a strong verbal psychism, and any above twenty reveal you as a high psychic in the visual capabilities. This test was designed to help you pinpoint your susceptibility to psychic invasion, as well as your intuitive potential.

To more thoroughly understand your visual gift and the type of intuitive development it might require, please respond to these questions:

1. Is my sixth chakra a strong, weak, or midrange chakra?
2. This chakra has created the following psychic vulnerabilities:
3. This chakra has provided me the following strengths and assets:
4. To better manage the information, psychic and sensory, that flows through this chakra, I must do the following:
    - Establish this protection:
    - Heal these issues:
    - Forgive the following people (may include the self):
    - Use this gatekeeper in this way:
    - Enjoy my gift in these ways:
5. I can enfold the gift inherent in this chakra in these ways:
    - In my personal life, I can. . .
    - In my relationships, I can. . .
    - In my professional life, I can. . .
    - In my health, I can. . .
    - In these additional ways, I can. . .
6. In summation, this chakra provides me the opportunity to do or become the following:

Chapter 10

From Psychic Sensitivity to Spiritual Vocation: Unfolding Your Destiny

> *The body is a unit, though it is made of many parts, and though all its parts are many, they form one body. . .*
> ~From *I Corinthians 12:12*

You have learned of the truth, and even the necessity, of being psychic. You have figured out how your psychic gifts have benefited or hurt you. You have committed to using these gifts to do more than survive. And so you have gone about the lengthy process of studying the intuitive system, of connecting the dots that walk from psychic to intuitive to spiritual.

Being intuitive is more a process of hard work and dedication than natural and easy gifts. It involves:

1. Accepting that you are psychic
2. Assessing the effects of the psychic sensitivities on your life to date
3. Honestly owning how you have hurt yourself and others with your uncontrolled psychic gifts
4. Learning that there is a different way to use your psychic gifts
5. Learning this way, called the intuitive system, by studying:
   - The science and spirituality of the invisible realms
   - The human energy system

- Universal energies
- The connection between your body, mind, soul, and spirit
- The various sources of psychic information
- Ways of connecting to each of these sources

6. Pinpointing your specific psychic gifts
7. Figuring out the exact locations and functions of your natural psychic gifts
8. Reading how to develop your specific psychic abilities into intuitive gifts
9. Practicing accessing your seventh sense to use information and energy

And now, you come full circle, back to the reason that you undertook this process in the first place.

If the Divine—or your own divinity—gave you these gifts, then the Divine and/or your own divine self must want you to use them.

You've walked the path from psychic to intuitive for this reason alone: to use your gifts and to uncover your spiritual destiny.

Your Destined Path

The Christian New Testament makes it clear that each person is expressly capable of miracles.

> *To one, the gift of manifesting, of making the world a more solid place.*
> *To another, the gift of compassion, of assisting those in need.*
> *To another, the gift of administration, of building systems for heaven.*
> *To yet another, the gift of healing, of making things better.*
> *And to others, the gifts of words, of prophecy and knowing, of enlightening and teaching, of holding and of forcing.*

Do these gifts only apply to Christians? No. During his life,

Christ always pointed to God, the One Above All, which in turn, looks back to us. We are all unified in the Presence, the One Spirit, or the All. We are all here to perform the miraculous, just as each of us, individually, is a miracle.

Your spiritual destiny is about reaping the fruits of your labors. This isn't a selfish endeavor. You are here to share your fruit with others! The insight provided through your gift might be the very one needed to save someone's life, heal an ill child, help the dying die peacefully, or make a person smile. Your psychic gifts must be pruned if they are to blossom into the **spiritual gifts**, the expressions of spirit that make your spiritual purpose concrete and valid.

Your Seventh Sense

If the goal is to create a little more heaven on earth, this means allowing your innate psychic sensitivities to evolve into the spiritual gifts. The **seventh sense** is the spiritual use of psychic sensitivities. When you use your sixth sense to carry out your divine mission, magic is sprinkled into the mix. The mysterious consciousness that most of us call God breathes the miraculous into you, and you become a conduit of miracles.

Miracles are nothing more than the creation of what is supposed to be—now. Your child might be sick, but this doesn't mean that the sickness is caused by a divine plan. By linking your intuitive healing powers with the Divine's healing energy, your child might experience a miraculous healing. Your child will experience that which is about his or her destiny. From a divine perspective, this healing isn't miraculous. It is simply the transformation of what is not supposed to be into what is supposed to be. Our limited human perspective adds the drama.

Miracles don't break natural reality. They create it.

The Spiritual Gifts

While the psychic gifts make sure that you survive
and the intuitive gifts help you thrive,
the spiritual gifts guarantee you divine protection and guidance so you can fulfill your spiritual destiny.

If you know your basic psychic gifts, you are halfway to understanding the nature of your spiritual gifts and, therefore, your spiritual destiny. When you surrender to the Ultimate, to whatever you call the Divine, your basic psychic gifts transform into your spiritual gifts.

When you invite the Divine Spirit to run your life, your own spirit will unfold in your body. You'll still be psychic. Your strongest chakra will still be your strongest chakra. But now the Divine can protect you from negative psychic information—you asked it to do so! It will make sure that you send positive psychic messages into the world. You won't be the victim of your programming or psychic gifts; you'll be the victor with your own spiritual destiny. And this is what your psychic and intuitive gifts will become:

Your twelfth-chakra gifts are individualized and unique to you. They transform throughout the entirety of your life, enabling you to reach the state of spiritual mastery.

What do these categories mean? Here are descriptions of each of the eleven basic psychic gifts and how they evolve from the sixth into the seventh sense.

Chakra and Auric Layer	Psychic Sensitivity	Intuitive Ability (Sixth Sense)	Spiritual Gift (Seventh Sense)
First	Physical sympathy	Physical empathy	Manifesting
Second	Feeling sympathy	Feeling empathy	Compassion/ Feeling
Third	Mental sympathy	Mental empathy	Thinking/ Administration
Fourth	Relational sympathy	Relational empathy	Healing
Fifth	Verbal sympathy	Verbal empathy	Divine Communicating
Sixth	Visual sympathy	Visual empathy	Visualizing
Seventh	Spiritual sympathy	Spiritual empathy	Spiritualism/ Prophecy
Eighth	Shadow sympathy	Shadow empathy	Power Shamanism
Ninth	Soul sympathy	Soul empathy	Idealism/Harmony
Tenth	Environmental sympathy	Environmental empathy	Natural Healing
Eleventh	Force sympathy	Force empathy	Commanding/ Transmutation

First Chakra

Psychic Gift: Physical Sympathy
You can take on others' physical problems.

Intuitive Ability: Physical Empathy
You can sense your own and others' physical needs and create a plan to meet them.

Spiritual Gift: Manifesting
You can make tangible products or services that are useful in this world and illustrative of heaven on earth.

By putting the Divine in charge of your life, this first chakra gift evolves from taking on physical energy to shaping physical energy. You become a Manifester.

Manifestation occurs when psychic energy is converted into physical energy. Individuals with a strong manifesting gift are the builders of the world. Their spiritual destiny involves using physical resources to create tangible products and services. These physical resources could include money, air, housing, clothing, water, or even the physical body. If you're a Manifester, you'll know it. You'll be driven to create something real and practical with tangible tools.

Second Chakra

Psychic Gift: Feeling Sympathy
You can feel what other people are feeling.

Intuitive Ability: Feeling Empathy
You can register and define others' feelings as well as your own.

Spiritual Gift: Compassion and Feeling
You help heal others' emotions through love and care, so they can use their emotions creatively. You might also express your feelings in artistic ways.

Compassion is an elevated way to deal with feeling sensitivities. The spiritual method for sensing feelings is to care about others' feelings without holding onto them. Then the Divine can transform the feelings into creative energy.

Mercy and compassion are two of the several spiritual gifts recognized in the Bible's New Testament and in religions everywhere. Both gifts relate to people who heal others' emotions. When you are merciful, you give others the gift of understanding. No matter what they've done wrong, you relate to why they behave negatively, even if you don't condone their behavior.

Compared to sympathizing with others' feelings, being compassionate involves feeling their feelings *with*—not *for*—them. You don't take over. You don't judge. You don't make it all better. You just act as a *feeling companion*. You are a Feeler. When people feel accepted, they are able to transform their feelings into creative energy, to make something good out of something that has been difficult. And guess what? You might be the person who uses his or her feelings creatively! Dancing, drawing, painting, decorating, composing, writing—the modes of creative expressions are endless. If you are a Feeler, know that you are one of the people warming this cold world and adding color to the black and white.

Third Chakra

Psychic Gift: Mental Sympathy
You know information without even knowing why you know it.

Intuitive Ability: Mental Empathy
You can organize sensory and psychic data so it can be utilized.

Spiritual Gift: Thinking and Administration
You receive and organize information and data so that spiritual goals can be delivered in the real world.

What's the natural application of the ability to access or organize information? The gift of thinking and administration.

Thinkers think. But what are they going to think? Thoughts, of course. Some thoughts come from logical and concrete sources, such as books and other people, but others are understood psychically. **Thinking** is uploading vast amounts of information, both psychic and sensory, and synthesizing it usefully. A typical result is the ability to administrate.

Administration is a spiritual act. You could say an Administrator is a minister of information. You organize the world for those of us who create chaos. You set up structures so that goal-setters can meet their goals. You make sure that the systems in place are running smoothly and ethically—and, in your spare time, you stack your clothing in neat piles and line up your cereal boxes in alphabetical order!

Many spiritual people think that spirituality is just about talking with the Divine, delivering great sermons, or tending to the poor. Who makes sure that the phone lines are operational so that the Divine can get through? Who answers emails so the preacher has time to work? Who lines up the delivery people so the starving can receive their food? Who runs the computer, information, and management operations of the world? The Administrators.

Fourth Chakra

Psychic Gift: Relational Sympathy
You always know what's really going on in others' relationships, often to the point of taking on others' relationship problems.

Intuitive Ability: Relational Empathy
You sense others' relationship needs and desires, as well as your own.

Spiritual Gift: Healing
You want to see people made whole and are willing to let the Divine use your skills toward this goal.

To heal means to make whole. The word ***healing*** indicates the ability to see what's broken and to help fix it. As a Healer, you open to the energy and information needed to help yourself and others move from brokenness to wholeness.

There are many forms of healing. Doctors, nurses, dentists, and other health-care professionals are often Healers, and therapists or hospital administrators can be, too. Nevertheless, salespeople, homemakers, and car mechanics can also be Healers. The real indicators of a destined Healer are that you:

- Are relationship-based
- Want to be used by the Divine to create positive change
- Let the Divine do the healing so you can concentrate on loving relationships

Fifth Chakra

Psychic Gift: Verbal Sympathy
You are capable of receiving audible messages from the invisible world.

Intuitive Ability: Verbal Empathy
You can understand and sort through the psychic verbal messages given to you.

Spiritual Gift: Divine Communicating
The Divine communicates higher messages and shares wisdom about the world through you, adding to humanity's spiritual knowledge, as well as your own.

An elevated fifth-chakra person is one devoted to **communicating truth**. He or she is a Communicator, one who receives and presents truths. You'll understand the truth you're sharing isn't personal to you, even though we all have our own personal truths. You're willing to allow the Divine access to your psychic gift so that you can share spiritual truths with the world. Because of this, the Divine provides you with **Words of Knowledge**, direct communication from the Divine and helpful sources. Communicators who work at this level often become authors, speakers, teachers, and presenters, or offer instruction as a mother or a father. Of course, not all communication is verbal. Music, tones, and any type of utterance come through the sixth chakra. All forms of communication serve the divine plan.

Sixth Chakra

Psychic Gift: Visual Sympathy
You receive visions or pictures about reality.

Intuitive Ability: Visual Empathy
You can understand yourself and others through the visions you receive.

Spiritual Gift: Visualizing
You visualize revelation so you can help guide people to make wise choices.

Once you elevate the standard of your intuitive visions from self-imaging to the Divine's imaging, you can automatically distinguish truth from illusion. You more clearly see all the choices involved in a decision and the projected outcomes of each choice. You become a Visualizer, someone who receives **revelation**, or the "revealed truth."

If your spiritual destiny is connected to visualizing, you'll probably find that many people seek your advice. Your gift makes you a likely candidate for positions requiring the use of strategy, visioning, and directing. Just remember that your connection to the world of possibilities makes it imperative that you qualify your statements; you need to ensure that people understand that there is free will and that they have to be responsible for their own actions.

Seventh Chakra

Psychic Gift: Spiritual Sympathy
You are sensitive to matters and energies of the spiritual realm.

Intuitive Ability: Spiritual Empathy
You can perceive spiritual reality and constantly seek to bring what's spiritually significant into the everyday world.

Spiritual Gift: Spiritualism and Prophecy
You have an innate knowledge of the divine plan for all and can help lead people to their destined paths.

If your destiny involves using your spiritualism, you'll eventually fit the job description of **prophet**. Ultimately, you are a Spiritualist, someone who can sense what's going on in your own or others' spirits.

Over the centuries, prophets have gotten somewhat of a bad reputation. Read the Bible. Most of the Biblical prophets were ostracized, excommunicated, killed, or at least seriously disliked. Prophecy needs to be better understood if it's to be better accepted. If you are a prophet, you are someone who can access the divine plan for an individual, a family, a community, or the world. You will know, sense, or feel what's on target and what's not. Prophets don't necessarily predict the future, although that might be a subspecialty. Rather, a prophet will help people adjust their expectations, actions, or attitudes so that they can meet their own divinely ordained destinies.

Eighth Chakra

Psychic Gift: Shadow Sympathy
You are a walker between worlds. Because of this, you can read dark as well as light energy.

Intuitive Gift: Shadow Empathy
As a shaman, you are able to direct dark and light energies toward a chosen end.

Spiritual Gift: Power Shamanism
You understand the responsibilities of power and are committed to using it only for higher ends.

The eighth-chakra shaman is naturally connected to the powers of the light and the dark. Not everything that is dark is evil. Not everything of the light is good. The ultimate power of those destined for the shamanic role is **power shamanism,** the ability to distinguish right and wrong and know when to wield force and when not to. Power Shamans understand that power is simply the application of energy to meet divine ends.

Real power isn't coercive. It isn't manipulative. Truly powerful people don't act out of accordance with divine will; in fact, if there's a question, they don't act at all! They seek to become less so that the All can become more. In the process, they become very powerful spiritual souls.

If you are destined to understand and wield power, you are on an interesting path indeed. There are people who like power. Usually, they rise to the top. But people who employ the spiritual gifts of power aren't always noticeable. True spiritual Power Shamans tend to disregard power in favor of love and only employ power and forces, or even prayer and advising, when all else has failed.

Ninth Chakra

Psychic Gift: Soul Sympathy
You can sense what is going on in others' souls.

Intuitive Ability: Soul Empathy
You can sense the soul purpose and needs of others.

Spiritual Gift: Idealism and Harmony
You make sure that everyone is seen as a child of God and deserves to be treated accordingly.

Idealists are able to see the best in themselves and others. They don't hold people to these ideals; rather, they apply the ideals like standards or templates for decision-making. You've probably experienced an Idealist, if you aren't one. Don't you do better when someone knows that you can? Idealism is a powerful gift.

When using his or her spiritual gift, an Idealist actually creates harmony and blessing between people. There are no "isms"—racism, sexism, fascism, or even idealism—in one who **harmonizes**, or is dedicated to the universal truth of oneness. Harmonizers are natural peacemakers.

At a family reunion, Harmonizers are the ones grouping everyone for the photo. At a party, Harmonizers make sure that the drinking partygoers don't drive. In the workplace, Harmonizers bring tranquility and serenity. They are the team players and the team organizers. They are the Girl and Boy Scout leaders who keep track of every child. They are the community activists, the public affairs experts, the ethics teachers, the caring parole officers, and the fundraisers of the world. They are the soul doctors. They are ones who want everyone to get that we are all in this world together.

Tenth Chakra

Psychic Gift: Environmental Sympathy
You can read nature and hear the ancestors.

Intuitive Ability: Environmental Empathy
Through your affinity with nature and the ancestral, you can sense what people need from nature and what nature might need from people.

Spiritual Gift: Natural Healing
You help heal others and the natural beings of the earth through your spiritual wisdom.

A **Natural Healer** is someone who is destined to employ his or her sensitivity to nature for positive ends.

If you are a Naturalist or a Natural Healer, you are attuned with all things natural and organic. You can hear messages on the wind, and you wonder at the meaning of a crow call. These innate sensitivities join you with nature, which, in turn, uses you to bring healing and balance into the natural world. You might have a green thumb or a way with plants or animals. You might be interested in herbal medicine, holistic chiropractic care, or farming. Whatever your interests, your spiritual calling will envelop a means for relating to nature and helping nature relate to people.

Do your bones hurt whenever the weather is going to change? Have you thought of being a meteorologist? How about being a crop duster or a firefighter? Are you in touch with the natural elements like wind, air, or fire? Do you receive divine omens through animals or birds? Do animals bring you messages in your dreams? You have the gift of bringing change and healing through your relationship with the Natural.

Eleventh Chakra
Psychic Gift: Force Sympathy
You are aware of the forces at play in any given situation.

Intuitive Ability: Force Empathy
You can command spiritual and energetic forces toward your chosen ends.

Spiritual Gift: Commanding and Transmutation
You can adjust forces to bring about good in alignment with divine plans.

A Commander is able to do just that—command! But what does an eleventh-chakra Commander command? Natural and supernatural forces. When you apply this ability according to divine will, you can:

- Intuit whether the forces involved in a given situation are right or wrong.
- Access divine power to use or change forces so the situation plays out according to divine will.
- Actually change one type of force into another, for higher ends. This is called transmutation.

To **transmute** means to modify a substance from one form or state to another. Transmuters are able to alter reality by moving forces around. A Transmuter can switch one force for another in order to bring about the desired change. However, he or she can also alter or adjust the present forces so they bring about a positive affect.

Transmuters can use words or paint pictures to make a point. They can employ ideas, writing, or feelings to command forces. They can also learn how to access physical forces to bring about a desired outcome. A Commanding Transmuter, under the right conditions, could even get a toaster to spit out apples—if the Divine calls for it!

Opening to Your Destiny

The spiritual gifts are actually encoded into your entire body, through both your energy system and your spirit. Your gifts are the tools needed to fulfill your destiny. They are the medium through which the Divine assists you and others in delivering the spiritual truths entrusted to you. Most people think that their destiny involves only career or workplace options. This isn't true. Your destiny is ultimately to be yourself—your true self. The expression of your self is the expression of your gifts.

Living in the seventh sense is not a religious undertaking. Nevertheless, it is a divine experience. Your destiny is all about the Divine—and the divine in, through, and around you. It's not about perfection, for who said that the divine is "perfect?" Rather, it is divine to be in a state of continual change, improvement, and growth, and that is ultimately what the seventh sense is all about. Your seventh sense is your link with the Divine, which already knows you as perfect—and perfectly able to continue becoming more of your self! And this is love, the acceptance of God's belief in our own beauty, goodness, and power. Once you know that you are a miracle, life becomes miraculous.

Endnotes

Introduction

1. Philip Goldberg, *The Intuitive Edge* (Los Angeles: Jeremy Tarcher, 1983), 40.

Chapter 1

1. Fred Alan Wolf, *Taking the Quantum Leap* (New York: Harper & Row, 1989), 182.

Chapter 2

1. Russell Targ and Jane Katra, *Miracles of the Mind* (Novato Calif.: New World Library, 1998), 1–2.
2. John M. Templeton and Robert L. Hermann, *The God Who Would Be Known*, (Philadelphia, Templeton Foundation Press, 1998), 37.
3. Charles Swindoll, *Flying Closer to the Flame* (Dallas: Word Publishing, 1993), 135.

Chapter 3

1. Victoria E. Slater, "Toward and Understanding of Energetic Healing: Part I," *Journal of Holistic Nursing* 13 (1995), 209–212.
2. Richard Gerber, *Vibrational Medicine* (Rochester, Vt.: Bear & Company, 2001.), 162.
3. Valerie V. Hunt, "Appendix, The Rolf Study," in Rosalyn L. Bruyere, *Wheels of Light* (Arcadia, Calif.: Bon Productions, 1989), 247–258.

Chapter 5

1. Larry Dossey, *Be Careful What You Pray For, You Just Might Get It* (New York: HarperCollins, 1997), 43.

Chapter 8

1. Morton Kelsey, *Companions on the Inner Way* (New York: Crossroad Publishing Company, 1996), 124.
2. Anaya Rudolfo, *Bless Me, Ultima* (New York: Warner Books, 1972), 120–121.

Chapter 9

1. Francis Crick, *The Astonishing Hypothesis: The Scientific Search for the Soul* (New York: Macmillan Publishing, 1994), 33.
2. Ibid., 33

Index

A

E

F

N

P

R

S

Also by Cyndi Dale

Books

Kundalini: Divine Energy, Divine Life (Llewellyn Worldwide, 2011)

The Everyday Clairvoyant (Llewellyn Worldwide, 2010)

The Complete Book of Chakra Healing (Llewellyn Worldwide, 2009; formerly *New Chakra Healing)*

The Subtle Body: An Encyclopedia of Your Energetic Anatomy (Sounds True, 2009)

Illuminating the Afterlife (Sounds True, 2008)

Attracting Your Perfect Body Through the Chakras (Crossing Press, 2006)

Advanced Chakra Healing: Heart Disease; The Four Pathways Approach (Crossing Press, 2006)

Advanced Chakra Healing: Energy Mapping on the Four Pathways (Crossing Press, 2005)

Advanced Chakra Healing: Cancer; The Four Pathways Approach (Crossing Press, 2005)

Attracting Prosperity Through the Chakras (Crossing Press, 2004)

E-books (available at www.cyndidale.com)

The Energy of You: Your Chakras

The Spirit's Diet: Part One Stop Waiting for Your Weight

The Spirit's Diet: Part Two Freedom of the Spirit

The You Around You: Your Auric Field

Walking the Planes of Light: Death, Dying and Life

Your 6th Sense

Zap! You Are a Teen, Now What? Part One: The Energy of You

Zap! You Are a Teen, Now What? Part Two: Uncovering Your Destiny

DVDs and CDs

Energetic Boundaries: How to Stay Protected and Connected in Work, Love, and Life (Sounds True, 2011)
Energy Clearing (Sounds True, 2009)
Healing Across Space & Time (Sounds True, 2009)
Advanced Chakra Wisdom (Sounds True, 2008)
Illuminating the Afterlife (Sounds True, 2008)
The Songbird Series (Essential Energy, 2008)

About the Author

Cyndi Dale is internationally recognized as an authority on energy healing. She is the author of several books on energy healing, including the original and revised *New Chakra Healing* (now entitled *The Complete Book of Chakra Healing*), which has been published in more than ten languages, and six other best-selling books on the topic, including *Advanced Chakra Healing, Illuminating the Afterlife, Kundalini: Divine Energy, Divine Life* and *The Subtle Body*.

Through her company, Essential Energy, she provides intuitive assessments and life-issues healing for thousands of clients a year, seeking always to uplift and inspire others toward their true purpose and personalities. Her enthusiasm and care ignite all who attend her workshops, trainings sessions, and college classes, which are offered around the world.

Cyndi has studied cross-cultural healing and energy systems and has led instructional classes in many countries, including Peru, Costa Rica, Venezuela, Japan, Belize, Mexico, Morocco, Russia and across Europe, as well as among the Lakota people and the Hawaiian kahunas. She currently lives in Minneapolis, Minnesota, with her two sons and various pets.

More information about Cyndi's classes, products and services is available at **www.cyndidale.com.**

Another Must-Have Book by Cyndi Dale

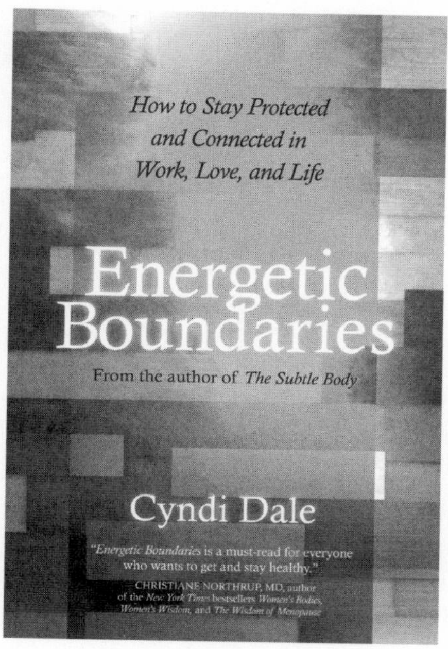

"Strong and flexible energetic boundaries allow us to share who we truly are with the world," teaches Cyndi Dale. Filled with insights, practical guidance, and easy-to-learn techniques, Energetic Boundaries is an indispensible tool for staying protected and connected in every aspect of life—in our relationships, career, and on our spiritual journey.